谨以此书纪念王世襄先生

In memory of Mr Wang Shixiang

伍 嘉 恩
GRACE WU

木 趣 居
家具中的嘉具

The Best of The Best
The
MQJ
Collection
of Ming Furniture

上
―――
Vol. 1

生活·讀書·新知 三联书店

目 录
CONTENTS

家具中的嘉具 / 伍嘉恩	9	The Best of the Best / GRACE WU
王世襄题字	16	Wang Shixiang Calligraphy
附：王世襄信札	18	Wang Shixiang Letter
王世襄"望江南"六阕	24	Wang Shixiang *ci*-poems *Wang Jiangnan*
附：王世襄信札	28	Wang Shixiang Letter
图录	62	Catalogue
版画索引	506	Woodblock Illustrations Index
引用文献	517	Books Cited

家具中的嘉具

从小喜欢古物，青少年时游走外国，对比下我对中国古物更觉好奇。20世纪70年代开始留意家具，遇上黄花梨家具，触动了我的心。继而全球搜索、寻觅、据为己有，启动了我收藏明式家具的旅程。

"木趣居"藏明式家具一百多件套，多为第一手、第二手从原产地得着。多在收藏明式家具的黄金时期20世纪80、90年代得着，秘藏至今，不少从未曝光。木趣居家具涵括明式家具的各种类别，入藏标准为造型美丽、结构卓越、状况良好、以及稀有、罕见。比如香几可能是明式家具传世品中最稀有的大种类，木趣居有四件，四件都异常美观、状况完美、设计优越，都不愧为经典的代表作；比如四件方桌的造型，结构都是难得一见的，其中两件更有可能是传世孤品；还有拔步床，世人所知的明代珍贵木材黄花梨制拔步床只有一例，在美国堪萨斯市纳尔逊-阿特金斯艺术博物馆。木趣居有一例，无论是结构、造型、状况，都比美国的更胜一筹。

"木趣居"的缘由

1985年，王世襄先生大作《明式家具珍赏》面世，掀起了明式家具热，市场上接二连三出现大量早期家具，热衷收藏的我无法以私人身份吸纳市场上众多精品，于是在1987年创办嘉木堂经营明式家具，适应市场的骤变。因为此举是我收藏活动的延续，便在力所能及的情况下收蓄所有达到我要求的标准的明式家具，不管大量购入能否售出。这样在六七年间便积累了几十件特别精美的存货。因为经手过眼多，所以充分知道什么是珍稀，留的都是较罕见的，这些珍品只有嘉木堂陈列室或定期举办的展览需要特别亮点时才会偶尔出现。

1995年，加州中国古典家具博物馆落实遣散其收藏的决定，因为当时全球没有别的一所对外开放的机构拥有一套较有代表性的明式家具收藏，王世襄先生的评语是"这套家具能留着一起就好了"。这话我听进心里，萌生了这工作由我担当的想法，组织一套有代表性的家具留在一起。王先生惠赐木趣居斋额、印章以及"望江南"六阕。而嘉木堂存的几十件明式家具精品，便成了木趣居的基础。自此我继续为木趣居收藏的提升与添加新品而努力，能够符合我定下入藏标准的都积极罗致，特别是嘉木堂已出手而木趣居未有的珍品若重现市场会争取买回。与木趣居失散的成对、成堂的椅子、凳子，也会尽力购回合成一对或一堂。

三十多年的经历，一个特别的时代，加上我个人特殊的机遇，成就了今天的木趣居。时势已过，机会不再，想再组织这样的一套明式家具收藏，恐怕是没有可能了。

  这三十多年我经手过眼的明式家具无数，他们教育了我，我吸收了常人所不了解的知识。以往编撰图录，为了传达这些知识，我会提点每件套之特征、为何与众不同，述其独特风格，如何在型、式、工方面臻至完美。以上这类文字在撰写《木趣居》时尽量略去，主要陈述家具的结构。这回我少说话，是希望以家具本身的线条、形状、颜色传达他们的本质与精神，让家具自己说话。

  感谢所有成全木趣居的人，特别是嘉木堂的团队，木趣居的收藏永远有你们的印记。此套图录从策划、摄影、撰写、设计至成书，酝酿多年，见证了所有参与者的耐力；而达到"让家具自己说话"，则考验了设计装帧的功力。

  建立木趣居的本意是组织一套有代表性的明式家具留在一起。坚持多年，初衷未变，我的希望是让木趣居的收藏一直在一起，给后代。

伍嘉恩

丙申岁晚

The Best of the Best

My interest in antiquities began at an early age and, in a curious way, the times spent abroad during my youth seemed to increase my affinity for "old things" from China. In the 1970s I began to look at furniture and discovered classical Chinese furniture – those amazing Ming period forms in *huanghuali*. I was captivated and began to seek high and low for them, to buy and to own them, thus beginning the journey of my Ming furniture collecting.

The *Muquju* Collection (木趣居; "Lodge of Wood Delights"), shortened to the MQJ Collection, comprises over one hundred pieces (sets) of Ming furniture. Most were acquired directly or second-hand from their places of origin and in the 1980s and 1990s, the golden period of Ming furniture collecting. The MQJ Collection was kept under wraps until now, with many examples never exposed before. The collection encompasses all types of Ming furniture and the criteria for selection was based on beautiful design, superb craftsmanship, excellent condition and rarity. For instance, among the major types of Ming furniture, incense stands maybe the rarest type in surviving examples - the MQJ Collection has four pieces. Each stand is of exquisite form and in perfect condition. Four square tables in the collection are unusual forms, two are possibly unique. And then there is the star of the collection.....the alcove bed. The only other example in precious *huanghuali* wood dated to the Ming known to the world is in the Nelson-Atkins Museum of Art in Kansas City. The design, construction and condition of the alcove bed in the MQJ Collection are all a notch above that of the Nelson-Atkins bed.

How the MQJ Collection came about

In 1985 Wang Shixiang (1914-2009) released his publication *Mingshi Jiaju Zhenshang* ("Appreciation of Ming Furniture") to wide acclaim and it triggered an immense interest in Ming furniture. The marketplace responded to this new level of awareness and large quantities of early furniture surfaced. As an avid collector I wanted to acquire all the wonderful pieces that were available but I realized this was too ambitious as a private collector. The solution was to open a gallery specializing in Ming furniture, so I founded the Grace Wu Bruce gallery in 1987. In reality this was an act that enabled me to continue collecting. I bought all that I was able to and all that met my collecting standard without considering whether my fervent buying might result in too many for the gallery to sell. Over the course of six or seven years I accumulated a sizable stock. The experience of handling large quantities of Ming furniture pieces has equipped me with knowing well what is rare, hence the stock comprised mostly rare pieces. These were intended for sale as gallery highlights or when they were needed for the exhibitions we mounted from time to time.

In 1995, the Museum of Classical Chinese Furniture in California made good its plans to disperse its collection. At the time there was no other institution open to the public that possessed such a sizable, representative collection of Ming furniture, and Mr Wang Shixiang made the comment that he wished the collection would be kept together. This inspired me to take on the task of forming a sizable, representative collection for keeping intact. Mr Wang honoured me with a collection name, *Muquju*, and gifted me a collection seal as well as six verses of *ci*-poems to the tune of *Wang Jiangnan* ("Dreaming of the South"). The accumulated rare and special pieces of the Grace Wu Bruce gallery became the foundation of *Muquju*, the MQJ Collection. Since then I have actively acquired Ming furniture pieces to add to the collection, particularly when precious examples previously sold by the gallery reappear on the market and when chairs and stools resurface to complete a pair or a set in the MQJ Collection.

The MQJ Collection, acquired over some thirty years during the golden

period of Ming furniture collecting, is the result of my deep involvement in the world of Ming furniture. It is the essence of the large body of early material that surfaced from the primary sources in the latter part of the last century. It was an unprecedented opportunity from a bygone era that will never be repeated.

The handling of numerous pieces of early furniture allowed me to gain knowledge and expertise that few have. In my previous exhibition catalogues it was customary to point out the special features that distinguished a piece and how the superlative design, balanced proportions and exquisite workmanship rendered them exceptional. I have however refrained from doing this for the MQJ Collection limiting the discussion to mainly construction reports. It is my hope that the quality and the spirit of the furniture will be conveyed through the design and the lines and by the colour of the wood. It is my hope that the furniture will speak for themselves.

Salute to everyone who was part of the collecting process, especially the Grace Wu Bruce gallery team. You have left an indelible mark on the MQJ Collection. The preparation of this publication from conception, photography, cataloguing to design has been in progress for many years. The results bear witness to the patience of the work team; and meeting the brief "to let the furniture speak for themselves" is a testament to the prowess of the design and production.

I began this journey with the intention of building a sizeable and representative repository of Ming furniture to be one entity. My vision has not changed. It is my wish that the MQJ Collection will be kept intact, for future generations.

Grace Wu
Spring 2017

居

乙亥六月暢安為嘉恩女史題

木趣

My Dearest Grace,

　　我這幾天一直在思考為你想一个室名或齋額。我竟覺得並不很容易。也許會不合你意。請坦率地告訴我。不合意我必再想。

　　首先我認為室名不宜長，字多了太囉嗦。三个字還是最好。

　　名稱在想來想去要切合傢具和美麗的木材还必須有一个木字。因為有关家具的其它字眼 如：家具、家私、木器、傢俱、器用、器物、家生、動使、家椿等之都夠格放進室名。放進字後都不像话，成了不倫不類的名堂。因此只能用一个"木"字。

　　為了和巳有的"嘉木堂"有區別，"木"准備作為首字。避免作為第三个字。

　　第二个字要和你本人結合得密切一些，也就是我上一信所谓的要 intimate 一些，要和彼 Gallery 的名稱(嘉木堂)不同，所以我別"趣"字。"趣"最容易譯成 interest。不過在漢語中"趣"有許多涵意。例如：

"巳卜耕鋤景趣深" 元潘音孫句 歸隱田園的樂趣

"悠然得趣聽鳴琴" 戴復古詩句 得音乐的樂趣

"個中妙趣真堪語，最是初醺未醉時。宋陸游诗句
　　　　　　　　　言酒之趣

清趣　　指超兒脫俗的趣味

"保自然之雅趣，鄙人间之荒雜" 江淹《傷心賦》

"素心自此得，真趣非外借" 李白诗句

"山水有真趣，琴书得自由。" 钱起诗句

"夜深人静月明中，方识荷花有真趣" 于石诗句

"忽然'怪'真趣，不觉成朝夕。" 朱熹诗句

"朝来上楼望，稍觉用得真趣" 贾岛诗句

总之"趣"字涵意包括对外象和内心的认识、理解、欣赏，和所得到的乐趣，甚至对真谛、真理的领悟。这就包括你对美术文理的欣赏，造形艺术的喜爱，及明式家具艺术的真正理解及对情的融汇合一 人与物

这样室名的第二个字为"趣"字。

第三个字不用堂、斋字，而需家庭化一些，也有 intimate 的意思。通俗一些的可用"居"字。有房舍之意。今解一些三联以下某个字更合一些。字宜用平声字，不宜用仄声字。只有平声才觉醒。

榭 即楼阁边的小屋 音 xiè

宧 室内的东北角为宧。即室内的某一部分。也音 yí。如住楼房用朱趣楼也可以

因此为你想的室名为：朱趣居 或 朱趣榭 或 朱趣宧。不知你喜欢哪一个？也许都不喜欢。再后变一个。请用中文回邮的信。你如满意，采用哪一

《文物》95年4期不知收到没有？身接到海关通知，把所寄出的文物扣了，因为它见国内版。以及'没给批人带了。祝你快乐！

王世襄 95/5/28

My Dearest Grace,

我这几天一直在思考为您想一个室名或斋额。我竟觉得并不很容易。也许会不合你意，请坦率地告诉我。不合意可以再想。

首先我认为室名不宜长，字多了太啰嗦。三个字还是最好。

为难在想来想去要切合家具和美丽的木材还只有一个"木"字。因为有关家具的其它字眼如：家具、家私、木器、长物、器用、器物、家生、动使、桌椅等等都无法放进室名，放进去后都不像话，成了不伦不类的名堂。因此只能用一个"木"字。

为了和已有的"嘉木堂"有区别，"木"准备作为首字。避免作为第二个字。

第二个字要和你本人结合得密切一些，也就是我上一信所谓的要 intimate 一些，要和做 Gallery 的名称（嘉木堂）不同，所以我想到"趣"字。"趣"最容易译成 interest。不过在汉语中"趣"有许多涵意。

例如：
"已卜耕锄乐趣深"　元潘音诗句　归隐田园的乐趣
"悠然得趣听鸣琴"　戴复古诗句　得音乐的乐趣
"个中妙趣真堪语，最是初醺未醉时。"　宋陆游诗句
　　　　　　　　　　　　　　　　　言酒之趣

清趣　指超凡脱俗的趣味

"保自然之雅趣，鄙人间之荒杂"　江淹《修心赋》
"素心自此得，真趣非外惜"　李白诗句

"山水有真趣，琴书得自由。" 舒逊诗句
"夜深人静月明中，方识荷花有真趣。" 于石诗句
"悠然惬幽趣，不觉几朝夕。" 朱熹诗句
"朝来上楼望，稍觉得幽趣。" 贾岛诗句

总之"趣"字涵意包括对外象和内心的认识、理解、欣赏和所得到的乐趣，甚至对真谛、真理的悟彻。这就包括你对美材文理的欣赏，造形、花纹的喜爱，及明式家具艺术的真正理解及人与物神情的融会合一。

这样室名的第二个字为"趣"字。

第三个字不用堂、斋等字，而要家庭化一些，也有 intimate 的意思。通俗一些的可用"居"字。有居家之意。冷僻一些可从以下几个字选一个。这个字宜用平声字，不宜用仄声字。只有平声才响亮。

移　即楼阁边的小屋　音 yi。

宧　室内的东北角为宧。即室内的某一部分。也音 yi。如住楼房用木趣楼也可以。

因此为你想的室名为：木趣居或木趣移或木趣宧。不知你喜欢哪一个？也许都不喜欢。再重想一个。请用中文回我的信。你如满意，我再写。

《文物》95 年 4 期不知收到没有？我接到海关通知，把我寄出的《文物》扣了，因为它是国内版。以后恐须托人带了。祝你快乐！

王世襄 95/5/28

28 May 1995

My Dearest Grace,

I have been thinking of a Chinese studio name or a plaque for you in the past few days. To my surprise, it turned out to be not that easy. Simply tell me if you don't like it. I can always find you another one.

First of all, I am not for a long one. Three Chinese characters would be best after all. Anything longer would be wordy.

The difficulty is there seems to be no other choice but the character "*mu* (wood)" if it has to be relevant to furniture and their beautiful material. There are many other related words or expressions but they just do not fit nicely into a studio name and would actually sound weird. So, I was left with this one single Chinese character.

And, for the sake of differentiation, I have decided to begin the name with "*mu*" instead of placing it in the middle as in Jiamutang, the existing Chinese name of your gallery.

As for the second character, it has to be personal, or "intimate" as I put it in my last letter, so as to be different from that for a gallery. This is when the character "*qu* (delight)" came up. Although it is often translated into English as "interest", it has many meanings in Chinese. Here are some examples:

"Working the land, as foretold, is to bring much delight." From a poem by Pan Yin of the Yuan dynasty to express the pleasure of retiring into farming.

"Delight is to be had listening to a sounding zither." From a poem by Dai Fugu to express how music delights.

"Who can ever describe the delight of delights / Of being tipsy but not yet drunk?" From a poem by Lu You of the Song dynasty to express the pleasure of drinking.

Pure delight means unworldly pleasure.

"Cherish the pristine delights by Nature. / Disdain the rank clutters by men." —Jiang Yan, "Cultivating the Heart"

"Purity of the heart is attainable nowhere else. / Delights of the truest kind evade everyone else."—Li Bai

"Mountains and waters offer true delights. / Books and zithers afford liberation." –Shu Xun

"Lotuses reveal their true delights / Only in the quiet of a moonlit night." –Yu Shi

"Days and nights pass unawares / Whilst delighting in leisure without a care." –Zhu Xi

"Leisurely delights begin to creep in / When dawn, from a height, is seen." –Jia Dao

Anyway, "*qu*" refers to the pleasure obtained from both mental and sensual acknowledgment, understanding and appreciation to the extent of enlightenment. In your case, it would include your appreciation of the wood grains, attraction to the designs and decorations, genuine understanding of the art of Ming-style furniture, and spiritual communion with objects.

Thus, "*qu*" is made the second character of your studio name.

The third character can neither be "*tang* (hall)" nor "*zhai* (studio)". There has to be more homeliness and hence intimacy to it. A relatively common character would be "*ju* (lodge)", which is associated with home. Less common ones are given below for you to choose from. By the way, a level tone is preferred to an oblique one if the name is to be resounding to the ear.

The first two are both pronounced as "*yi*", the first of which means a small side-room in a house and the second the north-eastern corner of an interior. The character "*lou*" would also do should you live in a storied building.

So, here are my suggestions: "Muquju" or "Muquyi", with either the first "*yi*" or the second. Which do you like best? Maybe none. In that case, I will give it some thought once again. Looking forward to your reply in Chinese. By the way, I will write out the one that you are most happy with.

Has Issue No. 4, 1995, of *Wenwu* arrived yet? I got this notification from the Customs that the one I sent by post had been seized since it was a domestic edition. I am afraid the journal would have to be delivered to you in the future.

Yours sincerely, Wang Shixiang 1995/5/28

Translated by Tina Liem

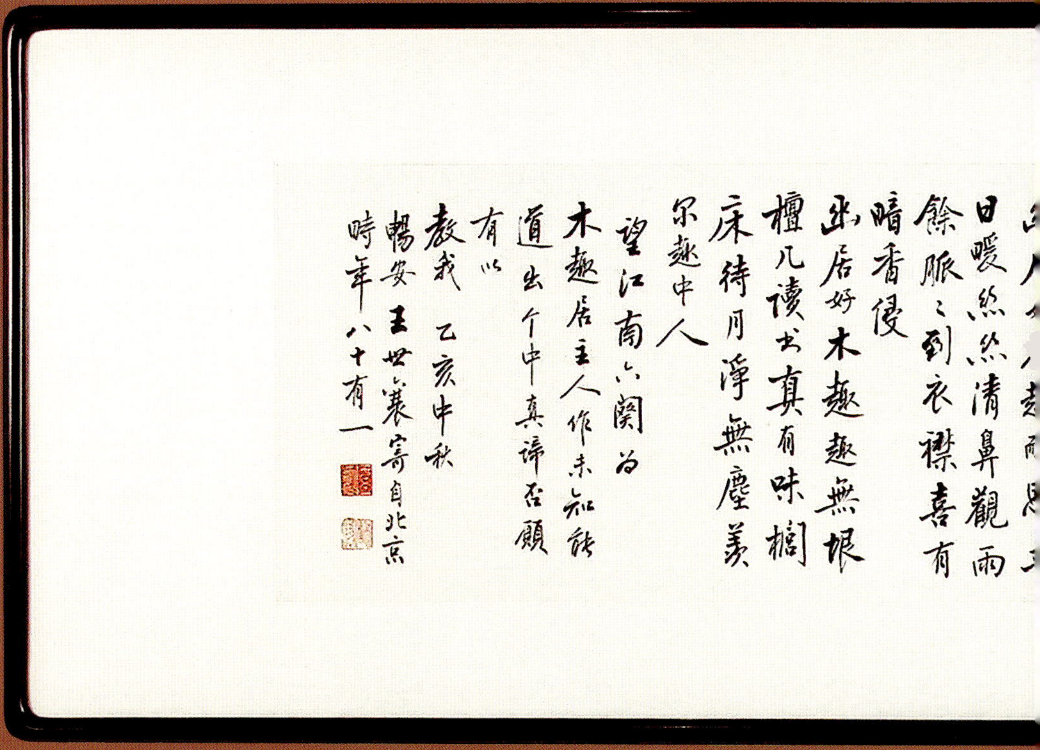

出人如八拱而思玉

日暖絮絮清鼻觀雨

餘脈脈到衣襟喜有

暗香侵

此居好木趣無垠

檀几讀書真有味榻

床待月淨無塵羨

尔趣中人

望江南六闋為

木趣居主人作未知能

道出个中真谛否願

有以

教我 乙亥中秋

暢安王世襄寄自北京

時年八十有一

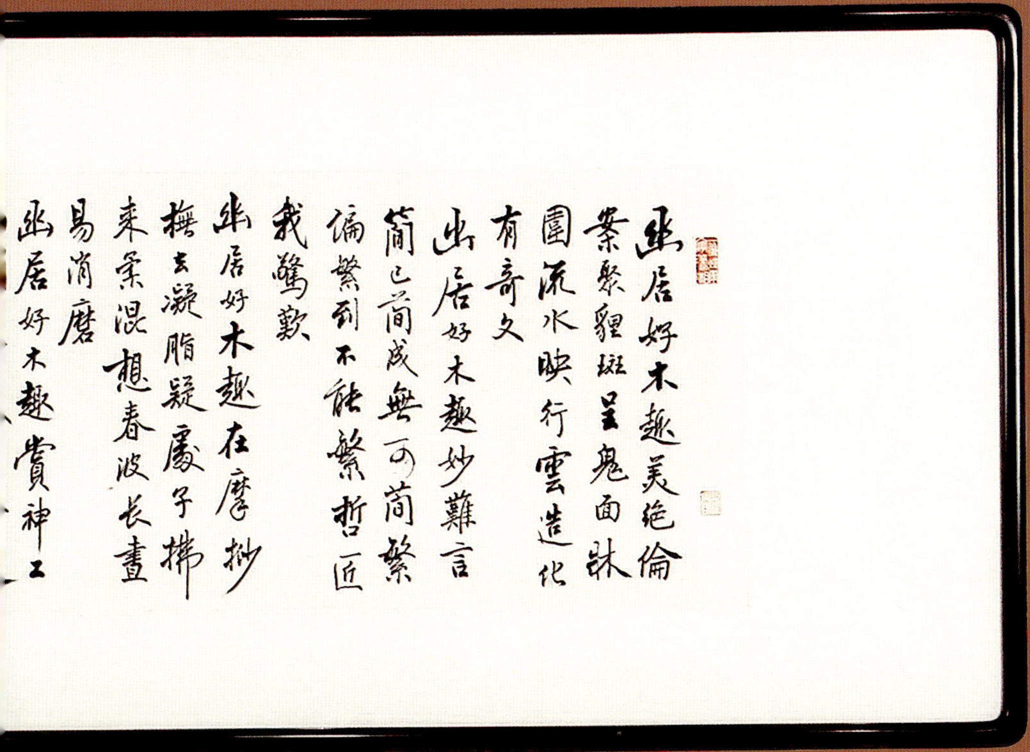

幽居好木趣美絶倫
纍纍貍斑呈鬼面
圍流水映行雲造化
有奇文
出居好木趣妙難言
簡已前成無可商繁
偏繁剗不能繁哲匠
我驚歎
出居好木趣在摩抄
樓玄凝脂疑厝子梯
來柴混想春波长畫
易消磨
幽居好木趣賞神工

望江南 為木趣居主人作

幽居好，木趣悅其真，案聚貍斑星兔面（古人稱黃花梨之斑紋曰貍斑，貍斑或兔面），牀圍流水映行雲，造化有奇文。

幽居好，木趣在摩抄，極去凝脂疑慶子，拂來柔混（木構件之西面曰混，見營造法式）想春波長，畫易消磨。

幽居好，木趣妙難言，簡已簡成無可簡，繁偏繁到不能繁（西方人士以往只驚歎其如……製亦有極高藝術價值，皆正明式家具之簡練），哲匠我驚歎。

幽居好，木趣賞神工，巧鬥寸材成卍亞（明式家具多以萬字不到頭空心十字為佛，皆用短材搭橙門而成，像卍字與亞字也），透鏤尺幅走螭龍，真個太玲瓏。

幽居好，木趣耐思尋，日暖徐徐清鼻觀，雨餘脈脈到衣襟，妻有暗香侵（黃花梨有異香成文），絆陣香木。

幽居好，木趣趣無垠，檀几讀古真有味，桐牀待月靜無塵，羨爾趣中人。

Lodged in tranquility is the best.
So is ravished by wood with grain sublime.
In this bench, spotted raccoons like mystic masks lurk.
In that bed, sprawling rivulets like streaky clouds gird.
How Nature leaves its heavenly marks!

Lodged in tranquility is the best.
So is ravished by wood of great design.
In the simple, simplicity in its sleekest is celebrated.
In the florid, floridity in its richest is manifested.
How craftsmen drive their lively minds!

Lodged in tranquility is the best.
So is ravished by wood with a touch defined.
The satin brings to mind the jade cheek of a fair maiden.
The creasy can be to a pond rippling in spring likened.
How long hours do fleetingly fly!

Lodged in tranquility is the best.
So is ravished by wood with carvings fine.
Dainty are Buddhist crosses no bigger than a fingernail.
Mighty are Chinese dragons in large openwork unveiled.
How adorable is artistry at its height!

Lodged in tranquility is the best.
So is ravished by wood with aroma divine
That wafts to waken nostrils through air that sizzles;
Else lingers to perfume clothing on days that drizzle.
How pleasurable is a faintly fragranced life!

Lodged in tranquility is the best.
So is ravished by wood till the end of time.
Reading good books at a *zitan* desk proffers much to savour.
Gazing at the moon in a *huali* bed transforms woes to vapour.
How enviable is lodging in wood delights!

Whether or not I have succeeded in conveying the true meaning will have to await enlightenment from the Master of the Lodge of Wood Delights, to whom these six *ci*-poems to the tune of *Peering at Jiangnan* are dedicated.

Best Wishes from Wang Shixiang, aged 81, in Beijing.
Mid-Autumn Festival, 1995.

Translated by Tina Liem

21th Sept. 1995

My Dearest Grace:

竹刻展片两盒皆已收到，拍得好極了。已去函向您和向攝影師道謝。想已收到。

大批 Chinese Classical Furniture 簽名本皮书也20本收到，謝之。将代為送给應該送的人。

台灣不少位收藏家送文物到故宫展覽，包括鴻禧美術館的廖桂英館長。我國內想给他一个 surprise，連夜寫了六首"望江南"當成橫幅，托她帶到香港付郵，或打電話請您派人去取。不知收到沒有？我想你会喜歡，完全從木板出發，真正為你而寫的。下面再想作一些講解，也许会多餘的，因為不请你也知道。

"望江南"是一个詞牌名，一般用"××好"開始，唐代和五代诗人喜歡用此詞寫词。其中三、四两句往往是一對對聯，末一句要總結全首詞意。

(一) 此紋好，enjoyment & pleasure of the grain
木紋美绝倫
眾黎<u>裡纹是鬼画</u> (見"研究"圖版卷 P.191 右欄)
林间流水映文雲，("研究"只文字卷 P.73 兩6 説明)
<u>造化方家文</u> nature creats beautiful grain

(二) 此居好，enjoyment & pleasure of the form of Ming furniture
木趣如佳音
商祀商戚蒡了商 (此两句对得很得意，没明明成多見東的商风五朝，右的商列也不要。远要歸功於古代的顯明之匠。)
輩僑擎刻不能歇，
<u>哲匠的蟹歌</u>！ (聲智之人 曰"哲")"款字既是平声字，又是仄声字。此處為平声，讀作 tén，不作 tén。)

(三) 此屠好，enjoyment & pleasure of the touch or texture
木趣在摩挲，
摩去<u>凝脂凝扇子</u> (故常用凝脂形嬰若美的肌膚。屠子即處女Virgin。故诗人极相信處女的肌膚最润滑。)

拼木条混着看波（拼拿和的部貝凸面。文研究文字見卷P.177
長畫易消磨. you may enjoy the polishing whole day long! 混面）convex moulding

(四) 出居好, the enjoyment or pleasure from beautiful carving
木塾堂神之 & sculting
巧門寸材咸巫亚 (亚指空心十字)
房鍵尺临支撐龍，
東恒大珍驪!

(三) 出居好!, the enjoyment & pleasure from the pleasant
木紋耐思孝. odour of the wood
日暖絲絲清鼻観, 〞鼻観指嗅覺〝有平声,有仄声.此
雨條脈脈朝不斷, 处讀 guàn, 不讀 guān. 仄声
試有暗香侵! （脈脈有含蓄有情之意）
(暗香 faint fragrance

(二) 出居好,
木紋徹無垠 (no limit, or endless 有眼結与有之竟
檀几讀古來加味,（你眼愛食出, 故云〝
摘味俗月浮气虚, "摘 見"研究"向册卷P.191, 即若花梨想
衷尔絨中人! 識你的美麗 的黃花梨大妹）
（你, 明你, 木塾居中的人)

21ˢᵗ Sept 1995

My Dearest Grace,

　　竹刻底片两盒先后收到，拍得好极了。已上函向您和向摄影师道谢。想已收到。

　　大作 Chinese Classical Furniture 签名本及另包 20 本已收到，谢谢。将代为送给应该送的人。

　　台湾不少位收藏家送文物到故宫展览，包括鸿禧美术馆的廖桂英馆长。我因为想给您一个 surprise，连夜写了六首"望江南"，写成横幅，托她带到香港付邮，或打电话请您派人去取。不知收到没有？我想你会喜欢，完全从木趣出发，真正为你而写的。下面我想作一些讲解。也许是多余的，因为不讲你也知道。

　　"望江南"是一个词牌名，一般用"××好"开始，唐代不少位诗人喜欢用此调写词。其中三、四两句往往是一副对联，末一句要总结全首词意。

（一）幽居好，enjoyment and pleasure of the grain
　　　木趣美绝伦
　　　案聚狸斑呈鬼面，（见《研究》图版卷 p.191 右栏）
　　　床围流水映行云，（见《研究》文字卷 p.73 丙 6 说明）
　　　造化有奇文 nature creates beautiful grain

（二）幽居好，enjoyment and pleasure of the form of Ming furniture
　　　木趣妙难言
　　　简已简成无可简，（此两句我很得意，说明明式家具有的简到无可简，
　　　繁偏繁到不能繁。　有的繁到无可繁。这要归功于古代的聪明工匠。）
　　　哲匠我惊叹！（贤智之人曰"哲"，"叹"字既是平声字，又是仄声字。
　　　　　　　　　此处为平声。读作 tán，不作 tàn。）

（三）幽居好，enjoyment and pleasure of the touch or texture
　　木趣在摩挲，
　　抚去凝脂疑处子（古人常用凝脂形容美的肌肤。
　　　　　　　　　处子即处女,Virgin,古代诗人相信处女的肌肤最润滑。）
　　拂来柔混想春波（指柔和的家具凸面。见《研究》文字卷 P.177 混面）
　　　　　　　convex moulding
　　长昼易消磨。You may enjoy the polishing whole day long!

（四）幽居好，the enjoyment or pleasure from beautiful carving and joining
　　木趣赏神工
　　巧斗寸材成卍亚（"亚"指空心十字）
　　透镂尺幅走螭龙，
　　真个太玲珑！

（五）幽居好，the enjoyment and pleasure from the pleasant odour of the wood
　　木趣耐思寻。
　　日暖丝丝清鼻观，（"鼻观"指嗅觉。"观"有平声，有仄声。此处读 guàn。
　　　　　　　　　　不读 guān。仄声）
　　雨余脉脉到衣襟，（脉脉有含蓄有情之意）
　　喜有暗香侵！（暗香 faint fragrance）

（六）幽居好，
　　木趣趣无垠（no limit or endless, 有总结六首之意。）
　　檀几读书真有味，　（你很爱念书，故云）
　　桐床待月净无尘，（"桐"见《研究》图版卷 p.191，即黄花梨。想起你的美丽的黄花梨大床）
　　羡尔趣中人！（尔,即"你"，木趣居中的人）

21ˢᵗ Sept 1995

My dearest Grace,

The two boxes of bamboo carvings transparencies have arrived, what an excellent job. Under separate cover, I have written to thank you and to ask you to convey my thanks to the photographer, trust it has already arrived.

Your new book *Classical Chinese Furniture*, a signed copy and a case of twenty copies also arrived, thank you. I will gift them to whom I think should have them.

Taiwan collectors have been coming to Beijing to deliver antique objects for the exhibition at the Gugong Palace Museum, and this drone includes the director of the Chang Foundation Museum, Liao Guiying. I wanted to give you a surprise, so overnight, composed six *ci*-poems to the tune of *Wang Jiangnan* "Dreaming of the South", styled them in a horizontal scroll and asked her to bring it to Hong Kong and send it by post to you or to telephone you to have it picked up. Have you received it? I am hoping you would be pleased, directed solely at the delights of wood, especially written for you. Let me explain. Perhaps it is superfluous because you would know even without explanation.

"Dreaming of the South" is a form of *ci*-poetry, usually with "XX is the best" to begin, quite a few Tang poets are fond of this tune to write *ci*-poems. The third and fourth line usually comprise a couplet, with the last line summarizing the meaning of the *ci*-poems.

1. Lodged in tranquility is the best.
   So is ravished by wood with grain sublime.
   In this bench, spotted raccoons like mystic masks lurk.
   (see "*Connoisseurship*" plates p.191 right)
   In that bed, sprawling rivulets like streaky clouds gird.
   (see "*Connoisseurship*" text p.73 C6 explanation)
   How Nature leaves its heavenly marks!

2. Lodged in tranquility is the best.
   So is ravished by wood of great design.
   In the simple, simplicity in its sleekest is celebrated. (I am very proud of these two lines exemplifying the art of ancient craftsmen in their creation of Ming Furniture)

In the florid, floridity in its richest is manifested.
How craftsmen drive their lively minds!(The last word is pronounced with the second tonation and not the fourth)

3 Lodged in tranquility is the best.
   So is ravished by wood with a touch defined.
   The satin brings to mind the jade cheek of a fair maiden.(ancients believe young maidens have silken skin)
   The creasy can be to a pond rippling in spring likened.(alludes to the gently convex moulding. See "*Connoisseurship*" text p. 177)
   How long hours do fleetingly fly! (you may enjoy the polishing whole day long!)

4 Lodged in tranquility is the best. (the enjoyment or pleasure from beautiful carving and joining)
   So is ravished by wood with carvings fine.
   Dainty are Buddhist crosses no bigger than a fingernail.(alludes to the hollow cross patterns)
   Mighty are Chinese dragons in large openwork unveiled.
   How adorable is artistry at its height!

5 Lodged in tranquility is the best.
   So is ravished by wood with aroma divine
   That wafts to waken nostrils through air that sizzles;(Pronounce here the fourth tonation and not the first)
   Else lingers to perfume clothing on days that drizzle.(lingering alludes also to feeling)
   How pleasurable is a faintly fragranced life!(faint fragrance)

6 Lodged in tranquility is the best.
   So is ravished by wood till the end of time.(no limit or endless, summarizing all 6 poems)
   Reading good books at a *zitan* desk proffers much to savour.(This is because you like to read)
   Gazing at the moon in a *huali* bed transforms woes to vapour.(see "*connoisseurship*" plates p.191, *lu* is *huanghuali*. Alludes to your excellent *huanghuali* canopy bed)
   How enviable is lodging in wood delights!(You, the person in the Lodge of Wood Delights)

幽居好木趣美絕倫
葉紮紫貍斑呈鬼面昧
園流水映行雲造化
有奇文

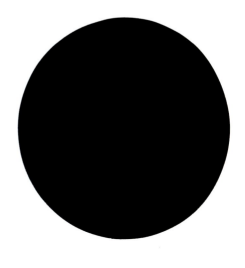

Lodged in tranquility is the best.

So is ravished by wood with grain sublime.

In this bench, spotted raccoons like mystic masks lurk.

In that bed, sprawling rivulets like streaky clouds gird.

How Nature leaves its heavenly marks!

出居好木趣妙難言
簡之簡成無可簡繁
偏繁到不能繁哲匠
我驚歎

Lodged in tranquility is the best.
So is ravished by wood of great design.
In the simple, simplicity in its sleekest is celebrated.
In the florid, floridity in its richest is manifested.
How craftsmen drive their lively minds!

幽居好木趣在摩抄
撫去凝脂疑處子揥
來紫混想春波長畫
易消磨

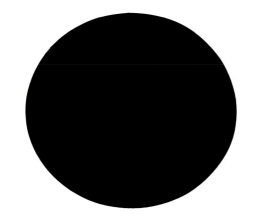

Lodged in tranquility is the best.
So is ravished by wood with a touch defined.
The satin brings to mind the jade cheek of a fair maiden.
The creasy can be to a pond rippling in spring likened.
How long hours do fleetingly fly!

幽居好木趣賞神工
巧鬥寸材成卍亞透
雕尺幅走螭龍真個
太玲瓏

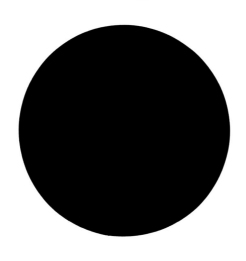

Lodged in tranquility is the best.
So is ravished by wood with carvings fine.
Dainty are Buddhist crosses no bigger than a fingernail.
Mighty are Chinese dragons in large openwork unveiled.
How adorable is artistry at its height!

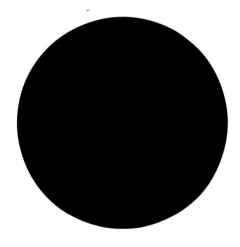

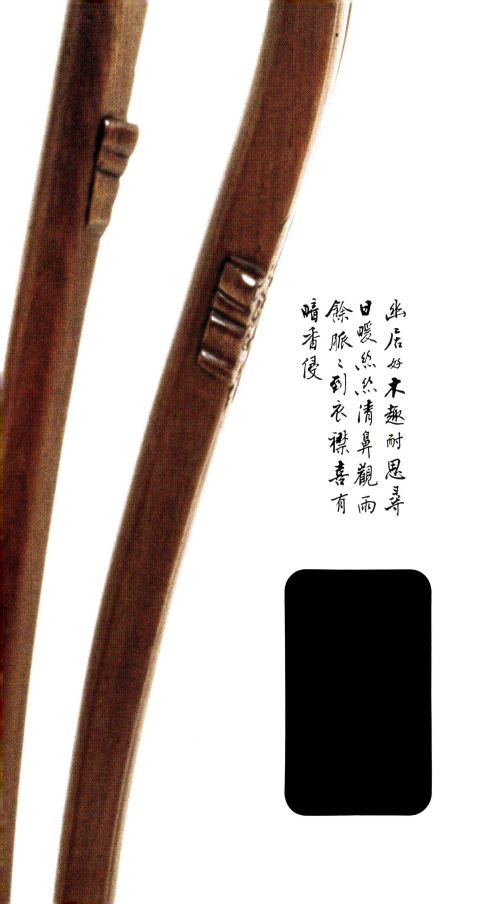

幽居好木趣耐思尋
日暖絲絲清鼻觀雨
餘脈脈到衣襟喜有
暗香侵

Lodged in tranquility is the best.
So is ravished by wood with aroma divine
That wafts to waken nostrils through air that sizzles;
Else lingers to perfume clothing on days that drizzle.
How pleasurable is a faintly fragranced life!

幽居好 木趣趣無根 檀几讀书真有味 榻床待月淨無塵 羡尔趣中人

Lodged in tranquility is the best.
So is ravished by wood till the end of time.
Reading good books at a zitan desk proffers much to savour.
Gazing at the moon in a huali bed transforms woes to vapour.
How enviable is lodging in wood delights!

图 录

香几

黄花梨五足三弯腿高圆香几 64
黄花梨四足叶纹八方高香几 70
黄花梨四足霸王枨马蹄足长方香几 74
紫檀木四足带底座长方香几 78

桌

紫檀木一腿三牙罗锅枨六仙方桌 86
黄花梨瓜棱腿霸王枨八仙方桌 90
黄花梨裹腿做高罗锅枨八仙方桌 94
黄花梨高罗锅枨霸王枨八仙方桌 98
黄花梨裹腿做直枨加矮老装卡子花半桌（成对） 102
黄花梨有束腰矮桌展腿式双龙纹半桌 106
黄花梨高束腰马蹄足霸王枨瘿木面小画桌 112
黄花梨无束腰马蹄足攒牙子琴桌 116
紫檀木壸门牙子霸王枨琴桌 120
黄花梨有束腰马蹄足壸门牙子罗锅枨条桌 126
黄花梨有束腰马蹄足卷纹角牙条桌 130
黄花梨有束腰马蹄足高罗枨画桌 134
黄花梨四面平马蹄足霸王枨条桌 138
黄花梨独板面霸王枨翘头桌 142
黄花梨三足月牙桌 148

案

黄花梨夹头榫小平头案 154
黄花梨夹头榫透锼卷云纹牙头瘿木面小画案 158
黄花梨夹头榫卷云纹牙头平头案 162
黄花梨夹头榫凤纹牙头瘿木面平头案 166
黄花梨夹头榫平头大画案 170
黄花梨夹头榫凤纹牙头长平头案 176
黄花梨夹头榫云纹牙头小翘头案 180
黄花梨活榫结构独板翘头案 184
黄花梨夹头榫带托子卍字纹独板翘头案 190

炕桌

黄花梨有束腰马蹄足小炕桌 196
黄花梨壸门牙子马蹄足小炕桌 198
黄花梨兽面虎爪梅枝纹炕桌 200
黄花梨壸门牙子叶纹卷球足炕桌 202

椅

黄花梨雕花圈椅（成对） 208
黄花梨攒靠背活屉圈椅（成对） 214
黄花梨高靠背四出头官帽椅 220
黄花梨素靠背雕花牙子四出头大官帽椅 224
黄花梨攒靠背凤凰麒麟龙纹四出头官帽椅（成对） 228
黄花梨方材高靠背四出头官帽椅（成对） 234
黄花梨高靠背四出头官帽椅（成对） 240
黄花梨素南官帽椅（成对） 246
黄花梨高靠背周制南官帽椅（成对） 250
黄花梨卡子花靠背玫瑰椅（成对） 256
黄花梨圈口靠背玫瑰椅四具成堂 260
黄花梨圆后背交椅 266

机凳

黄花梨有束腰雕龙纹三弯腿罗锅枨方凳（成对） 274
黄花梨有束腰马蹄足罗锅枨长方凳（成对） 278
黄花梨无束腰直足罗锅枨透雕牙条大方凳 280
黄花梨无束腰长方凳四张成堂 284
黄花梨四足带托泥圆凳（成对） 288
黄花梨有踏床交杌 290
黄花梨夹头榫卷云纹牙头带托子二人凳 294

脚踏

黄花梨有束腰三弯腿石面脚踏 300
黄花梨四面平马蹄足脚踏 302
黄花梨有束腰马蹄足脚踏（成对） 306
黄花梨案形井字面脚踏 310
黄花梨有束腰马蹄足滚凳脚踏 314

箱、橱、柜格

黄花梨衣箱 320
黄花梨大衣箱（成对）.................................. 324
黄花梨凤纹顶箱柜 328
黄花梨扛箱式带抽屉柜 332
黄花梨两开门扛箱式柜 336
黄花梨三层全敞带抽屉大架格 340
黄花梨大方角柜（成对）.............................. 344
黄花梨瘿木木轴门圆角柜（成对）.............. 350
黄花梨甜瓜棱木轴门圆角柜 354
黄花梨有柜膛方材大木轴门柜（成对）...... 358

床榻

黄花梨高束腰外翻马蹄足翘头榻 366
黄花梨有束腰马蹄足螭纹榻 370
黄花梨五屏风攒边装理石围子罗汉床 374
黄花梨三屏风攒接正卍字式围子卷球足罗汉床 .. 380
黄花梨四柱海棠十字纹架子床 384
黄花梨六柱透雕攒斗瑞兽凤鸟螭纹架子床 .. 390
黄花梨拔步床 398

其他

黄花梨六足高面盆架 408
黄花梨灵芝纹衣架 412
黄花梨升降式灯台（成对）.......................... 418
黄花梨折叠式琴架 422
黄花梨有束腰马蹄足矮火盆架 426
黄花梨嵌寿山石人物瑞兽图十二扇围屏 428

案头家具

黄花梨雕花卉笔筒 439
黄花梨葵瓣式笔筒 440
黄花梨素笔筒 441
紫檀葵瓣式嵌银笔筒 442
紫檀方形嵌银笔筒 443
紫檀雕花卉笔筒 444
紫檀方形笔筒 446
瘿木笔筒 447
黄花梨微型翘头案 448
黄花梨围棋子盒（成对）.............................. 450
黄花梨折叠棋盘 452
黄花梨三撞提盒 456
紫檀四撞提盒 458
黄花梨螭龙云纹折叠式镜架 462
黄花梨折叠式镜架 464
紫檀龙纹折叠式镜架 466
黄花梨宝座式镜台 468
紫檀官皮箱 470
黄花梨茶壶桶 474
黄花梨四足三弯腿圆盘几 476
黄花梨螺钿花盆 478
黄花梨鹌鹑笼箱 480
紫檀小箱 484
黄花梨小箱 486
黄花梨方箱 488
黄花梨带抽屉箱 490
黄花梨长箱 492
黄花梨画箱 494
黄花梨圆盒 496
紫檀轿箱 498
黄花梨天平架 500
黄花梨神龛 502
黄花梨理石大案屏 504

Catalogue

Incense stands
- Five-legged tall round incense stand 66
- Octagonal incense stand 72
- S-brace incense stand 76
- Rectangular incense stand 80

Zhuo Tables
- Yitui Sanya six-immortals table 88
- Lobed-shaped legs S-brace eight-immortals table... 92
- Bamboo style eight-immortals table 96
- Large eight-immortals table 100
- Pair of banzhuo side tables 104
- Carved dragon banzhuo table 108
- High-waist small painting table 114
- Open-work apron lute table 118
- Lute table...124
- Zhuo side table...................................128
- C-scroll spandrel table..............................132
- Painting table.....................................136
- Simianping long side table............................140
- Plank top qiaotou zhuo table.......................144
- Half-moon table....................................150

An tables
- Small pingtouan side table 156
- Small painting table 160
- Cloud-shaped spandrel pingtouan table........164
- Phoenix-spandrel pingtouan table..................168
- Large painting table 174
- Phoenix-spandrel large pingtouan table......178
- Small everted-end qiaotouan table 182
- Dismountable everted-end qiaotouan table ...186
- Plank top wan 卍 pattern everted-end qiaotouan table 192

Kang tables
- Small kang table with straight aprons 197
- Small kang table...199
- Kang table..201
- Kang table with ball feet.............................. 204

Chairs
- Pair of horseshoe armchairs...........................210
- Pair of horseshoe armchairs with removable seats 216
- High yoke back armchair 222
- Meditation chair..226
- Pair of carved phoenix and qilin yoke back armchairs 230
- Pair of square member high yoke back armchairs...236
- Pair of high yoke back armchairs 242
- Pair of continuous yoke back armchairs........248
- Pair of inlaid continuous yoke back armchairs 252
- Pair of rose chairs with inset struts and aprons 258
- Set of four rose chairs with inset aprons....262
- Folding horseshoe armchair 270

Stools
- Pair of carved square stools 276
- Pair of large rectangular stools 279
- Pair of large square stools 282
- Set of four rectangular stools 286
- Pair of round stools 289
- Folding stool 292
- Recessed-leg bench 296

Footstools

Footstool	301
Simianping footstool	304
Pair of footstools	308
Recessed-leg footstool	312
Massage stool & footrest	316

Chests, Shelves & Cabinets

Clothes Chest	322
Pair of large clothes chests	326
Phoenix-motif cabinet	330
Carry-type cabinet with drawers	334
Carry-type cabinet	338
Large bookcase	342
Pair of square-corner cabinets	346
Pair of sloping-stile wood-hinged cabinets	352
Sloping-stile wood-hinged cabinet	356
Pair of large sloping-stile wood-hinged cabinets	360

Beds

High waist daybed with everted ends	368
Daybed	372
Couch bed *luohan chuang* with marble panels	376
Couch bed *luohan chuang*	382
Four-post canopy bed	386
Six-post canopy bed	392
Alcove bed	402

Others

Tall basin stand	410
Clothes rack	414
Pair of lampstands	420
Musical instrument stand	424
Low brazier stand	427
Twelve-leaf folding screen	430

Table top furniture

Huanghuali carved brushpot	439
Huanghuali lobe-shaped brushpot	440
Huanghuali plain brushpot	441
Zitan lobe-shaped brushpot with silver inlay	442
Zitan square brushpot with silver inlay	443
Zitan carved brushpot	444
Zitan square brushpot	446
Burlwood brushpot	447
Huanghuali miniature *qiaotouan* table	449
Huanghuali pair of *weiqi* counter containers	451
Huanghuali folding game board	453
Huanghuali three-tier carry box	457
Zitan four-tier carry box	459
Huanghuali carved *chi*-dragon folding mirror stand	463
Huanghuali folding mirror stand	465
Zitan carved dragon folding mirror stand	467
Huanghuali throne-form mirror stand	468
Zitan table cabinet	472
Huanghuali teapot holder	475
Huanghuali Cabriole-leg round tray	477
Huanghuali mother-of-pearl inlaid flowerpot	479
Huanghuali quail cage	481
Zitan small box	485
Huanghuali small box	487
Huanghuali square box	489
Huanghuali box with drawers	491
Huanghuali long box	493
Huanghuali scroll box	495
Huanghuali round box	497
Zitan sedan chair box	499
Huanghuali balance stand	501
Huanghuali shrine	503
Huanghuali dali-marble table screen	505

香几

INCENSE
STANDS

黄花梨五足三弯腿高圆香几

晚明（1573–1644）

- 面径 38.2 厘米　腹径 49.5 厘米
- 托泥径 38.2 厘米　高 106 厘米

几面圆边框用楔钉榫五接，装独板活动心板，下安一根可装可卸的托带嵌入边框支承。几面冰盘沿自中部向下内缩至底起一窄边线。高束腰五接，混面圆润饱满，五个椭圆形开光内浮雕凤鸟纹，上连如屋檐状冰盘的几面，下接如台阶式起三道线脚的托腮。壸门轮廓牙子起线雕卷叶纹，以插肩榫造法与弯弧优雅的蜻蜓腿足结合。修长腿足顺势向外彭出，中部两侧突出雕攀龙纹，后婉转内收，至足端外卷成球终结，上翻花叶，足底承以一木连做的圆球，以榫卯插入带小足的托泥。圆形托泥以楔钉榫分五段相接，起三道阳线，最下线脚延续至小马蹄足。

传世黄花梨木制明代高圆香几屈指可数，异常珍稀。

此具五足圆香几含可装可卸活动心板，盖上心板时放置香炉、花樽或美石。卸下心板与托带，又让大花瓶安卧其中（看元末明初杂剧《玉壶春》插图）。到目前为止，传世黄花梨木制香几中，尚数孤例。

来源

北京大学工学院、北京工业建筑设计院杨耀教授 1978 前

香港 简氏兄弟贸易公司 1988

香港嘉木堂 1988

美国加州中国古典家具博物馆 1989–1993

出版

陈增弼《明式家具的功能与造型》，《文物》1981 年 3 月，北京，页 86

王世襄《明式家具研究》图版卷，香港，1989，页 74

Journal of the Classical Chinese Furniture Society, Winter 1990, Renaissance, California. 《中国古典家具学会季刊》1990 冬季刊，加州文艺复兴镇，封面

Grace Wu Bruce, "Sculptures To Use", *First Under Heaven: The Art of Asia*, London, 1997. 伍嘉恩《实用雕塑》，《天下第一：亚洲艺术》，伦敦，1997，页 82

Sarah Handler, *Austere Luminosity of Chinese Classical Furniture*, Berkeley, Los Angeles and London, 2001. 萨拉·汉德娜《中国古典家具的简朴光芒》伯克利，洛杉矶，伦敦，2001，页 299

伍嘉恩《明式家具二十年经眼录》北京，2010，页 20-21

《玉壶春》
Yu Hu Chun
The Romance of Yuhu

《北宋志传》
Bei Song Zhi Zhuan
Stories of the Northern Song

Five-legged tall round incense stand

Huanghuali wood
Late Ming (1573-1644)
Diameter top 38.2 cm (15 ¹⁵⁄₁₆″)   Chest 49.5 cm (19 ½″)
Base 38.2 cm (15 ¹⁵⁄₁₆″)   Height 106 cm (41 ¾″)

The top frame is of five sections, held together by pressure-pegged scarf joints with a single board centre panel, supported by an underneath brace resting on ledges in the frame members. Both the centre panel and support brace are removable. The edge of the frame moulds downwards from about half way down and again to end in a narrow banded edge. The high waist, comprised of five rounded members with oval-shaped medallions carved with stylised phoenix, join the eaves-like top and the terrace-like ridge with three-stepped mouldings below. The beaded-edged curvilinear-shaped aprons with stylised scrolling tendrils are mortised, tenoned and half-lapped on to the beautifully shaped legs which curve outwards and return to end in outward flaring knobs topped with openwork leaves, standing on ball pads which are made of one piece of wood as the legs. Each leg is carved with two stylised climbing dragons in mid section. At the bottom, the ball pads are tenoned into the circular base made in five sections, with pressure-pegged scarf joints, supported by five small feet. There are three line mouldings on the base, the bottom one extending down to the sides of the small hoof feet.

Extant examples of tall round stands made in *huanghuali* wood are extremely rare, with less than a handful known examples.

The present piece has a removable top panel which when in place serves as a stand for, an incense burner, a flower vase or a rock sculpture. When removed, a flower vase might be safely housed in the opening, as depicted in the illustration to the late Yuan early Ming drama, The Romance of *Yuhu*. In published *huanghuali* wood examples to date, this is unique.

Provenance

Yang Yao, professor, College of Engineering, Peking University, Beijing Industrial Architechture Designing and Researching Institute, before 1978

Kan & Brothers Tradings Co., Hong Kong, 1988

Grace Wu Bruce, Hong Kong, 1988

Museum of Classical Chinese Furniture, California, 1989-1993

Published

Chen Zengbi, *Mingshi Jiaju de Gongneng yu Zaoxing* (Functions and Styles of Ming Furniture), *Wenwu* (Cultural Relics), March 1981, Beijing, p. 86

Wang Shixiang, *Connoisseurship of Chinese Furniture: Ming and Early Qing Dynasties*, Vol. II: Plates, Hong Kong, 1990, p.74

Journal of the Classical Chinese Furniture Society, Winter 1990, Renaissance, California, Cover

Grace Wu Bruce, "Sculptures To Use", *First Under Heaven: The Art of Asia*, London, 1997, p. 82

Sarah Handler, *Austere Luminosity of Chinese Classical Furniture*, Berkeley, Los Angeles and London, 2001, p.299

Grace Wu Bruce, *Two Decades of Ming Furniture*, Beijing, 2010, pp. 20-21

椭圆形开光内浮雕凤鸟纹
oval-shaped medallions carved with stylised phoenix

壶门轮廓牙子起线雕卷叶纹
curvilinear-shaped aprons with stylised scrolling tendrils

腿足中部两侧突出雕攀龙纹
The leg is carved with two stylised climbing dragons in mid section

腿足婉转内收,至足端外卷成球终结,上翻花叶,足底承以一木连做的圆球,以榫卯插入带小足的托泥;圆形托泥以楔钉榫分五段相接,起三道阳线,最下线脚延续至小马蹄足

The legs curve outwards and return to end in outward flaring knobs topped with openwork leaves, standing on ball pads which are made of one piece of wood as the legs, the ball pads are tenoned into the circular base made in five sections, with pressure-pegged scarf joints, supported by five small feet. There are three line mouldings on the base, the bottom one extending down to the sides of the small hoof feet

几面冰盘沿自中部向下内缩至底起一窄边线;混面高束腰圆润饱满,上连如屋檐状冰盘的几面,下接如台阶式起三道线脚的托腮;壶门轮廓牙子起线雕卷叶纹,以插肩榫造法与蜻蜓腿足结合

The edge of the frame moulds downwards from about half way down and again to end in a narrow banded edge. Rounded members of the high waist join the eaves-like top and the terrace-like ridge with three-stepped mouldings below. The beaded-edged curvilinear-shaped aprons with stylised scrolling tendrils are mortised, tenoned and half-lapped on to beautifully shaped legs

几面圆边框用楔钉榫五接,装独板活动心板,下安一根可装可卸的托带嵌入边框支承

The top frame of five sections, held together by pressure-pegged scarf joints with a single board centre panel, supported by an underneath brace resting on ledges in the frame members
Both centre panel and support brace are removable

黄花梨四足叶纹八方高香几

晚明（1573–1644）

- 长 50.5 厘米　宽 37.7 厘米
- 高 103.3 厘米

八方几面攒边打槽平镶独板面心，下装一根穿带出梢支承。框面冰盘沿上部平直，自中上部下敛至底压窄平线。束腰与沿边起皮条线的叶形牙子一木连做，互相衔接，并向上与边框结合。四根修长的方材三弯腿足弧形舒敛有致，于底向外微翻出蹄足，足底出榫纳入带有小足支承于四角的微弧形长方托泥。

此香几造型独特，与前属王世襄先生收藏（王世襄 1985，页130），现归上海博物馆的高香几造型完全一样。原来是一对。

来源

香港敏求精舍成员钟华培先生 1990 – 1997

展览

香港、1994、"家具中的家具—明式家具私人珍藏精选"，香港嘉木堂

香港、1995、"敏求精舍三十五周年纪念展"，香港艺术馆

出版

香港艺术馆《好古敏求 敏求精舍三十五周年纪念展》香港，1995，页 281

R.P. Piccus, Conference and Exhibition Review, *Orientations*, February, 1995, Hong Kong. 毕格史《会议展览评论》，《东方艺术杂志》1995 年 2 月，香港，页 69

伍嘉恩《明式家具二十年经眼录》北京，2010，页 18-19

上海博物馆藏品 Shanghai Museum collection

Octagonal incense stand

Huanghuali wood
Late Ming (1573-1644)
Width 50.5 cm (19 ⅞″)   Depth 37.7 cm (14 ⅞″)
Height 103.3 cm (40 ⅝″)

The top is of frame construction with a single board flush, tongue-and-grooved floating panel supported by one dovetailed transverse stretcher below. The edge of the frame moulds downwards and inwards from about one third way down and then again to end in a very narrow flat band. The waist and the beaded-edged leaf-shaped aprons are made of one piece of wood. The four rectangular legs are shaped in a graceful curve to end in small outward hoofs which are tenoned to the slightly curved, rectangular base stretchers, with four small feet at the corners.

The shape of this incense stand is very unusual. It is identical to the piece that was in the collection of Wang Shixiang (Wang 1986, p 130) now in the collection of the Shanghai Museum, China. They were made as a pair.

Provenance

Hong Kong Min Chiu Society member Chung Wah Pui collection, 1990 - 1997

Exhibited

Hong Kong, 1994, "Best of the best - an exhibition of Ming furniture from private collections", Grace Wu Bruce Co Ltd

Hong Kong, 1995, "In Pursuit of Antiquities: Thirty-fifth Anniversary Exhibition of the Min Chiu Society", Hong Kong Museum of Art

Published

Hong Kong Museum of Art, *In Pursuit of Antiquities: Thirty-fifth Anniversary Exhibition of the Min Chiu Society*, Hong Kong, 1995, p. 281

R.P. Piccus, Conference and Exhibition Review, *Orientations*, February 1995, Hong Kong, p. 69

Grace Wu Bruce, *Two Decades of Ming Furniture*, Beijing, 2010, pp. 18-19

八方几面攒边打槽平镶独板面心

The top is of frame construction with a single board flush, tongue-and-grooved floating panel

束腰与沿边起皮条线的叶形牙子一木连做，互相衔接，并向上与边框结合

The waist and the beaded-edged leaf-shaped aprons are made of one piece of wood

黄花梨四足霸王枨马蹄足长方香几

晚明（1573–1644）
- 长 67 厘米　宽 39.1 厘米
- 高 82.6 厘米

几面以标准格角榫攒边框，平镶四角成圆弧形的独板面心，下装两根穿带出梢支承。抹头可见透榫。边抹立面上端平直后向下逐渐内缩至底压打洼儿的阳线。束腰与起边线的直牙条为一木连做，以抱肩榫与腿足、几面结合，腿足顶端出双榫纳入几面边框底部，下展至底以造型美好的马蹄足结束。牙条边线延至腿足一气呵成。腿足自肩部凿出一道凌厉的委角线，一路直落至马蹄足。四根菱形霸王枨下端以榫卯纳入四足，上端承托面板下穿带，用销钉固定。几面下原来的漆灰、糊织物与漆裹保存近乎完整。

此香几四腿向外微张，腿足肩部锼委角线，一路直落至马蹄足。挺拔干净利落。非常罕见。

来 源
香港嘉木堂 1990

出 版
从未发表

腿足自肩部凿出一道凌厉的委角线，一路直落至马蹄足

Wojiao grooved mouldings are cut into the corners of the legs, extending from the shoulders down to the hoof feet, highlighting the strong, clean line of the piece

S-brace incense stand

Huanghuali wood
Late Ming (1573-1644)
Width 67 cm (26 ⅜")   Depth 39.1 cm (15 ⅜")
Height 82.6 cm (32 ⁹⁄₁₆")

The top is of standard mitre, mortise and tenon frame construction with a single board, round-cornered, tongue-and-grooved, flush floating panel supported by two dovetailed transverse stretchers underneath. There are exposed tenons on the short sides of the frame top. The edge of the frame top begins in a flat surface, then moulds gently inwards and downwards to end in a grooved banded edge. The recessed waist and the beaded-edged straight apron, made of one piece of wood, is half-lapped, mortised and tenoned into the legs which are double-lock tenoned into the top and end in exquisitely drawn hoof feet. The beaded edges continue from the aprons down the legs. *Wojiao* grooved mouldings are cut into the corners of the legs, extending from the shoulders down to the hoof feet. Four square section S-braces are mortised and tenoned into the legs on one end and on the other, attached to the transverse stretchers underneath the top, secured by wood pins. The original clay, ramie and lacquer undercoating is almost completely intact.

The four legs of this stand slope gently outward in an almost imperceptible splay and there are *wojiao* grooved mouldings cut into the corners of the legs starting at the shoulders extending down to the hoof feet, highlighting the strong, clean line of the piece, very rare features.

Provenance

Grace Wu Bruce, Hong Kong, 1990

Published

Never published

几面以标准格角榫攒边框，平镶四角成圆弧形的独板面心

The top of standard mitre, mortise and tenon frame construction with a single board, round-cornered, tongue-and-grooved, flush floating panel

四根菱形霸王枨下端以榫卯纳入四足,上端承托面板下穿带,用销钉固定

Four square section S-braces are mortised and tenoned into the legs on one end and on the other, attached to the transverse stretchers underneath the top, secured by wood pins

几面下原来的漆灰、糊织物与漆裹

The original clay, ramie and lacquer undercoating

紫檀木四足带底座长方香几

晚明（1573–1644）

- 长 82 厘米　宽 38 厘米
- 高 84 厘米

此几比例协调匀称，几面为标准格角榫攒边框平镶独板瘿木面心，下装三根穿带出梢支承。独板面心采用的楠木瘿呈现其独特的葡萄纹。边抹冰盘沿立面上部平直，自中部下敛内缩至底起一边线。束腰与直素牙条以抱肩榫与腿足、几面结合。腿足顶端出双榫纳入几面边框底部，下展至底收成马蹄足。足底以榫卯与黄花梨底座接合，出透榫。底座以标准格角榫攒边框落堂装独板面心，抹头出透榫，下装两根穿带出梢支承。几面底部原来的漆灰、糊织物与漆裹尚存痕迹。

明式家具带托泥或底座的多为香几香案。托泥中镶心板成底座，传世香几中比带托泥的更罕见。紫檀木造明式家具又是黄花梨木造的千分之一二。此几集比例完美与珍稀于一身，其重要性可想而知。

来源

香港嘉木堂 1987

此具香几是嘉木堂 1987 年在香港中环毕打行开业首轮陈设之一（见页 83），上置灵璧赏石。

出版

Grace Wu Bruce, "Classic Chinese Furniture in Tzu-Tan Wood", *Arts of Asia*, November-December 1991, Hong Kong. 伍嘉恩《紫檀木造古典中国家具》,《亚洲艺术》1991 年 11-12 月，香港，页 144

伍嘉恩《中国古典紫檀家具—几件明及清初实例及其纵横探讨》,《中国古典家具研究会会刊》十二，1992 年 11 月，北京，页 45

伍嘉恩《从几件实例探讨中国古典紫檀家具》,《文物天地》第 213 期，中国文物报社，北京，2009 年 3 月，页 88

几面为标准格角榫攒边框平镶独板瘿木面心，独板面心采用的楠木瘿呈现其独特的葡萄纹

The frame top is of standard mitre, mortise and tenon construction with a single board burl wood, flush, tongue-and-grooved floating panel. The burl wood top is that of *nanmu*, a Chinese cedar, characterised by its grape-seed pattern

Rectangular incense stand

Zitan, burl and *huanghuali* wood
Late Ming (1573-1644)
Width 82 cm (32 ¼")   Depth 38 cm (14 15⁄16")
Height 84 cm (33 1⁄16")

This *zitan* stand is of almost perfect proportions. The frame top is of standard mitre, mortise and tenon construction with a single board burl wood, flush, tongue-and-grooved floating panel supported by three dovetailed transverse braces underneath. The burl wood top is that of *nanmu*, a Chinese cedar, characterised by its grape-seed pattern. The frame moulds gently downwards and inwards from about half way down and ends in a beaded edge. The recessed waist and the plain straight apron are half-lapped, mortised and tenoned into the legs which are double-lock tenoned to the top and end in beautifully drawn hoof feet. The feet are mortised and tenoned into a *huanghuali* wood base, the tenons exposed. The wood base of standard mitre, mortise and tenon frame construction, with an inset single board, tongue-and-grooved floating panel is supported by two dovetailed transverse stretchers underneath. There are exposed tenons on the short sides. Traces of ramie, clay and lacquer coating are on the underside.

Stands and small tables with floor stretchers, as well as base stands like the present piece, are usually incense stands or incense tables. Those with base stands are rarer than those with base stretchers in surviving examples dated to the classical period. In addition, Ming furniture made in *zitan* wood is not even point one or two percent of that made in *huanghuali* wood. This elegant stand is perfect in proportions and extremely rare, an important piece.

Provenance

GRACE WU BRUCE, Hong Kong, 1987

This piece was among the first display at the Grace Wu Bruce gallery when it commenced business in 1987 in Pedder Building, Hong Kong. A *lingbi* rock was placed on the stand. (see p. 83)

Published

Grace Wu Bruce, Classic Chinese Furniture in Tzu-Tan Wood, *Arts of Asia*, November-December 1991, Hong Kong, p.144

Grace Wu Bruce, *Zhongguo Gudian Zitan Jiaju - Jijian Ming ji Qing Chu Shili jiqi Zongheng Tantao* (Chinese Classic furniture in Zitan - Some Ming and Early Qing Examples and Their Exploration), *Zhongguo Gudian Jiaju Yanjiuhui Huikan* (Journal of the Association of Chinese Classical Furniture), No. 12, November 1992, Beijing, p.45

Grace Wu Bruce, *Cong Jijian Shili Tantao Zhongguo Gudian Zitan Jiaju* (Some Examples of Chinese Classic furniture in Zitan Wood and Their Study), *Cultural Relics World*, issue 213, Zhongguo Wenwu Baoshe, Beijing, March 2009, p. 88

几面下装三根穿带出梢支承；束腰与直素牙条以抱肩榫与腿足、几面结合，腿足顶端出双榫纳入几面边框底部；几面底部原来的漆灰、糊织物与漆裹尚存痕迹

The top is supported by three dovetailed transverse braces underneath. The recessed waist and the plain straight apron are half-lapped, mortised and tenoned into the legs which are double-lock tenoned to the top. There are traces of ramie, clay and lacquer coating on the underside

足底以榫卯与黄花梨底座接合，出透榫；底座以标准格角榫攒边框落堂装独板面心，下装两根穿带出梢支承

The feet are mortised and tenoned into a *huanghuali* wood base, the tenons exposed. The wood base of standard mitre, mortise and tenon frame construction, with an inset single board, tongue-and-grooved floating panel is supported by two dovetailed transverse stretchers underneath

嘉木堂1987年在香港中环毕打行开业首轮陈设
香几在其中，上置灵璧赏石

The first display at the Grace Wu Bruce gallery when it commenced business in 1987 in Pedder Building, Hong Kong
The incense stand was among the display, with a *lingbi* rock placed on it

桌

Zhuo
Tables

紫檀木一腿三牙罗锅枨六仙方桌

晚明（1573–1644）

- 长 85.3 厘米　宽 85 厘米
- 高 82.5 厘米

此桌为一腿三牙设计，桌面以标准格角榫攒边打槽平镶八拼面心板。下装两根穿带出梢支承，另加一根双十字形加强支撑力。抹头可见透榫。边抹线脚自中上部向下内缩，底加起阳线的垛边。圆材腿足内缩起侧脚，上以双榫纳入桌面。腿足间装有带牙头的牙条，其下安黄花梨高罗锅枨。罗锅枨接圆腿处，加销钉。内缩腿足与桌角相接处各安有一角牙。

此件体积不大的紫檀木六仙方桌面心板，竟以八块木拼成。紫檀木在明代的缺乏，可见一斑。

制于明代的紫檀家具相当稀少，比率不到黄花梨木制的千分之一二。此桌属典型明朝方桌设计，用紫檀配黄花梨，非常独特。

来源

香港嘉木堂 1994

比利时 布鲁塞尔 侣明室 1995-2005

展览

巴黎，2003，吉美国立亚洲艺术博物馆"明·中国家具的黄金时期"

出版

Grace Wu Bruce, *Living with Ming – the Lu Ming Shi Collection*, Hong Kong, 2000. 伍嘉恩《侣明室家具图集》香港，2000，页 140-141

Musée national des Arts asiatiques – Guimet, *Ming: l'Âge d'or du mobilier chinois. The Golden Age of Chinese Furniture*, Paris, 2003. 吉美国立亚洲艺术博物馆《明·中国家具的黄金时期》巴黎，2003，页 174-175

伍嘉恩《明式家具二十年经眼录之四 桌类》，《紫禁城》第 166 期，2008 年 11 月，北京，页 119

边抹线脚自中上部向下内缩，底加起阳线的垛边；圆材腿足内缩起侧脚，上以双榫纳入桌面；腿足间装有带牙头的牙条，其下安黄花梨高罗锅枨；罗锅枨接圆腿处，加销钉；内缩腿足与桌角相接处各安有一角牙

The edge of the frame moulds inwards and downwards from about one third way down and ends in an added strip with beading called *duobian*. The four round legs, recessed from the corners, splayed outwards, are double tenoned to the top. They are joined by a shaped, spandrelled apron and a hump-back shaped *huanghuali* stretcher below. There are wing-shaped spandrels at the corners where the recessed legs meet the top

《叮花魁》
Zhan Huakui
Tale of the Popular Courtesan

Yitui Sanya six-immortals table

Zitan and *huanghuali* wood
Late Ming (1573-1644)
Width 85.3 cm (33 9/16")   Depth 85 cm (33 7/16")
Height 82.5 cm (32 ½")

Of the design called *yitui sanya*, three apron-spandrel to one leg, the top is of standard mitre, mortise and tenon, flush tongue-and-grooved eight-board floating panel construction supported by two dovetailed stretchers underneath. There is an additional cross brace for further support. There are exposed tenons on the short sides of the frame top. The edge of the frame moulds inwards and downwards from about one third way down and ends in an added strip with beading called *duobian*. The four round legs, recessed from the corners, splayed outwards, are double tenoned to the top. They are joined by a shaped, spandrelled apron and a hump-back shaped *huanghuali* stretcher below. There are wing-shaped spandrels at the corners where the recessed legs meet the top.

This medium size *zitan* table requiring a composite of eight panels for its table top attests to the scarce supply of *zitan* wood during the Ming period.

Zitan furniture dated to the Ming dynasty is extremely rare, not even point one or two percent of those made in *huanghuali* wood. This piece in typical Ming square table design, is very unusual in that both *zitan* and *huanghuali* wood are used.

Provenance

Grace Wu Bruce, Hong Kong, 1994

The Lu Ming Shi Collection, Brussels, 1995 - 2005

Exhibited

Paris, 2003, Musée national des Arts asiatiques – Guimet, Ming: l'Âge d'or du mobilier chinois. The Golden Age of Chinese Furniture

Published

Grace Wu Bruce, *Living with Ming – the Lu Ming Shi Collection*, Hong Kong, 2000, pp. 140-141

Musée national des Arts asiatiques – Guimet, *Ming: l'Âge d'or du mobilier chinois. The Golden Age of Chinese Furniture*, Paris, 2003, pp. 174-175

Grace Wu Bruce, Two Decades of Ming Furniture Part IV: *Zhuo* tables, *Forbidden City*, issue 166, November 2008, Beijing, p. 119

桌面以标准格角榫攒边打槽平镶八拼面心板

The top is of standard mitre, mortise and tenon, flush tongue-and-grooved eight-board floating panel construction

桌面下装两根穿带出梢支承，另加一根双十字形加强支撑力

The top is supported by two dovetailed stretchers underneath. There is an additional cross brace for further support

黄花梨瓜棱腿霸王枨八仙方桌

晚明 (1573–1644)

- 长 94.3 厘米　宽 93.5 厘米
- 高 86.8 厘米

桌面标准格角榫攒边框，平镶取自一材的六拼面心，下装两根穿带加一根横贯托带交叉支承。抹头可见透榫。边抹立面自中部向下内缩至底压一窄边线。瓜棱腿线脚的腿足间安卷尾龙纹角牙的牙条。牙条下沿边起阳线。四根菱形霸王枨下以榫卯纳入四足，上交于桌面下两端的穿带，以销钉固定。桌底原来的漆灰、糊织物与漆裹保存近乎完整。

瓜棱腿线脚造工精细，不常见的卷尾龙纹造型俏丽。四根霸王枨在桌底划出弧形空间，凸显八仙方桌妍秀空灵。

六拼面心板，黄花梨桌案中不常见。细看下发现不但六拼板取自一材，连桌面边框，四腿足，四牙子等都属同一树材。是一木一器的制作。

来 源
| 香港嘉木堂 1988

出 版
| 从未发表

边抹立面自中部向下内缩至底压一窄边线；瓜棱腿线脚的腿足间安卷尾龙纹角牙的牙条；牙条下沿边起阳线

The edge of the frame moulds downwards from about half way down to end in a narrow flat band. The lobed-shaped legs carved with *gualeng* "melon ridge" mouldings, are fitted with aprons carved with stylised coiled dragons spandrels. There are raised beaded edges on the aprons

Lobed-shaped legs S-brace eight-immortals table

Huanghuali wood
Late Ming (1573-1644)
Width 94.3 cm (37 ⅛")   Depth 93.5 cm (36 ¹³⁄₁₆")
Height 86.8 cm (34 ³⁄₁₆")

The top is of standard mitre, mortise and tenon construction with a six-board floating panel tongue-and-grooved into the mitred frame, supported by two dovetailed transverse stretchers and an additional cross stretcher underneath. There are exposed tenons on the short sides of the frame top. The edge of the frame moulds downwards from about half way down to end in a narrow flat band. The lobed-shaped legs carved with *gualeng* "melon ridge" mouldings, are fitted with aprons carved with stylised coiled dragons spandrels. There are raised beaded edges on the aprons. Four square-section S-shaped braces are mortised and tenoned into the legs and lapped and wood-pinned to the stretchers at the ends of the underside of the table top. The original ramie, clay and lacquer undercoating are almost completely intact.

The lobe-shaped legs are finely carved with mouldings, the unusual shaped dragon spandrels beautifully rendered, and together with the S-braces that create a curved silhouette at the corners, they make this piece airy and gorgeous.

Huanghuali tables rarely have top panels with so many boards. Closer examination reveals that not only the six boards of the floating panels are cut from the same timber, so are the table top frame members, the four legs and the four aprons. In fact, the whole table was made from timber cut from one tree.

Provenance

Grace Wu Bruce, Hong Kong, 1988

Published

Never published

桌面标准格角榫攒边框，平镶取自一材的六拼面心

The top is of standard mitre, mortise and tenon construction with a six-board floating panel tongue-and-grooved into the mitred frame

桌面下装两根穿带加一根横贯托带交叉支承；桌底原来的漆灰、糊织物与漆裹保存近乎完整

The top is supported by two dove-tailed transverse stretchers and an additional cross stretcher underneath. The original ramie, clay and lacquer undercoating are almost completely intact

四根菱形霸王枨下以榫卯纳入四足，上交于桌面下两端的穿带，以销钉固定

Four square-section S-shaped braces are mortised and tenoned into the legs and lapped and wood-pinned to the stretchers at the ends of the underside of the table top

黄花梨裹腿做高罗锅枨八仙方桌

晚明（1573–1644）

- 长 95.7 厘米　宽 95.9 厘米
- 高 85.1 厘米

桌面以标准格角榫造法攒边框，打槽平镶两拼面心板，大边侧窄条是远年复修。下装三根穿带出梢支承，两侧两根出透榫。抹头亦可见明榫。桌面边抹立面劈料做起双混面。下装形状相似的双混面垛边牙子。垛边紧贴桌面。其下四角安单混面角牙，与垛边相同，皆为裹腿做。罗锅枨亦是劈料做起双混面裹腿接合腿足，中部紧贴垛边。圆材腿足以长短榫纳入桌面。

竹制或藤编家具常见于宋朝（960 – 1279）与明朝（1368 – 1644）绘画中。裹腿做是从竹制与藤编家具得到启发，运用到硬木家具中。此八仙桌以裹腿做，平面通起混面，圆形腿足，整体予人感觉如竹制家具。此种以珍贵木材仿制一般到处可见的竹材或藤编家具，反映明代文人追求内敛的心态。

此特殊设计半桌也有采用。故宫博物院收藏一具（朱家溍 2002，页 110）。

来源
香港嘉木堂 1995

出版
Grace Wu Bruce, "Sculptures To Use", *First Under Heaven: The Art of Asia*, London, 1997. 伍嘉恩《实用雕塑》，《天下第一：亚洲艺术》伦敦，1997，页 72

桌面边抹立面劈料做起双混面。下装形状相似的双混面垛边牙子；垛边紧贴桌面。其下四角安单混面角牙，与垛边相同，皆为裹腿做；罗锅枨亦是劈料做起双混面裹腿接合腿足，中部紧贴垛边；圆材腿足以长短榫纳入桌面

The edge of the frame top is carved to look like two rounded stretchers joined together. The similarly carved members underneath the frame appear to be its continuation but are actually the aprons and below them, fitted at the four corners, are spandrels carved to look like a rounded stretcher. Both aprons and spandrels meet each other in a "wrap around the legs" join, *guotui*. The similarly carved double-rounded hump-back stretchers below also wrap around the legs to join with each other, their middle sections reach up to meet with the aprons. The round legs are double tenoned into the frame top

Bamboo style eight-immortals table

Huanghuali wood
Late Ming (1573-1644)
Width 95.7 cm (37 ⅝") Depth 95.9 cm (37 ¾")
Height 85.1 cm (33 ½")

The top of standard mitre, mortise and tenon construction with a flush, tongue-and-groove two-board floating panel supported by three dovetailed stretchers underneath, two with exposed tenons. The narrow strip on the edge of the frame is an old restoration. There are exposed tenons also on the short sides of the frame top. The edge of the frame top is carved to look like two rounded stretchers joined together. The similarly carved members underneath the frame appear to be its continuation but are actually the aprons and below them, fitted at the four corners, are spandrels carved to look like a rounded stretcher. Both aprons and spandrels meet each other in a "wrap around the legs" join, *guotui*. The similarly carved double-rounded hump-back stretchers below also wrap around the legs to join with each other, their middle sections reach up to meet with the aprons. The round legs are double tenoned into the frame top.

Bamboo or cane furniture were often depicted in Song (960-1279) and Ming (1368-1644) paintings. *Guotui* or "wrap around the legs" method of making furniture with precious hardwood was inspired by their bamboo counterparts. This table with its rounded surfaces and round legs was designed to portray a bamboo table. The usage of precious hardwood to simulate common material illustrates the sensibilities of understatement considered high form by the Ming elite.

Banzhuo side tables of this special design are also known, an example is in the collection of the Palace Museum. (Zhu 2002, p. 110)

Provenance

Grace Wu Bruce, Hong Kong, 1995

Published

Grace Wu Bruce, "Sculptures To Use", *First Under Heaven: The Art of Asia*, London, 1997, p. 72

桌面以标准格角榫造法攒边框，打槽平镶两拼面心板，大边侧窄条是远年复修

The top of standard mitre, mortise and tenon construction with a flush, tongue-and-groove two-board floating panel. The narrow strip on the edge of the frame is an old restoration

桌面下装三根穿带出梢支承

The top is supported by three dovetailed stretchers underneath

黄花梨高罗锅枨霸王枨八仙方桌

晚明（1573–1644）

- 长 98.2 厘米　宽 98.2 厘米
- 高 84 厘米

用料厚实，桌面以标准格角榫造法攒边框，打槽平镶三片取自一材的面心板，下装三根穿带出梢支承，另外加两根横托穿带交叉贯穿直枨，加强支撑力。边抹冰盘沿上舒下敛，自三分之一处内缩至底压一窄边线。微起混面的牙条以榫卯接入粗壮的圆材腿足，腿足上端以双榫纳入桌面边框。牙子下方栽入铁钉，贯穿达面框底部加固连结。罗锅枨子两端出榫结合腿足，中部向上延伸紧贴牙子。四根霸王枨以钩挂垫榫接入腿足和桌面下尽端穿带，以销钉固定。桌底原来的漆灰、糊织物与漆裹保存近乎完整。

此桌选料比其他相似体型的家具要厚重实在，因此呈现出沉稳有力的气势。

此具八仙方桌采用铁钉加固牙条与桌面边框底部的连结。在最标准的明式家具设计平头案中，牙子栽入铁钉加固的造法屡见不鲜。虽然只是某种类别，但传说中国家具不采用铁钉的说法是不正确的。

来　源
香港嘉木堂 1987

出　版
从未发表

边抹冰盘沿上舒下敛，自三分之一处内缩至底压一窄边线；微起混面的牙条以榫卯接入粗壮的圆材腿足，腿足上端以双榫纳入桌面边框；罗锅枨子两端出榫结合腿足，中部向上延伸紧贴牙子

The edge of the frame top moulds downwards and inwards from about one third way down and ends in a narrow flat band. The gently rounded apron is half-lapped, mortised and tenoned to the strong round legs which are double tenoned to the top. Mortised and tenoned to the legs are hump-back shaped stretchers, the middle part reaching up to meet with the aprons

Large eight-immortals table

Huanghuali wood
Late Ming (1573-1644)
Width 98.2 cm (38 ¹¹⁄₁₆″)   Depth 98.2 cm (38 ¹¹⁄₁₆″)
Height 84 cm (33 ¹⁄₁₆″)

Of substantial material, the top of standard mitred, mortised and tenoned frame construction has a three matched board tongue-and-grooved, flush floating panel supported by three dovetailed transverse braces underneath. Two additional stretchers are tenoned through the transverse braces to the frame for further support. The edge of the frame top moulds downwards and inwards from about one third way down and ends in a narrow flat band. The gently rounded apron is half-lapped, mortised and tenoned to the strong round legs which are double tenoned to the top. Metal nails are applied to the undersides of the apron to further secure them to the frame top. Mortised and tenoned to the legs are hump-back shaped stretchers, the middle part reaching up to meet with the aprons. There are four S-shaped braces tenoned to the legs in a hook and pegged joint and pinned to the outside transverse braces underneath the top for further support. The original clay, ramie and lacquer undercoating is almost completely intact.

This table has members that are more substantial than other pieces of its size and exerts a strong powerful presence.

The aprons of this table are further secured to the top with metal nails. The usage of metal nails to further secure aprons to the frame tops of tables are found often on the most typical Ming design of recessed-leg *ping-touan* tables. While nails were sparingly used in other types of classical furniture, the conventional wisdom that no nails were ever used is erroneous.

Provenance
Grace Wu Bruce, Hong Kong, 1987

Published
Never published

桌面以标准格角榫造法攒边框，打槽平镶三片取自一材的面心板

The top of standard mitred, mortised and tenoned frame construction has a three matched board tongue-and-grooved, flush floating panel

桌面下装三根穿带出梢支承，另外加两根横托穿带交叉贯穿直枨，加强支撑力；牙子下方载入铁钉，贯穿达面框底部加固连结；桌底原来的漆灰、糊织物与漆裹保存近乎完整

The top is supported by three dovetailed transverse braces underneath. Two additional stretchers are tenoned through the transverse braces to the frame for further support. Metal nails are applied to the undersides of the apron to further secure them to the frame top; The original clay, ramie and lacquer undercoating is almost completely intact

罗锅枨子两端出榫结合腿足，中部向上延伸紧贴牙子；四根霸王枨以钩挂垫榫接入腿足和桌面下尽端穿带，以销钉固定

Mortised and tenoned to the legs are hump-back shaped stretchers, the middle part reaching up to meet with the aprons. There are four S-shaped braces tenoned to the legs in a hook and pegged joint and pinned to the outside transverse braces underneath the top for further support

黄花梨裹腿做直帐加矮老装卡子花半桌（成对）

晚明（1573–1644）

- 长 105 厘米　宽 52.4 厘米
- 高 88.4 厘米

桌面以标准格角榫造法攒边，打槽平镶木纹生动对称，取自一材的两拼面心板，下装三根穿带出梢支承，两根出透榫。抹头亦可见明榫。桌面边抹冰盘沿上压平线后微起混面，下安同样起混面的牙条垛边。其下直帐也起混面。垛边与帐子均以裹腿榫卯互相接合。垛边与帐子之间栽入矮老，隔出长方形空间，装入海棠形卡子花。圆材腿足以双榫纳入桌面边框底部。

如前例，此对半桌之设计亦是自竹制与藤编家具得到启发，运用到硬木家具中。裹腿做，平面通起混面，圆形腿足，卡子花如用竹、藤拗弯成圈的装饰，都给人感觉如竹制家具。此种以珍贵木材仿制一般到处可见的竹材或藤编家具，反映明代文人追求内敛的心态。

成对的明代制作黄花梨桌案，传世品十分稀少。笔者所知不过十对实例。

来源
| 香港嘉木堂 1991

出版
| 从未发表

Pair of *banzhuo* side tables

Huanghuali wood
Late Ming (1573-1644)
Width 105 cm (41 ⅜")   Depth 52.4 cm (20 ⅝")
Height 88.4 cm (34 ¾")

The top is of standard mitre, mortise and tenon construction with a flush, tongue-and-grooved, beautifully grained matching two-board floating panel supported by three dovetailed transverse stretchers underneath, two with exposed tenons. There are also exposed tenons on the short sides of the frame top. The edge of the frame begins with a raised edge and curves to form a gently rounded shape. Below the frame, a carved rounded stretcher appears to be its continuation but is actually the apron. Similarly shaped stretchers are dovetailed into and wrap around the legs to meet up with each other, in the same manner as the aprons. Pillar-shaped struts divide the space between the apron and the stretcher into rectangular openings, inset with begonia-shaped struts. The round legs are double tenoned into the frame top.

This pair is another example influenced by bamboo or cane furniture design. *Guotui* or "wrap around the legs" method of making furniture with precious hardwood was inspired by their bamboo counterparts. This table with its rounded surfaces and round legs as well as the inset struts being shaped like bent bamboo strips was designed to portray a bamboo table. The usage of precious hardwood to simulate common material illustrates the sensibilities of understatement considered high form by the Ming elite.

Pairs of tables made in *huanghuali* wood datable to the Ming are very rare. This author knows of only less than ten examples.

Provenance

Grace Wu Bruce, Hong Kong, 1991

Published

Never published

桌面以标准格角榫造法攒边,打槽平镶木纹生动对称,取自一材的两拼面心板

The top is of standard mitre, mortise and tenon construction with a flush, tongue-and-grooved, beautifully grained matching two-board floating panel

桌面下装三根穿带出梢支承

The top is supported by three dovetailed transverse stretchers underneath

黄花梨有束腰矮桌展腿式双龙纹半桌

晚明（1573–1644）

- 长 105.1 厘米　宽 63.2 厘米
- 高 80 厘米

桌面周缘起拦水线，标准格角榫攒边框，打槽平镶一材两拼面心，下装三根穿带出梢支承，皆出透榫。抹头亦可见明榫。边抹冰盘沿上舒下敛，自中上部内缩至底压窄平线。沿边起线的壸门式牙条，高浮雕双龙及卷草纹，与束腰一木连做，以抱肩榫与腿足、桌面接合。牙子的阳线顺势伸延至腿足。腿足上截造成如炕桌三弯腿，肩部延续牙条上的雕饰，垂下花叶，意在模仿金属包角。下则为光素圆材直腿。牙条下方与桌脚间安两卷相抵角牙。

矮桌展腿式半桌，较常见的造型是在现例基础下加装霸王枨。角牙与霸王枨，又常满刻雕饰，十分繁缛。一般在足底下，更加安鼓墩形的足套，与素圆腿足格格不入。此半桌是矮桌展腿式一个较清丽的展示。

来　源
香港嘉木堂 1990

出　版
从未发表

腿足上截造成如炕桌三弯腿，肩部延续牙条上的雕饰，垂下花叶，意在模仿金属包角；牙条下方与桌脚间安两卷相抵角牙

The legs are modelled as the feet of *kang* tables at the top section, the shoulders with carved patterns continuing from the aprons simulating metal mounts. There are carved shaped spandrels of curls meeting up at the corners between the legs

Carved dragon *banzhuo* table

Huanghuali wood
Late Ming (1573-1644)
Width 105.1 cm (41 ⅜")   Depth 63.2 cm (24 ⅞")
Height 80 cm (31 ½")

The lip-edged top is of standard mitre, mortise, tenon frame construction with a flush, tongue-and-grooved, two-board floating panel cut from the same timber supported by three transverse dovetailed stretchers underneath, all with exposed tenons. There are also exposed tenons on the short sides of the frame top. The edge of the frame moulds downwards and inwards from about one third way down to end in a narrow flat band. The recessed waist and the beaded-edged curvilinear apron, made of one piece of wood, carved in high relief with confronting dragons amidst tendrils are mortised, tenoned and half-lapped onto the legs, which are modelled as the feet of *kang* tables at the top section, the shoulders with carved patterns continuing from the aprons simulating metal mounts, and then extend down as plain round legs to the floor. There are carved shaped spandrels of curls meeting up at the corners between the legs.

The more often encountered examples of this design featuring a *kang* table with extended legs are usually fitted with S-braces in addition to the corner spandrels, and all are often heavily carved with decorations. The plain round legs are also frequently capped at the foot with a bulbous base, not altogether harmonious. The present piece is a more elegant and refreshing rendering of this design.

Provenance

Grace Wu Bruce, Hong Kong, 1990

Published

Never published

桌面周缘起拦水线，标准格角榫攒边框，打槽平镶一材两拼面心

The lip-edged top is of standard mitre, mortise, tenon frame construction with a flush, tongue-and-grooved, two-board floating panel cut from the same timber

桌面下装三根穿带出梢支承

The top is supported by three transverse dovetailed stretchers underneath

格角榫攒边框，打槽平镶面心，下装穿带 拆装连环图
Mitre, mortise and tenon frame construction with floating panel and transverse dovetailed stretchers joinery details

抱肩榫拆装连环图

Baojiansun, mitre, mortise, tenon and half-lap joinery details

黄花梨高束腰马蹄足霸王枨瘿木面小画桌

晚明（1573–1644）

- 长 106.2 厘米　宽 66.8 厘米
- 高 80.7 厘米

桌面以标准格角榫攒边框镶独板瘿木面心，下装三根出梢穿带加一根横托带交叉支承。独板面心为楠木瘿，呈现其特有的葡萄纹。边抹立面上部平直，下部打洼槽。高束腰嵌入如小方柱的外露腿足上截与桌面下的槽口，直碰在弧面牙条上。牙条以榫卯与腿足结合，长边牙条内有穿销贯过高束腰至桌面边框用以加强稳固性。牙条下沿微向外翻成碗口线，其势延顺至腿足，下展为形状有力的马蹄足。四根方材霸王枨下以榫卯纳入四足，上交于桌面下两端的穿带，以销钉固定。桌底原来的漆灰、糊织物与漆裹保存良好。

高束腰结构与霸王枨皆为明朝家具基本设计。外翻的碗口线脚就较特殊，只见于少数制于苏州一带的传世品，特别是高束腰家具上。

此具画桌镶楠木瘿心板。多年所见，黄花梨造楠木瘿心板家具均为上品。唯瘿木质软，纹理多旋转，容易沿着纹理爆裂，所以传世瘿木心板多破裂残缺。保存完好的比率较黄花梨硬木心板面的例子低很多。倍觉珍稀。

来源
| 香港嘉木堂 1990

出版
| 从未发表

《鲁班经匠家镜》
Lu Ban Jing Jiang Jia Jing
The Classic of Lu Ban and the Craftman's Mirror

《金田盒》
Jindian He
Inlaid Gold Box

边抹立面上部平直，下部打洼槽；高束腰嵌入如小方柱的外露腿足上截与桌面下的槽口，直碰在弧面牙条上，牙条以榫卯与腿足结合；牙条下沿微向外翻成碗口线，其势延顺至腿足

The edge of the frame is straight and flat on its upper part and the lower part, carved with a concave groove. The recessed high waist, tongue-and-grooved to the underside of the frame top as well as the pillar-like exposed top section of the legs, rests on the curved apron which is half-lapped, mortised and tenoned into the legs. The apron ends in an edge that is gently everted outwards and this moulding is continued onto the legs

High-waist small painting table

Huanghuali and burl wood
Late Ming (1573-1644)
Width 106.2 cm (41 13/16")   Depth 66.8 cm (26 5/16")
Height 80.7 cm (31 ¾")

The top is of standard mitre, mortise and tenon construction with a flush, single burl floating panel tongue-and-grooved into the mitred frame, supported by three dovetailed transverse stretchers and an additional cross stretcher underneath. The burl is that of *nanmu*, a Chinese cedar, characterised by its grape-seed pattern. The edge of the frame is straight and flat on its upper part and the lower part, carved with a concave groove. The recessed high waist, tongue-and-grooved to the underside of the frame top as well as the pillar-like exposed top section of the legs, rests on the curved apron which is half-lapped, mortised and tenoned into the legs. The aprons together with the waists are further secured to the frame top by a dovetailed peg on the long sides. The apron ends in an edge that is gently everted outwards and this moulding is continued onto the legs that terminate in strong hoof feet. There are four rectangular-section S-shaped braces, mortised and tenoned into the legs and lapped and wood-pinned to the stretchers at the ends of the underside of the table top. There are extensive traces of ramie, clay and lacquer undercoating.

High-waist construction and the usage of S-shaped braces are classic elements to Ming furniture design and construction. The special bead edge which everts outward is a type of moulding often associated with high-waist construction pieces, and seems to be found on extant examples in the Suzhou area only.

This painting table has an inset *nanmu* burl panel. *Huanghuali* furniture made with *nanmu* burl wood panels seen by this author have all been exceptionally refined. However, as burl wood is relatively soft by nature and their whirling patterns render them easily breakable along the grain, many examples encountered were badly damaged with large losses. Hence, the survival rate of burl wood panel pieces are much lower than those made with *huanghuali* panels, making them rarer and more precious.

Provenance

Grace Wu Bruce, Hong Kong, 1990

Published

Never published

桌面以标准格角榫攒边框镶独板瘿木面心，独板面心为楠木瘿，呈现其特有的葡萄纹

The top is of standard mitre, mortise and tenon construction with a flush, single burl floating panel tongue-and-grooved into the mitred frame. The burl is that of *nanmu*, a Chinese cedar, characterised by its grape-seed pattern

桌面下装三根出梢穿带加一根横托带交叉支承；桌底原来的漆灰、糊织物与漆裹保存良好

The top is supported by three dovetailed transverse stretchers and an additional cross stretcher underneath. There are extensive traces of ramie, clay and lacquer undercoating

四根方材霸王枨下以榫卯纳入四足，上交于桌面下两端的穿带，以销钉固定

There are four rectangular-section S-shaped braces, mortised and tenoned into the legs and lapped and wood-pinned to the stretchers at the ends of the underside of the table top

黄花梨无束腰马蹄足攒牙子琴桌

清前期（1644–1722）

- 长 122.6 厘米　宽 54.3 厘米
- 高 81.8 厘米

桌面以格角榫攒边平镶独板面心，下装三根穿带出梢支承。腿足肩部向外彭出成圆弧形，继而犀利有力向下直达地面，以形状美好但异于常态的马蹄足结束。腿足间用长短不一的沿边起线纵横枨作肩，构成圆角长方形空间。

此具攒牙子琴桌，是从明代标榫半桌演变而成，略去束腰与相连的牙子，用矮老连接枨子与桌面边抹形成空间。马蹄足也有变化，形状刚劲有力，弧度明显，着地处锼出垫子。

此例展示清前期家具造型之演变。

来　源
香港嘉木堂 1989

出　版
从未发表

腿足间用长短不一的沿边起线纵横枨作肩，构成圆角长方形空间

The aprons are made up of beaded-edged stretchers and struts that are mitred, mortised and tenoned to each other to form rectangular openings with round corners

Open-work apron lute table

Huanghuali wood
Early Qing (1644 - 1722)
Width 122.6 cm (48 ¼")   Depth 54.3 cm (21 ⅜")
Height 81.8 cm (32 3/16")

Of rectangular form, the top is of mitre mortise, tenon, single board, flush tongue-and-grooved floating panel construction supported by three dovetailed transverse stretchers underneath. The legs are carved to curve outwards at the shoulders, then downwards in a clean sharp line to finish in beautifully shaped variant hoof feet. The aprons are made up of beaded-edged stretchers and struts that are mitred, mortised and tenoned to each other to form rectangular openings with round corners.

The design of this table is a development from the classic *banzhuo* table of the Ming period. Dispensing with the waist and its connecting apron, struts are fitted to the stretcher below to connect it to the table top frame members to form openings. The hoof feet are powerfully drawn with a lower pad like section, also a development from the standard.

This piece demonstrates the change in furniture construction from the Ming to early Qing.

Provenance

Grace Wu Bruce, Hong Kong, 1989

Published

Never published

腿足以形状美好但异于常态的马蹄足结束

The legs finish in beautifully shaped variant hoof feet

桌面以格角榫攒边平镶独板面心，下装三根穿带出梢支承
The top is of mitre mortise, tenon, single board, flush tongue-and-grooved floating panel construction supported by three dovetailed transverse stretchers underneath

紫檀木壸门牙子霸王枨琴桌

晚明（1573–1644）

- 长 125.5 厘米　宽 50.5 厘米
- 高 80 厘米

桌面为格角榫攒边框，镶入圆角独板鸡翅木面心，下装四根穿带出梢支承。边抹立面上端平直，自中部向下逐渐内缩至底压一窄平线。造型优美的壸门式牙条沿边起线，牙条转弯与牙头接合处锼出两叶，两卷相抵。牙子两端出榫纳入腿足，上方齐头碰入桌面边框底部。菱形霸王枨下以钩挂垫榫纳入四足，上接桌面下穿带，以销钉固定。腿足外圆内方，交面处压平线。桌面下原来的漆灰、糊织物与漆裹保存近乎完整。

明代紫檀家具数量非常稀少，公开出版的例子屈指可数，传世品中比率不到黄花梨木制的千分之一二。

此具精美绝伦的琴桌与北京故宫博物院藏较短较窄不设霸王枨、圆腿的一件设计相同。（朱家溍 2002，页109）现例腿足外圆内方，长宽适中大方，比例匀称，相对更胜一筹。

来 源

香港嘉木堂 1987

出 版

Grace Wu Bruce, "Classic Chinese Furniture in Tzu-Tan Wood", *Arts of Asia*, November-December 1991, Hong Kong. 伍嘉恩《紫檀木造古典中国家具》，《亚洲艺术》1991 年 11-12 月，香港，页 143

伍嘉恩《中国古典紫檀家具—几件明及清初实例及其纵横探讨》，《中国古典家具研究会会刊》十二，1992 年 11 月，北京，页 44

伍嘉恩《从几件实例探讨中国古典紫檀家具》，《文物天地》第 213 期，中国文物报社，北京，2009 年 3 月，页 87

北京故宫博物院藏品
Palace Museum collection, Beijing

Lute table

Zitan and *Jichimu* wood
Late Ming (1573-1644)
Width 125.5 cm (49 7/16")   Depth 50.5 cm (19 7/8")
Height 80 cm (31 1/2")

The top is of mitre, mortise and tenon frame construction with a single board round-cornered *jichimu* floating panel tongue-and-grooved into the frame supported by four dovetailed transverse stretchers underneath. The edge of the frame is flat and moulds downwards and inwards from about half way down to end in a narrow flat band. The beaded-edged, exquisitely shaped curvilinear apron with two carved openwork leaves meeting each other at the ends, are tongue-and-grooved into the legs and butt-joined to the underneath of the frame top. There are square section S-shaped braces tenoned to the legs in a hook and pegged joint and pinned to the two end transverse stretchers. The legs are rounded on the outsides, squared on the insides and edged with a narrow band. The original clay, ramie and lacquer undercoating is almost completely intact.

Early furniture made in *zitan* wood datable to the Ming are extremely rare, with only a handful of known published examples. They are less than point one or two percent of those made in *huanghuali* wood.

This exquisite Ming lute table is very similar in design to a piece in the Palace Museum collection, Beijing. (Zhu 2002, p.109) However, the present piece with its moulded legs and being longer and deeper as well as inset with S-shaped braces, is of better proportion and more refined by comparison.

Provenance

Grace Wu Bruce, Hong Kong, 1987

Published

Grace Wu Bruce, Classic Chinese Furniture in Tzu-Tan Wood, *Arts of Asia*, November-December 1991, Hong Kong, p. 143

Grace Wu Bruce, *Zhongguo Gudian Zitan Jiaju - Jijian Ming ji Qing Chu Shili jiqi Zongheng Tantao* (Chinese Classic furniture in Zitan - Some Ming and Early Qing Examples and Their Exploration), *Zhongguo Gudian Jiaju Yanjiuhui Huikan* (Journal of the Association of Chinese Classical Furniture), No. 12, November 1992, Beijing, p.44

Grace Wu Bruce, *Cong Jijian Shili Tantao Zhongguo Gudian Zitan Jiaju* (Some Examples of Chinese Classic Furniture in *Zitan* Wood and Their Study), *Cultural Relics World*, issue 213, Zhongguo Wenwu Baoshe, Beijing, March 2009, p. 87

桌面为格角榫攒边框，镶入圆角独板鸡翅木面心

The top is of mitre, mortise and tenon frame construction with a single board round-cornered *jichimu* floating panel tongue-and-grooved into the frame

桌面下装四根穿带出梢支承；桌面下原来的漆灰、糊织物与漆裹保存近乎完整

The top is supported by four dove-tailed transverse stretchers underneath. The original clay, ramie and lacquer undercoating is almost completely intact

菱形霸王枨下以钩挂垫榫纳入四足，上接桌面下穿带，以销钉固定

There are square section S-shaped braces tenoned to the legs in a hook and pegged joint and pinned to the two end transverse stretchers

边抹立面上端平直，自中部向下逐渐内缩至底压一窄平线；造型精美的壸门式牙条沿边起线，牙条转弯与牙头接合处锼出两叶，两卷相抵。牙子两端出榫纳入腿足，上方齐头碰入桌面边框底部

The edge of the frame is flat and moulds downwards and inwards from about half way down to end in a narrow flat band. The beaded-edged, exquisitely shaped curvilinear apron with two carved openwork leaves meeting each other at the ends, are tongue-and-grooved into the legs and butt-joined to the underneath of the frame top

黄花梨有束腰马蹄足壶门牙子罗锅枨条桌

晚明（1573–1644）

- 长 140 厘米　宽 59.5 厘米
- 高 87.5 厘米

桌面为标准格角榫攒边打槽平镶两拼面板。面心板纹理对称，取自一材，下装四根穿带出梢支承，皆出透榫。抹头亦可见明榫。边抹线脚中部打洼槽，向下内缩至底压窄边线。沿边起线的壶门式牙条与束腰一木连做，以抱肩榫与腿足及桌面结合。牙条阳线顺势伸延至腿足。腿足上端纳入桌面边框底部，下展至底成优美的马蹄足。牙条下安沿边起线的罗锅枨作肩纳入四足，均出透榫。

桌面下穿带出透榫的造法，是年代的标志，还是工场作坊的特征，又或两者皆是，现在还待考。至于罗锅枨出透榫，与腿足结合的造法，需从更多实例中探索，寻求答案。

来　源
香港东泰商行 1985

展　览
香港，1986，"香港东方陶瓷学会—文玩萃珍"，香港大学 冯平山博物馆

出　版
香港东方陶瓷学会《文玩萃珍》香港，1986，页 248-249

Zhuo side table

Huanghuali wood
Late Ming (1573-1644)
Width 140 cm (55 ⅛") Depth 59.5 cm (23 ⁷⁄₁₆")
Height 87.5 cm (34 ⁷⁄₁₆")

The table is of standard mitre, mortise and tenon frame and flush, tongue-and-grooved, matching two-board floating panel construction supported by four dovetailed transverse stretchers underneath, all with exposed tenons. The tenons are also exposed on the short rails of the frame top. The edge of the frame is carved with a groove in the middle, and then moulds downwards and inwards to end in a narrow flat band. The recessed waist and the beaded-edged curvilinear apron, made of one piece of wood, is mitred, mortised and tenoned into and half-lapped onto the legs which double-lock tenoned to the underside of the mitred frame and terminate in well drawn hoof feet. Below the aprons are beaded-edged hump-back shaped stretchers, mitred, mortised and tenoned into the legs, with exposed tenons.

Whether the method of making transverse stretchers underneath table tops with exposed tenons is an indication of their period of manufacture or particular workshop characteristics or both, needs further research. As to the same query regarding hump-back shaped stretchers joining legs with exposed tenons, the observation of more surviving examples is necessary.

Provenance

Eastern Pacific Co. Hong Kong 1985

Exhibited

Hong Kong, 1986, "Arts from the scholars studio: The Oriental Ceramic Society of Hong Kong," The Fung Ping Shan Museum, University of Hong Kong.

Published

The Oriental Ceramic Society of Hong Kong, *Arts from the Scholar's Studio*, Hong Kong, 1986, p. 248 - 249

桌面为标准格角榫攒边打槽平镶两拼面板；面心板纹理对称，取自一材

The top is of standard mitre, mortise and tenon frame and flush, tongue-and-grooved, matching two-board floating panel construction

桌面下装四根穿带出梢支承

The top is supported by four dovetailed transverse stretchers underneath

黄花梨有束腰马蹄足卷纹角牙条桌

晚明至清前期（1600–1700）
- 长 157 厘米　宽 61 厘米
- 高 88.5 厘米

桌面为标准格角榫攒边打槽平镶独板面心，下装四根穿带出梢支承，近框边两根出透榫。抹头可见明榫。桌面边抹冰盘沿上舒下敛，自三分之一处内缩至底压窄平线。束腰与起阳线的直牙条为一木连做，以抱肩榫与腿足及桌面结合。牙条阳线顺势伸延至腿足。腿足上端纳入桌面边框底部，下展为马蹄足。造型美观的两卷相抵角牙出榫些微退后接入牙条下方与腿足。

《中国花梨家具图考》中的条桌（艾克 1962，图版14），与现例如出一辙，疑是一对。唯独书中记录尺码深度与现例有出入，不知记录是否有误。多年经眼过手明式家具中，从未遇见两具结构、造型雷同而不是成对同时生产的例子。

来 源
| 香港嘉木堂 1991 – 1995

出 版
| Grace Wu Bruce Co Ltd, *Ming Furniture*, Hong Kong, 1995. 嘉木堂《中国家具精萃展》香港，1995，页 14-15

造型美观的两卷相抵角牙出榫些微退后接入牙条下方与腿足

Beautifully shaped spandrels in the shape of multiple C scrolls are slightly set back and tenoned to the underside of the aprons and the legs

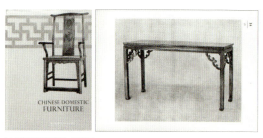

《中国花梨家具图考》中的条桌
A table published in *Chinese Domestic Furniture*

C-scroll spandrel table

Huanghuali wood
Late Ming to early Qing (1600-1700)
Width 157 cm (61 13/16")   Depth 61 cm (24")
Height 88.5 cm (34 7/8")

The top is of standard mitre, mortise and tenon frame construction with a single board tongue-and-grooved, flush floating panel supported by four dovetailed transverse stretchers underneath, the two end ones with exposed tenons. There are also exposed tenons on the short sides of the frame top. The edge of the frame moulds inwards and downwards from about one third way down and again to end in a narrow flat band. The recessed waist and the beaded-edged apron, made of one piece of wood, is half-lapped, mortised and tenoned into the beaded-edged legs which are double-lock tenoned to the top and terminate in well-drawn hoof feet. Beautifully shaped spandrels in the shape of multiple C scrolls are slightly set back and tenoned to the underside of the aprons and the legs.

A table published in *Chinese Domestic Furniture* (Ecke 1962, plate 14) is almost identical to the present piece but the printed measurements for its depth is different. This author queries whether there was a misprint because in the many years of handling Ming furniture, there seemed not to have been two pieces identical in their design and construction that were not made as a pair, at the same time.

Provenance

Grace Wu Bruce, Hong Kong, 1991 – 1995

Published

Grace Wu Bruce Co Ltd, *Ming Furniture*, Hong Kong, 1995, pp. 14-15

桌面为标准格角榫攒边打槽平镶独板面心

The top is of standard mitre, mortise and tenon frame construction with a single board tongue-and-grooved, flush floating panel

桌面下装四根穿带出梢支承

The top is supported by four dovetailed transverse stretchers underneath

黄花梨有束腰马蹄足高罗锅枨画桌

晚明（1573–1644）

- 长 172.4 厘米　宽 77.5 厘米
- 高 81.6 厘米

桌面为标准格角榫攒边平镶独板面心，心板上髹黑漆，下装六根穿带出梢支承。边抹立面平直，一木连做的束腰与直素牙条立面也平直，以抱肩榫与腿足接合。腿足上以长短榫与桌面边框接合，下展为造型优美的矮马蹄足。牙条下的高罗锅枨立面也平直。上部紧贴牙子，两端以榫卯些微后退安装入四足。桌底原来的漆灰、糊织物与漆裹保存近乎完整。

明代桌案超过一定深度适合书桌用途者，称为画桌或画案。传世品稀少。高罗锅枨紧贴桌面，可提供座位较充裕的足部伸展空间，尤为适合作书桌使用。

弥足珍贵的是画桌的明制黑漆面心几乎完好无缺，精光内含，色泽奇古。

来源

| 香港嘉木堂 2004

出版

| 从未发表

《画中人》
Huazhong Ren,
Beauty from the Hanging Scroll

《牡丹亭还魂记》
Mudanting Huanhun Ji,
The Peony Pavilion: Return to the Living

《鼓掌绝尘》
Guzhang Juechen,
Fantastic tales of Society

Painting table

Huanghuali wood
Late Ming (1573-1644)
Width 172.4 cm (67 ⅞") Depth 77.5 cm (30 ½")
Height 81.6 cm (32 ⅛")

The top is of standard mitre, mortise and tenon frame construction with a flush, tongue-and-groove, single board floating-panel supported by six dovetailed transverse braces underneath. Black lacquer covered the entire top panel. The edge of the frame is completely flat as is the recessed waist and the plain straight apron, which are made of one piece of wood. It is mitred, mortised and tenoned into and half-lapped onto the legs which are double-lock tenoned to the mitred frame and terminate in well drawn low hoof feet. Below the aprons are hump-back shaped stretchers, also completely flat, slightly set back from the edges. The original clay, ramie and lacquer undercoating is almost completely intact.

Ming tables more than a certain depth making them suitable for usage as desks are referred to as painting tables. Surviving examples are rare. The present design with the high hump-back shaped stretchers reaching up to connect with the table top is particularly suitable as a desk, allowing more leg room to sit in.

The black lacquered surface, exuding an antique glow from within, is nearly perfectly preserved, very rare in extant example.

Provenance

Grace Wu Bruce, Hong Kong, 2004

Published

Never published

边抹立面平直，一木连做的束腰与直素牙条立面也平直，以抱肩榫与腿足结合；牙条下的高罗锅枨立面也平直。上部紧贴牙子，两端以榫卯些微后退安装入四足；桌底原来的漆灰、糊织物与漆裏保存近乎完整

The edge of the frame is completely flat as is the recessed waist and the plain straight apron, which are made of one piece of wood. It is mitred, mortised and tenoned into and half-lapped onto the legs. Below the aprons are hump-back shaped stretchers, also completely flat, slightly set back from the edges. The original clay, ramie and lacquer undercoating is almost completely intact

桌面为标准格角榫攒边平镶独板面心，心板上髹黑漆

The top is of standard mitre, mortise and tenon frame construction with a flush, tongue-and-groove, single board floating-panel. Black lacquer covered the entire top panel

桌底下装六根穿带出梢支承；桌底原来的漆灰、糊织物与漆裹保存近乎完整

The top is supported by six dovetailed transverse braces underneath. The original clay, ramie and lacquer undercoating is almost completely intact

黄花梨四面平马蹄足霸王枨条桌

晚明（1573–1644）

- 长 193.1 厘米　宽 53 厘米
- 高 83.2 厘米

造型精致优美，桌面边抹与牙条和腿足皆平齐相接成为四面平式。桌面为格角榫攒边框，平镶三拼面板。面心板木纹华美生动，取自一材，下装五根穿带出梢支承。边框下的牙条，沿边起线，与边抹和腿足上端以棕角榫接合。牙条背面装燕尾形穿销上贯边框底部，使牙条固定贴紧。腿足亦沿边起线，下展为兜转有力的马蹄足。菱形霸王枨下端使用钩挂垫榫纳入腿足，上端交于面板下两端穿带，用销钉固定。

四面平式结构为标准明朝家具造法之一，但此设计之传世作品极为稀少。虽非定律，但霸王枨惯用于四面平式桌具。

来　源
| 香港嘉木堂 1993

出　版
| 从未发表

《西厢记》
Xi Xiang Ji
The West Chamber

《水浒传》
Shuihu Zhuan
Outlaws of the Marsh

SIMIANPING LONG SIDE TABLE

Huanghuali wood
Late Ming (1573-1644)
Width 193.1 cm (76″) Depth 53 cm (20 ⅞″)
Height 83.2 cm (32 ¾″)

The long side table is of exquisite form where the top, aprons and legs are set flush with each other forming a flat surface on all sides. The frame top of mitre, mortise and tenon construction has a beautifully figured, flush, three-board, tongue-and-grooved floating panel supported by five dovetailed transverse stretchers underneath. The aprons, which appear to be the continuation of the frame but are actually separate members, end in a beaded edge and together with the frame top, are pyramid joined to the legs, also with beaded edges, which terminate in well drawn hoof feet. Wedge-shaped pegs further secure the aprons to the frame on the insides. Square section S-braces are mortised and tenoned to the legs in a hook and pegged joint and wedged into the end supporting transverse stretchers of the top, secured by wood pins.

Simianping, four-sides-flushed construction is a typical Ming furniture design although surviving examples are very rare. S-braces *bawangchang*, are often although not always associated with *simianping* tables.

PROVENANCE

GRACE WU BRUCE, Hong Kong, 1993

PUBLISHED

Never published

边框下的牙条，沿边起线，与边抹和腿足上端以粽角榫接合；腿足亦沿边起线

The aprons, which appear to be the continuation of the frame but are actually separate members, end in a beaded edge and together with the frame top, are pyramid-joined to the legs, also with beaded edges

牙条背面装燕尾形穿销上贯边框底部，使牙条固定贴紧；菱形霸王枨下端使用钩挂垫榫纳入腿足，上端交于面板下两端穿带，用销钉固定

Wedge-shaped pegs further secure the aprons to the frame on the insides. Square section S-braces are mortised and tenoned to the legs in a hook and pegged joint and wedged into the end supporting transverse stretchers of the top, secured by wood pins

桌面为格角榫攒边框,平镶三拼面板;面心板木纹华美生动,取自一材

The frame top of mitre, mortise and tenon construction has a beautifully figured, flush, three-board, tongue-and-grooved floating panel

桌面下装五根穿带出梢支承

The top is supported by five dovetailed transverse stretchers underneath

黄花梨独板面霸王枨翘头桌

晚明（1573–1644）
- 长 198.6 厘米　宽 45.8 厘米
- 高 88.9 厘米

选料厚实的独板桌面木纹生动华美，两端嵌入小翘头，向下延伸接入独板桌面成为抹头。独板立面平直。素直牙子紧贴独板，作肩以粽角榫与结实的腿足相接。腿足上端与桌面接合，下端伸展为有力的矮马蹄足。牙子下方用铁钉贯穿上达独板面加固。四角有方材霸王枨以钩挂垫榫接入腿足，上方交独板底，用销钉固定。

"桌"在明式家具词汇中，指四腿足安在四角的，而腿足从四角内缩安装则称"案"。桌案面板两端高出上翘成翘头，在传世品中多采用四足内缩安装的造法，所以翘头案是明式家具的一大类。而"翘头桌"就十分罕见，传世品中只有屈指可数的几例。虽然明代翘头桌没有太多实例能留传至今，但从晚明插图本百科全书《三才图会》中，能见到称为"燕几"的翘头桌图例，就知道它们必是当时桌案造型标准系列之一。

来 源

Gangolf Geis 藏品 至 2003

纽约 佳士得 2003 年 9 月 18 日

出 版

Christie's, *The Gangolf Geis Collection of Fine Classical Chinese Furniture*, New York, 18 September 2003. 佳士得《Gangolf Geis 收藏之中国古典家具珍品图册》纽约，2003 年 9 月 18 日，编号 44

伍嘉恩《明式家具二十年经眼录之四　桌类》，《紫禁城》第 166 期、2008 年 11 月，北京，页 135

《三才图会》
Sancai Tuhui,
Pictorial Encyclopedia of Heaven, Earth and Man

Plank top *qiaotou zhuo* table

Huanghuali wood
Late Ming (1573-1644)
Width 198.6 cm (78 ³⁄₁₆″) Depth 45.8 cm (18 ¹⁄₁₆″)
Height 88.9 cm (35″)

Of substantial material, the single plank top of well-figured wood has small inset shaped everted flanges which return down the outside edges of the plank as a bread board end piece. The edge of the plank is completely flat. The massive legs into which the aprons are set flush in a mortise and tenon pyramid joint are mortised and tenoned to the top and end in strong low hoof feet. Metal nails applied to the underside of the plain straight aprons further secure them to the top. There are square section S-braces mortise and tenoned to the legs in a hook and pegged joint and pinned to the underside of the plank top.

Ming tables are divided into two main types, those with legs at the four corners, *Zhuo*, and those with recessed legs called *An*. Tables with tops that end with everted flanges usually have recessed legs and there is a large body of surviving Ming examples. Everted end tables with legs at the four corners like the present piece are very rare, with only a few extant examples. However, the design is illustrated in the Ming book *Sancai Tuhui*, Pictorial Encyclopedia of Heaven, Earth and Man and is refered to as "*Yanji*", so it must have been a main category of the time.

Provenance

Gangolf Geis Collection, to 2003

Christie's New York, 18 September 2003

Published

Christie's, *The Gangolf Geis Collection of Fine Classical Chinese Furniture*, New York, 18 September 2003, no. 44

Grace Wu Bruce, Two Decades of Ming Furniture Part IV: *Zhuo* tables, *Forbidden City*, issue 166, November 2008, Beijing, p. 135

选料厚实的独板桌面木纹生动华美，两端嵌入小翘头

Of substantial material, the single plank top of well-figured wood has small inset shaped everted flanges

牙子下方用铁钉贯穿上达独板面加固；四角有方材霸王枨以钩挂垫榫接入腿足，上方交独板底，用销钉固定

Metal nails applied to the underside of the plain straight aprons further secure them to the top. There are square section S-braces mortised and tenoned to the legs in a hook and pegged joint and pinned to the underside of the plank top

独板面两端嵌入小翘头，向下延伸接入独板桌面成为抹头；素直牙子紧贴独板，作肩以棕角榫与结实的腿足相接；腿足上端与桌面结合，下端伸展为有力的矮马蹄足；四角有方材霸王枨以钩挂垫榫接入腿足，上方交独板底，用销钉固定

The top has small inset shaped everted flanges which return down the outside edges of the plank as a bread board end piece. The massive legs into which the aprons are set flush in a mortise and tenon pyramid joint are mortised and tenoned to the top and end in strong low hoof feet. There are square section S-braces mortised and tenoned to the legs in a hook and pegged joint and pinned to the underside of the plank top

牙子与腿足相接榫卯细看

Details of the apron-leg join

翘头抹头与独板面交接榫卯面底看

Top and bottom view of the joinery of the everted end bread board with the plank top of the table

黄花梨三足月牙桌

晚明（1573–1644）

- 长 90.2 厘米　宽 44.8 厘米
- 高 86.4 厘米

木纹清晰华美的独板桌面喷面安装，些微盖过其下之牙条。前方二弧形牙条与后方直牙条皆以插肩榫造法与腿足和桌面接合。腿足下展为线条优美的马蹄足。牙条下安罗锅枨纳入腿足。后腿是前腿厚度的一半，背面在枨子下方有两个堵塞了的榫眼，原是为容纳栽榫以连结两张月牙桌拼接成一圆桌。

月牙桌，又名半月桌，两张合拢成圆形，成对制造。有关其形制的文字载录于万历版《鲁班经匠家镜》。然而，于至今出版的例子中，尚未见有成对明制实例传世，就连单品，亦极为罕见。世界各大博物馆中国家具藏品中也不含黄花梨月牙桌，包括北京故宫博物院、上海博物馆、美国明尼阿波利斯艺术博物馆与1966年已辟专室展示明式家具的纳尔逊-阿特金斯艺术博物馆。上世纪末在美国加州成立专馆收藏中国明式家具的中国古典家具博物馆，也未能收到一例。月牙桌之罕有，可见一斑。明代小说《清夜钟》版画插图中，能见室内放一件月牙桌，上置香炉。

来源
香港嘉木堂 1999

出版
从未发表

《清夜钟》
Qing Ye Zhong
Alarm Bell on a Still Night

《西湖二集》
Xihu Erji
Two Collections of Stories of the West Lake

Half-moon table

Huanghuali wood
Late Ming (1573-1644)
Width 90.2 cm (35 ½") Depth 44.8 cm (18 ⅝")
Height 86.4 cm (34")

The top is of a solid plank of well figured wood set to slightly overhang the plain aprons, two curved ones in front, one straight one in the back and all are mortised and tenoned into and half-lapped onto the legs which end in beautifully drawn hoof feet. Below the aprons are hump-back shaped stretchers. The two hind legs are half the depth of the front leg and there are two filled mortises on the back of the hind legs below the stretcher, marking the location where the live-pegs join the existing table to its mate.

Half moon tables derive their name from their shape and when paired, become a round table. They were recorded in the fifteenth century carpenter's manual *Lu Ban Jing Jiang Jia Jing* as a standard type in furniture making. There are no published examples of an extant Ming pair known and even single examples like the present piece are extremely rare. Museums worldwide with Ming furniture collections lack an example, including the Palace Museum, the Shanghai Museum, the Minneapolis Institute of Art as well as the Nelson-Akins Museum of Art, Kansas City, which in 1966 has already installed special galleries to feature Ming furniture. Even the Museum of Classical Chinese Furniture in California, set up at the end of the last century to specially collect Ming furniture, failed to acquire an example. The rarity of the type cannot be over emphasised. In an illustration to the Ming period drama *Qing Ye Zhong*, Alarm Bell on a Still Night, a single half-moon table is shown being in use with an incense burner placed on top.

Provenance

Grace Wu Bruce, Hong Kong, 1999

Published

Never published

独板桌面木纹清晰华美

The top of solid plank of well figured wood

牙条下安罗锅枨纳入腿足；后腿是前腿厚度的一半，背面在枨子下方有两个堵塞了的榫眼，原是为容纳栽榫以连结两张月牙桌拼接成一圆桌

Below the aprons are hump-back shaped stretchers. The two hind legs are half the depth of the front leg and there are two filled mortises on the back of the hind legs below the stretcher, marking the location where the live-pegs join the existing table to its mate

案

AN TABLES

黄花梨夹头榫小平头案

晚明（1573–1644）

- 长 88.7 厘米　宽 34.3 厘米
- 高 75.4 厘米

案面以标准格角榫攒边，打槽装木纹生动、四角弧形的独板面心，下有三根穿带出梢支承。边抹冰盘沿微向下内缩至底压窄平线。带侧脚的圆材腿足上端开口嵌夹带耳形牙头的素牙条，再以双榫纳入案面边框底部。腿足间安两根底部削平的椭圆形梯枨。

此典型平头案设计源自古代中国建筑大木梁架的造型与结构。20世纪家具专家学者关注明式家具，最早着眼于这样外形简约光素、线条清爽的平头案设计。这一设计现被视为明朝家具典范。

来源

香港嘉木堂 1995

出版

从未发表

《赵盼儿风月救风尘》
Zhao Paner Fengyue Jiu Fengchen
Rescue of Prostitute by Zhao Paner

案面以标准格角榫攒边，打槽装木纹生动、四角弧形的独板面心

The top is of standard mitre, mortise and tenon construction with a well-figured single board, round-cornered tongue-and-grooved, floating panel

案面下有三根穿带出梢支承

The top is supported by three dovetailed transverse stretchers underneath

Small *Pingtouan* Side Table

Huanghuali wood
Late Ming (1573-1644)
Width 88.7 cm (34 15/16")   Depth 34.3 cm (13 ½")
Height 75.4 cm (29 ⅝")

The top is of standard mitre, mortise and tenon construction with a well-figured single board, round-cornered tongue-and-grooved, floating panel supported by three dovetailed transverse stretchers underneath. The edge of the frame moulds gently downwards and ends in a narrow flat band. The round legs are cut to house the plain shaped spandrelled apron and are double tenoned into the top. Between the legs at each end are two oval stretchers, flattened on the underside.

This classic design has its origin in ancient Chinese architecture in wood. Completely plain, this simple form with pure lines is what first captures the attention of twentieth century furniture historians. The design is now considered quintessential Ming.

Provenance

Grace Wu Bruce, Hong Kong, 1995

Published

Never published

夹头榫细看：带侧脚的圆材腿足上端开口嵌夹带耳形牙头的素牙条，再以双榫纳入案面边框底部
Details of *Jiatousun*, elongated bridle join: the round legs are cut to house the plain-shaped spandrelled apron and are double tenoned into the top

黄花梨夹头榫透锼卷云纹牙头瘿木面小画案

晚明（1573–1644）

- 长 115.3 厘米　宽 75 厘米
- 高 84 厘米

案面为标准格角攒边平镶独板瘿木面心，下装四根出梢穿带支承。两端的穿带与抹头间加装短托带加强支承。木纹华美的面心板是楠木瘿，呈现其独特的葡萄纹。边抹冰盘沿自中上部向下逐渐内缩至底起阳线。带侧脚的长方材腿足混面起边线，中部锼一柱香线脚。腿足上端开口，嵌夹沿边起灯草线的牙条，以双榫纳入案面边框。在腿足上端左右的牙条牙头上各透锼卷云一朵，圆转简洁，牙头向下以叶状轮廓结束。腿足间各安两根上下削平的椭圆梯枨，上下起线，中部锼一柱香线。案面底部罩一层薄麻纱，原来的漆灰与漆裏尚存痕迹。

明代桌案较宽，如现例的75厘米，适合看书写字用途者称为画桌或画案。传世品稀少。

此具画案镶楠木瘿心板。多年所见，黄花梨造楠木瘿心板家具均为上品。唯瘿木质软，纹理多旋转，容易沿着纹理爆裂，所以传世瘿木心板多破裂残缺。保存完好的比率较黄花梨硬木心板面的例子低很多。倍觉珍稀。

来源
香港嘉木堂 1989

出版
从未发表

《养正图解》
Yangzheng Tuje Illustrated book of Educational Legends

长方材腿足混面起边线，中部锼一柱香线脚；腿足上端开口，嵌夹沿边起灯草线的牙条，以双榫纳入案面边框；在腿足上端左右的牙条牙头上各透锼卷云一朵，圆转简洁，牙头向下以叶状轮廓结束

The rectangular legs, decorated with a raised central beading on its rounded surface and ending in beaded edges, are cut to house the openwork cloud-spandrelled, beaded-edged aprons and are double tenoned into the top

Small painting table

Huanghuali wood and burl wood
Late Ming (1573-1644)
Width 115.3 cm (45 ⅜")   Depth 75 cm (29 ½")
Height 84 cm (33 ¹⁄₁₆")

The top is of standard mitre, mortise and tenon construction with a single burl plank, tongue-and-grooved floating panel supported by four dovetailed transverse stretchers underneath. An additional stretcher is joined to the end brace and the short side of the frame on each end for further support. The beautifully figured top panel is the burl of *nanmu*, a Chinese cedar, characterised by its grape-seed pattern. The edge of the mitred frame moulds inwards from about a third way down, and again to end in a beaded edge. The splayed rectangular legs, decorated with a raised central beading on its rounded surface and ending in beaded edges, are cut to house the openwork cloud-spandrelled, beaded-edged aprons and are double tenoned into the top. Between the legs at each end are two oval section stretchers, flattened on the top and bottom, similarly decorated with beaded edges and a central beading. The underside is completely covered with a gauze-like material. There are traces of clay and lacquer.

Ming tables of a certain depth like the preset piece of 75 cm deep making them suitable for usage as desks are termed painting tables. Surviving examples are rare.

This painting table has an inset *nanmu* burl panel. *Huanghuali* furniture made with *nanmu* burl wood panels seen by this author has all been exceptionally refined. However, as burl wood is relatively soft by nature and their whirling pattern renders them easily breakable along the grain, many examples encountered were badly damaged with large losses. Hence, the survival rate of burl wood panel pieces is much lower than those made with *huanghuali* panels, making them rarer and more precious.

Provenance

Grace Wu Bruce, Hong Kong, 1989

Published

Never published

案面为标准格角攒边平镶独板瘿木面心，木纹华美的面心板是楠木瘿，呈现其独特的葡萄纹

The top is of standard mitre, mortise and tenon construction with a single burl plank, tongue-and-grooved floating panel. The beautifully figured top panel is the burl of *nanmu*, a Chinese cedar, characterised by its grape-seed pattern

案面下装四根出梢穿带支承；两端的穿带与抹头间加装短托带加强支承；案面底部罩一层薄麻纱，原来的漆灰与漆裹尚存痕迹

The top is supported by four dovetailed transverse stretchers underneath. An additional stretcher is joined to the end brace and the short side of the frame on each end for further support. The underside is completely covered with a gauze-like material. There are traces of clay and lacquer

黄花梨夹头榫卷云纹牙头平头案

晚明（1573–1644）

- 长 166.8 厘米　宽 53 厘米
- 高 80.7 厘米

案面以格角榫造法攒边框，打槽平镶木纹华美的独板面心，下装五根穿带出梢支承。抹头可见透榫。边抹冰盘沿上舒下敛，自中上部内缩至底压窄平线。带侧脚的圆材腿足上端打槽嵌装锼出卷云纹牙头的牙条，以双榫纳入案面边框底部。腿足两旁的卷云纹牙头隆起混面。两腿间安两根底面削平的椭圆梯枨。案面底部原来的漆灰、糊织物与漆裹保存近乎完整。

平头案比例协调匀称，卷云纹牙头隆起混面，在简约造型中见制作的细腻精致。牙头隆起混面的造法，十分特别，是笔者经手经眼中的孤例。

来源

香港嘉木堂 1998

出版

Grace Wu Bruce, *Ming Furniture, Selections from Hong Kong & London Gallery*, Hong Kong, 2000. 嘉木堂《明朝家具香港伦敦精选》香港，2000，页 13

带侧脚的圆材腿足上端打槽嵌装锼出卷云纹牙头的牙条，以双榫纳入案面边框底部；腿足两旁的卷云纹牙头隆起混面

The splayed round legs are cut to house the cloud-shaped, spandrelled apron and are double tenoned to the underside of the top. The surfaces of the spandrels are gently curved

Cloud-shaped spandrel *pingtouan* table

Huanghuali wood
Late Ming (1573-1644)
Width 166.8 cm (65 11/16")   Depth 53 cm (20 7/8")
Height 80.7 cm (31 3/4")

The top is of mitre, mortise and tenon frame construction with a well-grained single board tongue-and-grooved, flush floating panel supported by five dovetailed transverse stretchers underneath. There are exposed tenons on the short members of the mitred frame which moulds downwards and inwards from about one third way down and ends in a narrow flat band. The splayed round legs are cut to house the cloud-shaped, spandrelled apron and are double tenoned to the underside of the top. The surfaces of the spandrels are gently curved. Between the legs at each end are two oval section stretchers, flattened on the underside. The original clay, ramie and lacquer coating on the underside of the table is almost completely intact.

Of simple form and perfect balance, the gently curved surfaces of the cloud-shaped spandrels highlight the subtle refinement in the making of Ming furniture. This feature is very special, the only example encountered to date by this author.

Provenance

Grace Wu Bruce, Hong Kong, 1998

Published

Grace Wu Bruce, *Ming Furniture, Selections from Hong Kong & London Gallery*, Hong Kong, 2000, p. 13

案面以格角榫造法攒边框，打槽平镶木纹华美的独板面心

The top is of mitre, mortise and tenon frame construction with a well grained single board tongue-and-grooved, flush floating panel

案面下装五根穿带出梢支承；案面底部原来的漆灰、糊织物与漆裹保存近乎完整

The top is supported by five dovetailed transverse stretchers underneath. The original clay, ramie and lacquer coating on the underside of the table is almost completely intact

黄花梨夹头榫凤纹牙头瘿木面平头案

晚明（1573-1644）

- 长 182.4 厘米　宽 57.7 厘米
- 高 82.6 厘米

案面以标准格角榫造法攒边框，内侧打槽容纳独板瘿木面心，下装五根穿带出梢支承。抹头可见透榫。花纹细密瑰丽的板心为楠木瘿子，呈现其独特的葡萄纹。边抹冰盘沿自中上部内缩至底压一边线。带侧脚长方材腿足中部凸起洼儿宽皮条线，两侧起混面压阔边线，上端打槽嵌装透雕凤纹牙头的牙条，以双榫纳入案面边框。牙条下沿边起皮条线。牙子用铁钉加固。腿足间安两根上下削平的椭圆梯枨，皆压边线。案面下原来的漆灰、糊织物与漆裹保存近乎完整。

传世黄花梨平头案以素牙子装耳形牙头为最常见的形式。其次是云纹牙头，再其次就是凤纹。收藏古物重珍稀，物以罕为贵。其他条件等同，凤纹家具的收藏价值就较前两种更高。

来源

香港嘉木堂 1987

香港 罗伯特·毕格史 1987-1997

纽约 佳士得 1997 年 9 月 18 日

出版

Curtis Evarts, "Classical Chinese Furniture in the Piccus Collection", *Journal of the Classical Chinese Furniture Society*, Autumn 1992, Renaissance, California. 柯惕思《毕格史收藏中国古代家具》，《中国古典家具学会季刊》1992 年秋季刊，加州文艺复兴镇，页 20

Christie's, *The Mr & Mrs Robert P. Piccus Collection Fine Classical Chinese Furniture*, New York, 18 September 1997. 佳士得《毕格史伉俪藏中国古代家具精品》纽约，1997 年 9 月 18 日，编号 15

带侧脚长方材腿足中部凸起洼儿宽皮条线，两侧起混面压阔边线，上端打槽嵌装透雕凤纹牙头的牙条，以双榫纳入案面边框

The splayed rectangular legs, carved with a raised wide, thumb-moulded band in the centre, with curved surfaces on both sides which finish with a banded edge, are cut to house the openwork stylised phoenix spandrelled aprons and are double tenoned into the top

Phoenix-spandrel *pingtouan* table

Huanghuali and burl wood
Late Ming (1573-1644)
Width 182.4 cm (71 ¹³⁄₁₆″)   Depth 57.7 cm (22 ¹¹⁄₁₆″)
Height 82.6 cm (32 ½″)

The top is of standard mitre, mortise and tenon frame construction with a single burl wood plank, tongue-and-grooved to the floating panel supported by five dovetailed transverse stretchers underneath. There are exposed tenons on the short sides of the frame top. The beautifully figured panel is the burl of *nanmu*, a Chinese cedar, characterised by its grape-seed pattern. The edge of the mitred frame moulds downwards and inwards from about a third way down and ends in a narrow flat band. The splayed rectangular legs, carved with a raised wide, thumb-moulded band in the centre, with curved surfaces on both sides which finish with a banded edge, are cut to house the openwork stylised phoenix spandrelled aprons and are double tenoned into the top. The aprons are edged with flat wide bands. Metal nails pin them to the underside of the table top for reinforcement. Between the legs at each end are two oval section stretchers, flattened on the top and the bottom, both with moulded edges. The original clay, ramie and lacquer undercoating is almost completely intact.

Recessed-leg tables *pingtouan* fitted with plain ear-shaped spandrels are the most numerous in extant examples. Those with cloud-spandrels are rarer and those with phoenix-spandrels like the present piece are the rarest of the three. As rarity is an important criterion of collecting, it would follow that tables with phoenix-spandrels are more precious, given all else being equal.

Provenance

Grace Wu Bruce, Hong Kong, 1987

Robert P. Piccus collection, Hong Kong, 1987-1997

Christie's, New York, 18 September 1997

Published

Curtis Evarts, Classical Chinese Furniture in the Piccus Collection, *Journal of the Classical Chinese Furniture Society*, Autumn 1992, Renaissance, California, p. 20

Christie's, *The Mr & Mrs Robert P. Piccus Collection Fine Classical Chinese Furniture*, New York, 18 September 1997, no. 15

案面以标准格角榫造法攒边框，内侧打槽容纳独板瘿木面心

The top is of standard mitre, mortise and tenon frame construction with a single burl wood plank, tongue-and-grooved to the floating panel

案面下装五根穿带出梢支承；牙子用铁钉加固；案面下原来的漆灰、糊织物与漆裏保存近乎完整

The top is supported by five dovetailed transverse stretchers underneath. Metal nails pin the aprons to the underside of the table top for reinforcement. The original clay, ramie and lacquer undercoating is almost completely intact

黄花梨夹头榫平头大画案

晚明（1573–1644）

- 长 227.3 厘米　宽 98.5 厘米
- 高 83 厘米

案面以格角榫攒边打槽装纳三板拼接、木纹对称生动华美的面心，下有六根出梢穿带加两根横贯托带交叉支承。案面做窄边框，四角内缘造成圆弧形。边抹冰盘沿上舒下敛至底压窄平线。带侧脚的椭圆腿足上端打槽嵌装耳形牙头的牙条，再以双榫纳入案面边框。牙子下用铁钉贯穿上达案面边框加固。腿足间安两根圆材梯枨。案面底部仍保留大部分的漆灰与漆裹。

此画案长逾二米二十厘米，近一米宽，腿足直径逾十厘米。体积这般庞大在传世黄花梨桌案中十分罕见。此案选料佳，制作极精美。全部构件都用取自同一棵树的金黄色的木材。案面边框非常窄，四角内缘更造成圆弧形。

该画案造型雄伟而细部又极圆熟，加以色泽温润，古趣盎然，耐人观赏，是明式家具之上上品。

来 源
| 香港嘉木堂 1995

出 版
| 从未发表

椭圆腿足上端打槽嵌装耳形牙头的牙条，再以双榫纳入案面边框

The oval legs are cut to house the shaped, spandrelled aprons and are double tenoned into the top

Large painting table

Huanghuali wood
Late Ming (1573-1644)
Width 227.3 cm (89 ½")   Depth 98.5 cm (38 ¾")
Height 83 cm (32 ¹¹⁄₁₆")

The top is of mitre, mortise and tenon narrow frame construction with a well-figured, matching three-board, round-cornered floating panel tongue-and-grooved into the mitred frame supported by six dovetailed transverse stretchers and two additional cross stretchers underneath. The edge of the mitred frame is gently moulded and ends in a narrow flat band. The splayed oval legs are cut to house the shaped, spandrelled aprons and are double tenoned into the top. Metal nails pin the aprons to the top for further reinforcement. Between the legs at each end are two round stretchers. There are extensive traces of clay, ramie and lacquer undercoating.

It is very rare to see *huanghuali* tables of this large size, its length exceeding two metres twenty centimeters and nearly one metre deep with legs that are over ten centimeters in diameter. Finely crafted with choice timber, the golden brown *huanghuali* used for each component of the table is cut from the same tree, and the table top frame of narrow construction is carved with rounded corners.

This table is powerful with presence, yet imbued with fine details. The colour is a soft golden hue. The table is an all time classic, a Ming masterpiece.

Provenance

Grace Wu Bruce, Hong Kong, 1995

Published

Never published

案面以格角榫攒边打槽装纳三板拼接、木纹对称生动华美的面心；案面做窄边框，四角内缘造成圆弧形

The top is of mitre, mortise and tenon narrow frame construction with a well-figured, matching three-board, round-cornered floating panel tongue-and-grooved into the mitred frame

案面下有六根出梢穿带加两根横贯托带交叉支承；牙子下用铁钉贯穿上达案面边框加固

The top is supported by six dovetailed transverse stretchers and two additional cross stretchers underneath. Metal nails pin the aprons to the top for further reinforcement

黄花梨夹头榫凤纹牙头长平头案

晚明（1573–1644）

- 长 242 厘米　宽 54.5 厘米
- 高 86.7 厘米

案面以格角榫造法攒边框，打槽平镶木纹生动华美的独板面心，下装六根穿带出梢支承。边抹冰盘沿上舒下敛，自中部内缩至底压窄平线。抹头可见双透榫。带侧脚圆材腿足上端打槽嵌装透雕凤纹牙头的牙条，并以双榫纳入案面边框。腿足间安两根底部削平的椭圆梯枨。案面下与牙条背面仍保留大部分原来的漆灰与漆裹。

传世黄花梨平头案以素牙子装耳形牙头为最常见的形式。其次是云纹牙头，再其次就是凤纹。现例的凤纹牙头，与前例不同，各有千秋。木趣居集两例罕见的凤纹牙头案子，难能可贵。

来 源
| 香港嘉木堂 1999

出 版
| 从未发表

案面边抹冰盘沿上舒下敛，自中部内缩至底压窄平线；带侧脚圆材腿足上端打槽嵌装透雕凤纹牙头的牙条

The edge of the frame moulds gently downwards and inwards from about half way down to end in a narrow flat band. The splayed round legs are cut to house the openwork stylised phoenix spandrelled apron and are double tenoned to the underside of the top

Phoenix-spandrel large *pingtouan* table

Huanghuali wood
Late Ming (1573-1644)
Width 242 cm (95 ¼") Depth 54.5 cm (21 ⁷⁄₁₆")
Height 86.7 cm (34 ⅛")

The top is of mitre, mortise and tenon frame construction with a well-figured single board, tongue-and-grooved, flush floating panel supported by six dovetailed transverse stretchers underneath. The edge of the frame moulds gently downwards and inwards from about half way down to end in a narrow flat band. There are double exposed tenons on the short sides of the frame top. The splayed round legs are cut to house the openwork stylised phoenix spandrelled apron and are double tenoned to the underside of the top. Between the legs at each end are two oval section stretchers, flattened on the underside. There are extensive traces of the original lacquer on the underside and on the aprons.

Recessed-leg tables *pingtouan* fitted with plain ear-shaped spandrels are the most numerous in extant examples. Those with cloud-spandrels are rarer and those with phoenix-spandrels like the present piece are the rarest of the three. The phoenix-spandrels here are rendered in a different manner than the previous example, both attractive and elegant. To be able to have two rare phoenix-spandrel tables in one collection is rather precious.

Provenance

Grace Wu Bruce, Hong Kong, 1999

Published

Never published

抹头可见双透榫
There are double exposed tenons on the short sides of the frame top

案面以格角榫造法攒边框，打槽平镶木纹生动华美的独板面心

The top of mitre, mortise and tenon frame construction with a well-figured single board, tongue-and-grooved, flush floating panel

案面下装六根穿带出梢支承；案面下与牙条背面仍保留大部分原来的漆灰与漆裹

The top is supported by six dovetailed transverse stretchers underneath. There are extensive traces of the original lacquer on the underside and on the aprons

黄花梨夹头榫云纹牙头小翘头案

晚明（1573–1644）
- 长 76 厘米　宽 41.1 厘米
- 高 81.2 厘米

案面格角攒边平镶木纹华美独板面心，下装两根穿带出梢支承。抹头可见明榫。两端形状美好的小翘头与案面抹头一木连做。微带侧脚的圆材腿足上端开口，嵌夹镂出云纹牙头的起线牙条，以双榫纳入案面。腿足间安两根底部削平的椭圆梯枨。

传世明式翘头案两腿间一般安档板，腿间装枨子的不常见。翘头案又以较长的例子居多。这具安梯枨小翘头案属非常稀少的传世实例。

来 源
| 香港嘉木堂 1989-2003

出 版

Grace Wu Bruce, "Sculptures To Use", *First Under Heaven: The Art of Asia*, London, 1997.
伍嘉恩《实用雕塑》，《天下第一：亚洲艺术》伦敦，1997，页 75

嘉木堂《中国家具・文房清供》香港，2003，封面，页 15

微带侧脚的圆材腿足上端开口，嵌夹镂出云纹牙头的起线牙条，以双榫纳入案面

The gently splayed round legs, cut to house the beaded-edged, cloud-shaped spandrelled apron, are double-tenoned to the top

Small everted-end *qiaotouan* table

Huanghuali wood
Late Ming (1573-1644)
Width 76 cm (29 ⅞")   Depth 41.1 cm (15 ¾")
Height 81.2 cm (32")

The frame top is of standard mitre, mortise and tenon construction with a single board, well-figured, flush, tongue-and-grooved floating panel supported by two dovetailed transverse stretchers underneath. There are exposed tenons on the short sides of the frame. The small beautifully shaped everted flanges are carved from the same piece of wood as the short members of the frame. The gently splayed round legs, cut to house the beaded-edged, cloud-shaped spandrelled apron, are double-tenoned to the top. Between the legs are two oval section stretchers, flattened on the underside.

Extant *qiaotouan* tables with everted ends dated to the Ming usually have inset panels between the legs. Those constructed like the present piece with stretchers are not often seen. In addition, *qiaotouan* tables usually are quite long and small size piece like this is very rare.

Provenance

Grace Wu Bruce, Hong Kong, 1989 – 2003

Published

Grace Wu Bruce, Sculptures To Use, *First Under Heaven: The Art of Asia*, London, 1997, p. 75

Grace Wu Bruce, *Chinese Furniture. Wenfang Works of Art*, Hong Kong, 2003, cover and p. 15

抹头可见明榫
There are exposed tenons on the short sides of the frame

案面格角攒边平镶木纹华美独板面心　　案面下装两根穿带出梢支承

The frame top is of standard mitre, mortise and tenon construction with a single board, well-figured, flush, tongue-and-grooved floating panel　　The top is supported by two dovetailed transverse stretchers underneath

黄花梨活榫结构独板翘头案

晚明（1573-1644）

- 长 218.5 厘米　宽 40.5 厘米
- 高 82.7 厘米

活动式独板案面两端嵌入小翘头。独板木纹华美生动。小翘头与抹头一木连做。案面边抹立面平直，至底内敛压窄边。栽入独板底面的四个小榫头卡在腿子上端的空间，将案面固定。方材腿足看面平直两边起混面压窄边线。上端开口嵌夹卷云纹牙头的起线牙子，一木连做。长牙子与抹头下的短牙条和案面下的四根托带为活动式，可装可卸。腿足下端出榫与托子上的卯眼拍合。腿足间档板的起线开光内透雕花卉图纹，其下卷纹相抵出尖的牙子十分美观。装入腿足高于托子部位，留出空间。此具可开可合活榫结构的翘头案能拆卸成十一件构件。

传统家具中有一组数目相当的平头案折叠式构造，可供组装拆卸，专为方便储藏或用于出游旅行而造。翘头案活榫结构传世品也有一定数目，他们虽然也是可装可卸，但与折叠式平头案构造有别。现例翘头案能简易地拆卸成十一件构件，但不具备方便携带的条件，构件有六根小枨，需要包扎，搬运时才不易失散，独板案面厚重，更不利搬运。而卸下的长牙条，更要小心放置才不会折断，所以可开合的活榫结构的桌案，不是为出游或方便储藏而制，而是为特大或特重的家具，比较容易由作坊运送到用家才装组而设，与架子床床座上部构件均可拆卸的结构理念一致。

来　源
| 香港嘉木堂 1994

出　版
| 从未发表

Dismountable everted-end *qiaotouan* table

Huanghuali wood
Late Ming (1573-1644)
Width 218.5 cm (86")   Depth 40.5 cm (15 15/16")
Height 82.7 cm (32 ¾")

The removable, beautifully-figured single plank top ends in small everted flanges carved from the same piece of wood as the mitred bread board ends. The edge of the plank top is flat and ends in a moulded edge with a narrow flat band. Four small tenons fitted to the underside of the plank top at positions near the upper ends of the legs hold the top in place. The rectangular legs with a flat centre and narrow rounded edges rimmed by a small flat band are cut to house the cloud-shaped beaded-edged spandrelled aprons, made of one piece of wood. These long aprons together with the small end aprons and the four transverse stretchers underneath the top, are dismountable. The legs are tenoned into shoe-type feet, decorated with line mouldings. An openwork panel carved with stylised floral patterns enclosed in a beaded edge is inset into the space between the legs and the beautifully shaped stretcher carved to appear as curled elements meeting up with each other below. These stretchers join the legs above the shoe-type feet, leaving an empty space in between. This dismountable everted-end *qiaotouan* table dissembles to 11 components.

There is a body of extant recessed-leg *pingtouan* tables that is constructed with folding mechanisms, and they can be dismantled and assembled at will. These were made for easy storage or for travelling. Several other everted-end *qiaotouan* tables with removable parts constructed like the present piece are known. Although they can also be dismantled at will, they seem not to be constructed for easy carriage. The small stretchers, like the six pieces in the present example, need to be bound or packaged to prevent them from being misplaced in transit; and the long aprons, when dismantled, are bendy and need special care to avoid damage; not to mention the solid plank top, which is very heavy and most inconvenient for carrying around. Dismountable pieces like this *qiaotouan* table, were then made to facilitate a labour-saving way to deliver heavy pieces from the workshop to their patrons, as they could be transported in components, like canopy beds where all the components above the seats are removable, to be assembled on site.

Provenance

Grace Wu Bruce, Hong Kong, 1994

Published

Never published

案面边抹立面平直，至底内敛压窄边；
方材腿足看面平直两边起混面压窄边线

The edge of the plank top is flat and ends in a moulded edge with a narrow flat band. The rectangular legs with a flat centre and narrow rounded edges rimmed by a small flat band are cut to house the cloud-shaped beaded-edged spandrelled aprons, made of one piece of wood

活动式独板案面两端嵌入小翘头；独板木纹华美生动

The removable, beautifully-figured single plank top ends in small everted flanges

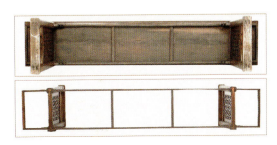

长牙子与抹头下的短牙条和案面下的四根托带为活动式，可装可卸

These long aprons together with the small end aprons and the four transverse stretchers underneath the top, are dismountable

小翘头与抹头一木连做；腿足下端出榫与托子上的卯眼拍合；腿足间档板的起线开光内透雕花卉图纹，其下卷纹相抵出尖的牙子十分美观；装入腿足高于托子部位，留出空间

Small everted flanges carved from the same piece of wood as the mitred bread board ends; The legs are tenoned into shoe-type feet, decorated with line mouldings. An openwork panel carved with stylised floral patterns enclosed in a beaded edge is inset into the space between the legs and the beautifully shaped stretcher carved to appear as curled elements meeting up with each other below. These stretchers join the legs above the shoe-type feet, leaving an empty space in between

此具可开可合活榫结构的翘头案能拆卸成十一件构件

This dismountable everted-end *qiaotouan* table dissembles to 11 components

黄花梨夹头榫带托子卍字纹独板翘头案

晚明（1573–1644）

- 长 228.5 厘米　宽 42.8 厘米
- 高 82.3 厘米

木纹生动华美的独板案面，两端有圆弧形的小翘头。小翘头向下延伸与抹头一木连做。案面冰盘沿上端平直，自中部下敛至底压边线。方材腿足立面平扁，边起委角线，上端开口嵌夹镂云纹牙头的起线牙子，以双榫纳入案面，下端出榫与托子上的卯眼拍合。案面下腿足间各安一长方枨。其下装纵横短材攒接之卍字纹档板。

用纵横短材攒接成卍字纹图案一般用于架子床与罗汉床围子，其他类家具中非常罕见。此具卍字纹档板翘头案是笔者所知的孤例。

来 源
| 香港嘉木堂 2000

出 版
| 从未发表

方材腿足立面平扁，边起委角线，上端开口嵌夹镂云纹牙头的起线牙子，以双榫纳入案面

The legs, flat in the centre, beaded on both edges, cut to house the beaded-edged cloud motif spandrelled aprons are double mortised and tenoned to the top

Plank top *wan* 卍 pattern everted-end *qiaotouan* table

Huanghuali wood
Late Ming (1573-1644)
Width 228.5 cm (89 ¹⁵⁄₁₆″)   Depth 42.8 cm (16 ⅞″)
Height 82.3 cm (32 ⅜″)

The top is of a well-figured single plank with small rounded, shaped everted flanges which are made from the same piece of wood as the bread board ends. The edge of the plank top moulds downwards and inwards from about half way down and again to end in a beaded edge. The legs, flat in the centre, beaded on both edges, cut to house the beaded-edged cloud motif spandrelled aprons are double mortised and tenoned to the top and tenoned into transverse shoe-type feet below. A rectangular stretcher is mortised and tenoned into the legs where they meet the top and below this is an open-work panel which comprises of small mitred members forming the *wan* 卍 pattern inset into the legs and shoe feet.

Small mitred members joined together forming *wan* 卍 pattern panels can be found on the railings of canopy beds, *luohan* beds but rarely on any other types of furniture. This is the only *qiaotouan* table with *wan* 卍 pattern inset panel known to this author.

Provenance

Grace Wu Bruce, Hong Kong, 2000

Published

Never published

小翘头向下延伸与抹头一木连做；案面冰盘沿上端平直，自中部下敛至底压边线；方材腿足下端出榫与托子上的卯眼拍合；案面下腿足间各安一长方枨。其下装纵横短材攒接之卍字纹档板

Small rounded, shaped everted flanges are made from the same piece of wood as the bread board ends. The edge of the plank top moulds downwards and inwards from about half way down and again to end in a beaded edge. The legs are tenoned into transverse shoe-type feet below. A rectangular stretcher is mortised and tenoned into the legs where they meet the top and below this is an open-work panel which comprises of small mitred members forming the *wan* 卍 pattern inset into the legs and shoe feet

木纹生动华美的独板案面,两端有圆弧形的小翘头
The top is of a well-figured single plank with small rounded, shaped everted flanges

炕桌

Kang tables

黄花梨有束腰马蹄足小炕桌

晚明（1573–1644）
- 长 52.2 厘米　宽 41.9 厘米
- 高 22.1 厘米

桌面为标准格角榫攒边框，平镶独板面心，下装两根穿带出梢支承。抹头可见明榫。边抹冰盘沿上舒下敛，自上中部内缩至底压窄平线。束腰与素面直牙条一木连做，以抱肩榫与腿足及桌面结合，腿足下端以马蹄足结束。

传世品中炕桌的标准尺码约90多厘米，小型如现例较为罕见。基本常见式为三弯腿式、壸门牙子。马蹄足设计的并不多。小型炕桌除了适用于炕上外，亦可置于榻、罗汉床及架子床上。

来 源
香港嘉木堂 2001

出 版
从未发表

桌面为标准格角榫攒边框，平镶独板面心，下装两根穿带出梢支承

The top is of standard mitre, mortise and tenon frame construction with a tongue-and-grooved, flush, single board floating panel supported by two dovetailed transverse stretchers underneath

SMALL *KANG* TABLE WITH STRAIGHT APRONS

Huanghuali wood
Late Ming (1573-1644)
Width 52.2 cm (20 9/16")   Depth 41.9 cm (16 ½")
Height 22.1 cm (8 11/16")

The top is of standard mitre, mortise and tenon frame construction with a tongue-and-grooved, flush, single board floating panel supported by two dovetailed transverse stretchers underneath. There are exposed tenons on the short sides of the frame top. The edge of the frame moulds inwards and downwards from about a third way down to end in a narrow flat band. The recessed waist and the plain, straight apron, made of one piece of wood, are mitred, mortised, tenoned and half-lapped to the legs which terminate in well drawn hoof feet.

The most often encountered *kang* tables is that of curvilinear-shaped aprons and cabriole legs and their size is usually like the previous examples, approximately ninety some centimeters. The present piece, smaller than usual and with straight aprons and hoof feet is a rare example. Small size *kang* tables are suitable for use on couch beds, canopy beds as well as on the *kang*.

PROVENANCE

GRACE WU BRUCE, Hong Kong, 2001

PUBLISHED

Never published

黄花梨壸门牙子马蹄足小炕桌

晚明（1573–1644）
- 长 55.7 厘米　宽 41.8 厘米
- 高 24.1 厘米

桌面为标准格角榫攒边平镶木纹华美独板面心，下装两根穿带出梢支承。抹头可见明榫。边抹冰盘沿上舒下敛，自中上部内缩至底压窄平线。牙条锼壸门轮廓，束腰牙条一木连做，以抱肩榫与腿足、桌面结合。腿足下端伸展为有力的马蹄足。

此桌线条优美，充满蓄势待发之力。体积较小适用于炕，亦可放置于榻、罗汉床与架子床上。

来 源
香港嘉木堂 2001

出 版
从未发表

桌面为标准格角榫攒边平镶木纹华美独板面心，下装两根穿带出梢支承

The top is of standard mitre, mortise and tenon frame construction with a tongue-and-grooved flush well-figured single board floating panel supported by two dovetailed transverse stretchers underneath

Small kang table

Huanghuali wood
Late Ming (1573-1644)
Width 55.7 cm (21 15/16")   Depth 41.8 cm (16 7/16")
Height 24.1 cm (9 ½")

The top is of standard mitre, mortise and tenon frame construction with a tongue-and-grooved flush well-figured single board floating panel supported by two dovetailed transverse stretchers underneath. There are exposed tenons on the short sides of the frame top. The edge of the frame moulds gently downwards and inwards from about one third way down and again to end in a narrow flat band. The recessed waist and the beautifully shaped curvilinear aprons, made of one piece of wood, are mitred, mortised, tenoned and half-lapped to the legs which terminate in well-drawn hoof feet.

This beautifully shaped table seems imbued with energy as if about to spring. Smaller than the standard size, it was made for use on a daybed, *luohan* bed or canopy bed as well as on the *kang*.

Provenance

Grace Wu Bruce, Hong Kong, 2001

Published

Never published

黄花梨兽面虎爪梅枝纹炕桌

晚明至清前期（1600–1700）
- 长 97 厘米　宽 62.8 厘米
- 高 27.9 厘米

桌面外围起拦水线，标准格角榫攒边框，打槽平镶独板面心，下装三根穿带出梢支承，两端两根出透榫。抹头亦可见明榫。边抹冰盘沿立面上端平直，自中上部内敛至底压窄平线。弧型牙条，沿边起线雕梅枝，与束腰一木连做，以齐牙条结构与桌面及三弯腿结合。腿子肩部刻兽面，足端刻虎爪抓球。

此具制作精美的炕桌为典型明朝家具造型，但炕桌牙子上刻串枝梅花，似未有其他发表别例。梅花纹雕饰较常用于镜台、架子床或是万历柜的绦环板。

来源
香港嘉木堂 1988

出版
从未发表

Kang table

Huanghuali wood
Late Ming to early Qing (1600-1700)
Width 97 cm (38 ³⁄₁₆")   Depth 62.8 cm (24 ¾")
Height 27.9 cm (11")

The lip-edged top of standard mitred, mortised and tenoned frame construction with a single board, flush floating panel supported by three dovetailed transverse stretchers underneath, two with exposed tenons. There are also exposed tenons on the short sides of the frame top. The edge of the frame moulds downwards from about a third way down and again to end in a narrow flat band. The recessed waist and the curvilinear, beaded-edged apron, carved with branches of flowering prunus, are made of one piece of wood, and are mortised and tenoned to the cabriole legs, carved on the shoulders with animal masks ending in claw-and-ball feet.

This well-modelled *kang* table is a classic Ming type but motifs of flowering prunus are rare in *kang* tables, more often seen as *taohuanban*, inset panels of mirror stands, beds or display cabinets.

Provenance

Grace Wu Bruce, Hong Kong, 1988

Published

Never published

桌面周边起拦水线，标准格角榫攒边框，打槽平镶独板面心，下装三根穿带出梢支承

The lip-edged top of standard mitred, mortised and tenoned frame construction with a single board, flush floating panel supported by three dovetailed transverse stretchers underneath

边抹冰盘沿立面上端平直，自中上部内敛至底压窄平线；弧型牙条，沿边起线雕梅枝，与束腰一木连做，以齐牙条结构与桌面及三弯腿结合；腿子肩部刻兽面，足端刻虎爪抓球

The edge of the frame moulds downwards from about a third way down and again to end in a narrow flat band. The recessed waist and the curvilinear, beaded-edged apron, carved with branches of flowering prunus, are made of one piece of wood, and are mortised and tenoned to the cabriole legs, carved on the shoulders with animal masks ending in claw-and-ball feet

黄花梨壸门牙子叶纹卷球足炕桌

晚明（1573–1644）

- 长 104.1 厘米　宽 75.2 厘米
- 高 26.7 厘米

桌面外围起拦水线，标准格角榫攒边框，打槽平镶三拼面心，下装三根穿带出梢支承。抹头内另加短托带贯穿两端的穿带加固。边抹冰盘沿上舒下敛，自中部内缩至底压窄平线。抹头可见明榫。沿边起线的壸门式牙条铩出大弧形轮廓，两旁出尖，与束腰一木连做，以抱肩榫与腿足、桌面结合。牙子背面加燕尾梢，贯上桌面边框下部加固，长边两枚，短边各一。牙条上的阳线延续至腿足，下端外翻出叶纹卷球足，着地处以方形足承作结束，一木连做。腿子上截与牙子连接部位雕出漂亮的卷叶纹。

大弧形轮廓壸门式牙子，三弯腿外翻叶纹卷球足踏足承的炕桌，可能是炕桌中最优美的设计。至今仅知另外一例（王、袁 1997，页 55），是前加州中国古典家具博物馆的旧藏。

来　源
| 香港嘉木堂 1998

出　版
| 从未发表

前加州中国古典家具博物馆旧藏
Formerly in the collection of the Museum of Classical Chinese Furniture

Kang table with ball feet

Huanghuali wood
Late Ming (1573-1644)
Width 104.1 cm (41")   Depth 75.2 cm (29 ⅝")
Height 26.7 cm (10 ⅛")

The lip-edged top is of standard mitre, mortise and tenon frame construction with a three-board tongue-and-grooved, flush floating panel supported by three dovetailed transverse stretchers underneath. There is an additional short stretcher tennoned to the short sides of the frame, through the transverse stretcher at either end for further support. The edge of the frame moulds downwards and inwards from about half way down to end in a narrow flat band. There are exposed tenons on the short rails of the mitred frame. The recessed waist and the deep curvilinear-shaped beaded-edged apron with pointed curls on each end, are made of one piece of wood and are mitred, mortised, tenoned and half-lapped to the legs. On the back of the aprons are wedge-shaped pegs, two on the long sides and one on each short side, joining them to the top for further reinforcement. The beaded edge continues down the elegantly shaped cabriole legs which end in leaf-and-ball feet with square pads below, made from the same piece of wood. There are beautifully shaped pointed curls where the legs meet the aprons.

Kang tables of this design with deep curvilinear-shaped apron, cabriole legs and leaf-and-ball feet on pads are perhaps the most beautiful of all extant *kang* table designs. Only one other published example comes to mind, the very similar but smaller piece (Wang et al. 1995, p.83)

Provenance

Grace Wu Bruce, Hong Kong, 1998

Published

Never published

边抹冰盘沿上舒下敛,自中部内缩至底压窄平线;抹头可见明榫;沿边起线的壶门式牙条镂出大弧形轮廓,两旁出尖,与束腰一木连做,以抱肩榫与腿足、桌面结合;牙条上的阳线延续至腿足,下端外翻出叶纹卷球足,着地处以方形足承作结束,一木连做;腿子上截与牙子连接部位雕出漂亮的卷叶纹

The edge of the frame moulds downwards and inwards from about half way down to end in a narrow flat band. There are exposed tenons on the short rails of the mitred frame. The recessed waist and the deep curvilinear-shaped beaded-edged apron with pointed curls on each end, are made of one piece of wood and are mitred, mortised, tenoned and half-lapped to the legs. The beaded edge continues down the elegantly shaped cabriole legs which end in leaf-and-ball feet with square pads below, made from the same piece of wood. There are beautifully shaped pointed curls where the legs meet the aprons

桌面周边起拦水线,标准格角榫攒边框,打槽平镶三拼面心,下装三根穿带出梢支承;抹头内另加短托带贯穿两端的穿带加固

The lip-edged top is of standard mitre, mortise and tenon frame construction with a three-board tongue-and-grooved, flush floating panel supported by three dovetailed transverse stretchers underneath. There is an additional short stretcher tennoned to the short sides of the frame, through the transverse stretcher at either end for further support

椅

Chairs

黄花梨雕花圈椅（成对）

晚明（1573–1644）

- 长 61.3 厘米　宽 47 厘米
- 高 101 厘米

扶手以楔钉榫五接，两端出头回转收尾成圆钮形。一弯靠背板上端两侧锼出弧形窄托角牙子，中央雕如意头形开光，内刻团花卷草纹。后腿穿过椅盘上承扶手。三弯形鹅脖出榫纳入扶手和椅盘，扶手与鹅脖间打槽嵌入小角牙。扶手左右支以大三弯形上细下大的圆材联帮棍。椅盘格角攒边，抹头见透榫，下有双托带支承。边抹冰盘沿自中上部内缩至底压窄平线。四框内缘踩边打眼造软屉，现用旧席是更替品。座面下壶门券口牙子雕卷草纹，沿边起线，上齐头碰椅盘下方，两侧嵌入腿足，底端出榫纳入踏脚枨。左右两侧装起线洼膛肚牙子，后方则为短素牙条。前腿间下施踏脚枨，两侧与后方安步步高赶枨。左右两边方材混面，后方椭圆，均出透榫。脚踏及两侧管脚枨下各安一素牙条。

圈椅是明朝家具主要椅型之一。这种唯独中国家具有的圈形弯弧扶手设计，令20世纪家具设计师得到启发，创作出各种现代椅子，广为人知。

此对椅子圆背下，鹅脖内缩，出榫纳入扶手和椅盘而非穿过椅盘成为前腿足，其弧形增添椅子整体的美感。明朝椅具传世品中，这类形制较为少见。

来源
香港嘉木堂 1989

出版
从未发表

四框内缘踩边打眼造软屉，现用旧席是更替品

椅盘下有双托带支承

The seat frame was drilled for soft seat construction and has been restored with old mat

There are two transverse stretchers underneath

Pair of horseshoe armchairs

Huanghuali wood
Late Ming (1573-1644)
Width 61.3 cm (24 ⅛")   Depth 47 cm (18 ½")
Height 101 cm (39 ¾")

The arm of five sections, joined by overlapping pressure-pegged scarf joints, begins and ends in returning rounded handgrips. The C-curved back splat has narrow curvilinear flanges and a carved *ruyi*-shaped medallion with a flower amidst entwining tendrils. The stiles are tenoned into the horseshoe-shaped arm and pass through the seat frame to become the legs. There are elongated S-shaped posts in front that are socketed into the underside of the arm and seat frame. Small cloud-shaped spandrels are tongue-and-grooved into the posts and the arm where they meet. There are tapering, accentuated S-shaped braces supporting the arm. The seat frame, of mitre, mortise and tenon construction with exposed tenons on the short rails has two transverse stretchers underneath. The edge of the frame moulds downwards and inwards from about one third way down and again to finish on a narrow flat band. It was drilled for soft seat construction and has been restored with old mat. The curvilinear-shaped, beaded-edged front apron carved with tendrils, is butt-joined to the underside of the seat frame, tongue-and-grooved to the legs and tenoned into the footrest. Curved beaded-edged aprons are on the sides while the one in the back is plain and high. The legs are joined in front by a shaped footrest and on the sides, rectangular stretchers with rounded outside edges, and the back an oval one, all with exposed tenons. There are plain shaped aprons below the footrest and the side stretchers.

Horseshoe armchairs are a main type of Ming chairs. In the history of furniture design, the unique horseshoe shape of Chinese chairs has inspired various twentieth century furniture designers to create well-known modern examples.

Horseshoe armchairs where the front posts arch backward into sockets in the seat frame rather than pass through the seat to become the front legs are very much rarer in surviving examples of Ming chairs. Their curve silhouette is an attractive addition to the chair form.

Provenance

Grace Wu Bruce, Hong Kong, 1989

Published

Never published

一弯靠背板上端两侧镂出弧形窄托角牙子，中央雕如意头形开光，内刻团花卷草纹

The C-curved back splat has narrow curvilinear flanges and a carved *ruyi*-shaped medallion with a flower amidst entwining tendrils

黄花梨攒靠背活屉圈椅（成对）

晚明（1573–1644）

- 长 61.6 厘米　宽 43.9 厘米
- 高 91.8 厘米

圈椅扶手以楔钉榫三接，两端出头回转收尾成扁圆钮形。后腿上承扶手，下穿过椅盘成为腿足，一木连做。大三弯形鹅脖出榫纳入扶手和椅盘，交接处各嵌入起边线的角牙。靠背板三段攒框装板做，由两根直材出榫纳入扶手和椅盘后框，中以二根横枨作肩出透榫接入直材将靠背一分为三。上段落堂作地透雕云纹，中段平镶木纹生动心板，下段则为落堂起线亮脚牙子。靠背板背面皆髹有厚黑褐漆。椅盘为标准格角攒边框起边线，抹头见透榫，四框内缘踩边出子口承可装可卸活动式屉面。腿足外圆内方，前腿内缘起线，上端以双榫纳入椅盘边框。座面下安沿边起线带牙头牙条嵌入腿足间，上齐头碰椅盘下方，两侧相同，后安素牙子。前腿间施一踏脚枨，下安一牙子，其余三面安椭圆枨。椅盘边框底面，牙条及踏脚枨背面均保存原有黑褐漆。枨子间用木制销钉加固。

这对圈椅尺寸相当标准，但造型与结构有别于一般。构件纤细，但攒框装板做的靠背板较宽，背后更髹厚黑褐漆。三弯形鹅脖曲度也较大，且上下附有一双角牙，令整体效果特殊。而活动屉面的造法，虽然在架子床常见，椅座就十分罕见。

此对圈椅设计与数件已发表例子如出一辙，如安思远旧藏中的一堂四张（Ellsworth 1971，图版15）。另一对为伦敦私人收藏，源自伦敦嘉木堂1998年开幕展览（Wu Bruce 1998，页17），亦载录于《明式家具二十年经眼录》（伍嘉恩 2010，页100–101）。

来源
| 香港嘉木堂 1994

出版
| 从未发表

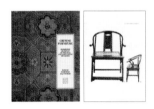

安思远旧藏
Ex R. H. Ellsworth collection

伦敦私人收藏
Private collection, London

Pair of horseshoe armchairs with removable seats

Huanghuali wood
Late Ming (1573-1644)
Width 61.6 cm (24 ¼")   Depth 43.9 cm (17 ¼")
Height 91.8 cm (36 ⅛")

The arm of three sections, joined by overlapping pressure-pegged scarf joints, begins and ends in a curve with flattened rounded knob-shaped handgrips. Into this horseshoe-shaped arm are mortised and tenoned the stiles which continue through the seat frame to become the back legs. The backward arched S-shaped posts, mortised and tenoned to the arm and the seat frame, each has two beaded-edged spandrels tongue-and-grooved to it, one where it meets the arm and the other where it meets the seat frame. The back splat, formed by two shaped upright members mortised and tenoned into the underside of the arm and the back of the seat frame has two mitred horizontal stretchers dividing it into three sections. The tenons of the horizontal stretchers are exposed. The top section is an inset openwork beaded-edged panel of cloud motif, the central one a single well-figured board set flush with the uprights and horizontal members and the lower section a beaded-edged apron in the form of a wide inverted U. The back of the splat is completely covered by a thick brownish black lacquer. The beaded-edged seat frame, of standard mitre, mortise and tenon construction with exposed tenons on the short rails has a ledge cut on the inside to house the removable seat. The legs are round on the outsides and squared on the insides. The front ones, beaded on the insides, are double tenoned to the seat frame. Between the legs in front and on the sides, are beaded-edged, spandrelled aprons. The back one is plain without beading. The legs are joined in front by a shaped footrest with an apron underneath and slightly oval stretchers on the sides and back. The underside of the seat frame, the back of the aprons and the footrests all retain their brownish black lacquer. Wood pins were applied to the mortise and tenon joints of all the stretchers.

This pair of horseshoe chairs, although quite standard in size, are unusual in their design and construction. Their members are slender, yet the back splat is wider than normal and a thick lacquer coating is applied on its back, not often seen on other Ming chairs. The

Provenance

Grace Wu Bruce, Hong Kong, 1994

Published

Never published

椅盘为标准格角攒边框起边线，四框内缘踩边出子口承可装可卸活动式屉面

The beaded-edged seat frame, of standard mitre, mortise and tenon construction has a ledge cut on the inside to house the removable seat

posts arch backward in an exaggerated curve and are fitted with a pair of spandrels, also an unusual feature. The removable seats are also unusual, although found in canopy beds, they are rarely used for chairs.

These exquisite chairs are identical in design to a number of known examples, notably the set that was in the R.H.Ellsworth collection, illustrated in Robert Hatfield Ellsworth *Chinese Furniture: Hardwood Examples of the Ming and Early Ching Dynasties*, 1971, plate 15, and the pair in a private collection in London, acquired from the Grace Wu Bruce 1998 London gallery inaugural exhibition, published in *On the Kang and Between the Walls : the Ming Furniture Quietly Installed*, p. 17, also illustrated in Grace Wu Bruce, *Two Decades of Ming Furniture*, 2010, pp. 100-101.

黄花梨高靠背四出头官帽椅

晚明（1573-1644）

- 长 58.3 厘米　宽 48.2 厘米
- 高 117.5 厘米

体形硕大结实，选材考究，搭脑造型弧度有力，两端上翘，中成枕形。后腿上截出榫纳入搭脑，下穿椅盘与后腿一木连做。三弯素面靠背板嵌入搭脑下方与椅盘后框。三弯弧形的扶手以飘肩榫与后腿上截与鹅脖接合。鹅脖大弧弯形向内插入椅盘抹头。扶手与鹅脖交接处各嵌入小角牙。椅盘格角攒边，四框内缘踩边打眼造软屉，现用旧席是更替品，下有一根托带支承。抹头可见透榫。边抹冰盘沿上舒下敛，自中上部内缩至底压窄平边线。前腿上端出双榫纳入椅盘边框。座面下安窄素面券口牙子，上齐头碰椅盘下方，两侧嵌入腿足。左右两面及后方则为短牙条，皆一木取材。腿足间施脚踏及椭圆管脚枨，用销钉加固，踏脚枨下安牙子。

高靠背四出头官帽椅，搭脑两端翘头和收尾圆润如此件，为传世明朝官帽椅中最稀有的类型。

后腿上段，扶手与鹅脖弯弧线条流畅，搭脑枕部与上翘的两端成大拱形，加上靠背板强而有力的大弯弧度，如箭在弦，充满动力。

来 源

伦敦嘉木堂

马尼拉私人藏品 1998 – 2000

出 版

Grace Wu Bruce, *On the Kang and Between the Walls : the Ming Furniture Quietly Installed*, Hong Kong, 1988. 嘉木堂《炕上壁间》香港，1998，页 12-15

椅盘四框内缘踩边打眼造软屉，现用旧席是更替品，下有一根托带支承

The seat frame was drilled for soft seat construction and is now restored with old matting, supported by one transverse brace underneath

High yoke back armchair

Huanghuali wood
Late Ming (1573-1644)
Width 58.3 cm (22 15/16")   Depth 48.2 cm (19")
Height 117.5 cm (46 ¼")

The armchair is of substantial size and excellent material, with a vigorously shaped top rail comprising a headrest with everted ends into which are tenoned the stiles which continue through the seat frame to become the back legs. The S-curved plain back splat is tongue-and-grooved into the top rail and the back of the seat frame. The elongated S-shaped arms are mitred, mortised and tenoned into the stiles and also the S-shaped front posts, which arch backward to fit into sockets in the seat frame. Small spandrels are tongue-and-grooved to the underside of the arms where they meet the posts. The seat frame of mitre, mortise and tenon construction, was drilled for soft seat construction and is now restored with old matting, supported by one transverse brace underneath. There are exposed tenons on the short rails. The edge of the frame moulds inwards and downwards from about a third way down and again to end in a narrow flat band. The front legs are double tenoned into the seat frame. Beneath the seat is a plain shaped narrow apron tongue-and-grooved to the legs and butt-joined to the underside of the seat frame. The side and back aprons, made of one piece of wood are plain and high. The legs are joined by a footrest in front and on the sides and back, oval stretchers, all further secured by wood pins. There is a shaped apron underneath the footrest.

Provenance

Grace Wu Bruce, London

Private collection, Manila, 1998-2000

Published

Grace Wu Bruce, *On the Kang and Between the Walls: the Ming Furniture Quietly Installed*, Hong Kong, 1998, pp. 12-15

Perhaps the rarest form of Ming yoke back armchairs in surviving examples is the high back with rounded everted ends type like the present piece.

The sweeping curves of the stiles, front posts, arms and the top rail with everted ends, as well as the accentuated arch of the back splat all combine to create a tension in the formation of this piece, as if about to spring, rendering it like a powerful sculpture.

黄花梨素靠背雕花牙子四出头大官帽椅

晚明（1573–1644）

- 长 70.8 厘米　宽 49.7 厘米
- 高 108.6 厘米

搭脑形状优美，中部出枕两端微弯上翘。三弯形的靠背板嵌装入搭脑下方与椅盘大边槽内。后腿上穿椅盘，出飘肩榫纳入搭脑。鹅脖亦穿过椅盘成为前腿足，构造相同。三弯弧形扶手与后腿上截及鹅脖接合，下承三弯形上细下大的圆材联帮棍。椅盘格角攒边，抹头见透榫，下有两根托带支承。冰盘沿上舒下敛底压平窄边线。椅盘四框内缘踩边打眼造软屉，现用旧席是更替品。座面下安壸门式券口牙子，沿边起线雕卷草花纹，上齐头碰椅盘下方，两侧嵌入腿足，底端出榫纳入踏脚枨。左右两面也安类似壸门式刻卷草纹券口牙子，后方则为素短牙条。前腿间施一脚踏，其他三边安起混面管脚赶枨。除了前腿，其他部位均出透榫。脚踏与管两侧脚枨下安一素牙子。

此张椅面宽大，足以容人盘腿而坐。大型椅具常于古画中见为僧侣坐具。明朝文献称之为禅椅或仙椅。

来 源
香港嘉木堂 1996

出 版
从未发表

椅盘四框内缘踩边打眼造软屉，现用旧席是更替品，下有两根托带支承

The seat was drilled for soft seat construction and is now restored with old matting. There are two transverse braces underneath

Meditation chair

Huanghuali wood
Late Ming (1573-1644)
Width 70.8 cm (27 ⅞") Depth 49.7 cm (19 %")
Height 108.6 cm (42 ¾")

The elegantly shaped top rail comprises a headrest and gently everted ends. The S-shaped curved back splat is tongue-and-grooved into the underside of the top rail and the back member of the seat frame. The stiles are tenoned into the top rail and like the front posts pass through the seat to become the legs. The elongated S-shaped arms, mortised and tenoned into the stiles and the posts are supported by tapering S-shaped braces of circular section socketed into the seat frame and the underside of the arm. The mitred, mortised and tenoned seat frame, with exposed tenons on the short rails, has two transverse braces underneath. The edge of the seat frame moulds downwards and inwards to end in a narrow flat band. It was drilled for soft seat construction and is now restored with old matting. Below the seat is a curvilinear beaded-edged apron carved with scrolling tendrils. There are curved beaded-edged aprons, also carved with tendrils on the sides while the back one is plain and high. The legs are joined by a shaped footrail in front and rectangular side and back stretchers, rounded on the outsides, all with exposed tenons except not through the front legs. There are plain shaped aprons below the footrest and side stretchers.

This type of chairs, large enough to sit cross-legged on, is often depicted as seats for monks in period paintings and illustrations. Ming texts recorded these chairs as *chanyi*, meditation chairs or *xianyi*, sages' chairs.

Provenance

Grace Wu Bruce, Hong Kong, 1996

Published

Never published

黄花梨攒靠背凤凰麒麟龙纹四出头官帽椅（成对）

晚明至清前期（1600–1700）

- 长 65.4 厘米　宽 49.6 厘米
- 高 108.6 厘米

圆材搭脑两端上翘，后腿穿过椅盘上截出榫纳入搭脑，连接处装有起线小角牙。一弯弧靠背板三段攒框打槽装板。两根起线弯材出榫纳入搭脑和椅盘后框，中以两根横枨作肩出榫接入将靠背一分为三。上段大圆开光内高浮雕飞凤团花，中段为梅下麒麟图，下段嵌入卷草纹亮脚雕游龙，均落堂装嵌。三弯弧形的扶手，作肩以榫卯接合后腿上截与鹅脖，鹅脖向下穿过椅盘成为前腿足，扶手与鹅脖接合处安起线小角牙。扶手中间装有竹节葫芦形联帮棍。椅盘为格角榫攒边，四框内缘踩边打眼造软屉，现用旧席是更替品，下有一双托带支承。抹头见透榫。座面下安直牙条，沿边起线，上齐头碰椅盘下方，两侧嵌入腿足，底端出榫纳入踏脚枨。左右两面及后方装起线短牙条。前腿间施一踏脚枨，下安小牙子，左右两边与后面为下方削平的椭圆形管脚枨。

此对椅子座面较典型官帽椅宽，其体积颇大。椅背上刻的凤、麒麟与龙均两首双向。传世明朝家具中，满雕华美装饰的靠背板见于圆后背交椅，不常用在其他椅具上。此设计主题与明清宫廷服饰补服上的补子近似，为朝臣、贵族与皇室成员所用。凤凰纹贵为皇后、公主专用。此对凤凰兼麒麟与龙纹雕刻的椅子，想必为御用器。

椅子原为四具一堂。其他一对，一具在2001年秋季纽约佳士得上拍（Christie's 2001，编号277）。另一具出现于中国嘉德香港2012年秋季拍卖会（中国嘉德2012，编号361）。

来源

纽约 苏富比 2002 年 3 月 20 日

出版

Sotheby's, *Fine Chinese Ceramic and Works of Art*, New York, June 3, 1992. 苏富比《中国陶瓷与工艺精品》纽约，1992 年 6 月 3 日，编号 329；Sotheby's, *Fine Chinese Ceramic and Works of Art*, New York, March 20, 2002. 苏富比《中国陶瓷与工艺精品》纽约，2002 年 3 月 20 日，编号 319

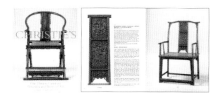

纽约佳士得 9/2001
Christie's New York 9/2001

香港嘉德 10/2012
China Guardian Hong Kong 10/2012

Pair of carved phoenix and *qilin* yoke back armchairs

Huanghuali wood
Late Ming to early Qing (1600 – 1700)
Width 65.4 cm (25 ¾") Depth 49.6 cm (19 ½")
Height 108.6 cm (42 ¾")

The round top rail is with everted ends into which are tenoned the stiles which continue through the seat frame to become the back legs. There are small beaded-edged spandrels where the top rail meets the stiles. The C-shaped back splat, formed by two shaped beaded-edged uprights mortised and tenoned into the underside of the top rail and the back of the seat frame has two mitred horizontal stretchers dividing it into three sections, the top one an inset panel with a large round medallion enclosing a phoenix amidst foliage and a peony, the central one carved with an open-mouthed mystical animal *qilin* under a plum tree in bloom, and the lowest one a beautiful *kunmen* shaped inset apron carved with a lively coiled dragon, all carved in high relief. The elongated S-shaped arms are mitred, mortised and tenoned into the stiles and the front posts, which continue through the seats to become the front legs. There are bamboo, gourd-shaped supports below the arms and beaded-edged spandrels where the arms meet the front posts. The seat frame, of mitred, mortised and tenoned construction was drilled for soft seat construction and now has been restored with old matting, supported by two transverse braces underneath. There are exposed tenons on the short sides of the seat frame. Beneath the seat is a beaded-edged, straight long apron in front. The ones on the sides and back are simple and high with beaded edges. The legs are joined by a shaped footrest in front with a shaped apron underneath and on the sides and back, by oval stretchers, flattened on the underside.

Provenance

Sotheby's New York, 20 March 2002

Published

Sotheby's, *Fine Chinese Ceramic and Works of Art*, New York, June 3, 1992, no. 329, and Sotheby's, *Fine Chinese Ceramic and Works of Art*, New York, March 20, 2002, no. 319

扶手与鹅脖接合处安起线小角牙；扶手中间装有竹节葫芦形联帮棍

There are bamboo, gourd-shaped supports below the arms and beaded-edged spandrels where the arms meet the front posts

一弯弧靠背板三段攒框打槽装板；两根起线弯材出榫纳入搭脑和椅盘后框，中以两根横枨作肩出榫接入将靠背一分为三；上段大圆开光内高浮雕飞凤团花，中段为梅下麒麟图，下段嵌入卷草纹亮脚雕游龙，均落堂装嵌

The C-shaped back splat, formed by two shaped beaded-edged uprights mortised and tenoned into the underside of the top rail and the back of the seat frame has two mitred horizontal stretchers dividing it into three sections, the top one an inset panel with a large round medallion enclosing a phoenix amidst foliage and a peony, the central one carved with an open-mouthed mystical animal *qilin* under a plum tree in bloom, and the lowest one a beautiful *kunmen* shaped inset apron carved with a lively coiled dragon, all carved in high relief

These chairs are wider than standard Ming chairs, which makes them quite large in scale. The phoenix, *qilin* and dragon on each chair splat were carved so that they face each other. Back splats with extensive carvings are usually associated with folding chairs and are rare in other types of Ming chairs. The carved motifs of these chairs bear close relationship to those depicted on rank badges of the Ming and Qing dynasties court robes worn by officials, nobles and the royal family. The insignia of phoenix, reserved for high ranking female members of the imperial family, in combination with *qilin* and dragon motif would almost certainly mean these chairs have imperial provenance.

Original a set of four, the other two appeared separately, one in the autumn auction at Christie's New York in 2001 (Christie's 2001, no. 277) and the other in the China Guardian Hong Kong autumn sale of 2012 (China Guardian 2012, no. 361)

黄花梨方材高靠背四出头官帽椅（成对）

晚明（1573–1644）

- 长 62.1 厘米　宽 46.7 厘米
- 高 119.4 厘米

四出头官帽椅用浑面方材做，后腿上截穿过椅盘作肩出榫纳入弯弧搭脑，一木连做。鹅脖前腿足也是相同造法。素面三弯靠背板嵌入搭脑下方与椅盘后大边槽口。三弯弧形的扶手作肩接入后腿上截与前腿鹅脖，中承三弯形方材联帮棍。椅盘格角榫攒边，四框内缘踩边打眼造软屉，现用旧席是更替品，下有一根托带支承。冰盘沿平直，自中下部内敛以阔平边结束。座面下安直牙子格肩接入腿足，下有高罗锅枨加两根短矮老。左右及后方皆为相同造法。前腿间施一方材格肩枨当脚踏，左右两边与后方安同样方材管脚赶枨。脚踏枨及管脚枨下各装一素牙子。

虽然传世明式家具中有相当数量方材造家具，特别是方柱造木轴圆角柜，方材四出头官帽椅却十分罕见。

此对方材高靠背四出头官帽椅，原属一组八具成套。英国国立维多利亚与艾尔伯特博物馆藏有一对（Clunas 1988，页18）、香港罗启妍旧藏一对（毛岱康 1998，页117）、菲律宾藏家购自英国嘉木堂另一对。八具的设计以及椅座尺码均相同，唯独椅子通高有别。现例高119.4厘米。其他三对分别为104厘米、114厘米、117.5厘米高，疑他们的椅背曾被截断改动。

来源

哈佛燕京学社 James R. Hightower (1915–2006)，1948 年购自北京

波士顿 斯金纳 2004 年 7 月 17 日

出版

Skinner, *European & Asian Furniture & Decorative Arts Featuring Fine Ceramics*, Boston, July 17, 2004. 斯金纳《欧洲与亚洲家具及装饰艺术并瓷器精品》波士顿，2004 年 7 月 17 日，编号 1178

英国国立维多利亚与艾尔伯特博物馆藏品
Victoria and Albert Museum collection, London

Pair of square member high yoke back armchairs

Huanghuali wood
Late Ming (1573-1644)
Width 62.1 cm (24 ⁷⁄₁₆")   Depth 46.7 cm (18 ⅜")
Height 119.4 cm (47")

The chair is of thumb-moulded square-section members, the shaped top rail into which are mitred, mortised and tenoned two stiles which continue through the seat frame to become the back legs. The front posts are similarly constructed, continuing through the seat to become the front legs. The plain, S-curved back splat is tongue-and grooved into the top rail and the back of the seat frame. The elongated S-shaped arms, mitred, mortised and tenoned into the stiles and the front posts, are supported by tapering S-shaped braces, also of square-sections. The seat, of mitre, mortise and tenon frame construction, was drilled for soft seat construction and now has been restored with old matting, supported by one transverse brace underneath. The edge of the seat frame is flat and moulds inwards from about two third way down to end in a wide band. Below the seat is a straight apron-stretcher, mitred, mortised and tenoned into the legs, and below it, a mitred hump-back shaped stretcher with two upright mitred struts in between. There are similar apron, stretcher and struts on the sides as well as the back. The legs are joined by a mitred stretcher in front serving as footrest, and similar stretchers are on the sides and back, also of square-sections. Underneath the footrest and the side stretchers are plain shaped aprons.

Provenance

Professor James R. Hightower (1915–2006), Harvard-Yenching Institute, purchased in Beijing in 1948

Skinner, Boston, July 17, 2004

Published

Skinner, *European & Asian Furniture & Decorative Arts Featuring Fine Ceramics*, Boston, July 17, 2004, no. 1178

椅盘格角榫攒边，四框内缘踩边打眼造软屉，现用旧席是更替品，下有一根托带支承

The seat, of mitre, mortise and tenon frame construction, was drilled for soft seat construction and now has been restored with old matting, supported by one transverse brace underneath

Square member yoke back armchairs are very rare in surviving examples of Ming chairs although there is quite a large body of other types of Ming furniture made with square stiles, notably sloping-stile wood-hinge cabinets.

This pair of square member high yoke back armchairs is from a set of eight. One pair is in the collection of the Victoria and Albert Museum (Clunas 1988, p. 18), another previously owned by Ka-Yin Lo (Maudsley 1998, p. 117) and the third pair in a Philippine collection purchased from the London Grace Wu Bruce gallery. All eight are identical in design as well as the seat sizes being similar. The only difference is their overall height, the present pair at 119.4 cm, the other three pairs respectively at 104, 114 and 117.5 cm high. It is suspected that the chair backs of these three pairs have been reduced.

黄花梨高靠背四出头官帽椅（成对）

晚明（1573–1644）

- 长 60.2 厘米　宽 47 厘米
- 高 122.5 厘米

此对椅子构件线条舒展流畅，造型优美，椅背比例高挑。素面三弯靠背板两端嵌入搭脑下方与椅盘后框大边。后腿穿过椅盘上出飘肩榫纳入搭脑，前腿亦为相同作法。三弯弧形的扶手作肩以榫卯接合后腿上截与鹅脖，中承三弯圆材联帮棍。扶手与鹅脖交接处嵌入小角牙。椅盘格角攒边框，内缘踩边打眼造软屉，现用旧席为更替品，下有两根托带支承，抹头可见透榫。座面下安起线的券口牙子。左右两面相同，后方安短牙条。腿足间施脚踏，两侧安长方起混面管脚枨，后方为椭圆枨。脚踏枨与左右枨子下安一小牙条。

高四出头官帽椅可能是明朝椅具中最经典、最优秀的设计。传世品中他们亦为椅类中数量最稀少的品种。

现例用粗大木材裁成弯度大并具流动感的构件，达到柔婉动人的特殊效果，是一件艺术价值很高的明代家具。

来　源

伍嘉恩女士藏品 1986

出　版

Michael Markbreiter, The Grace Wu Bruce Collection of Chinese Furniture, *Arts of Asia*, November – December 1987, Hong Kong.

迈克·马克布赖特《伍嘉恩中国家具藏品》,《亚洲艺术》1987 年 11-12 月，香港，页 137

椅盘格角攒边框，内缘踩边打眼造软屉，现用旧席为更替品，下有两根托带支承

The seat was drilled for soft seat construction and has now been restored with old matting. There are two transverse braces underneath

Pair of high yoke back armchairs

Huanghuali wood
Late Ming (1573-1644)
Width 60.2 cm (23 7/16") Depth 47 cm (18 ½")
Height 122.5 cm (48 ¼")

With fluid members of sweeping curves, the back of this pair of beautifully modeled chairs is proportionately extremely high. The plain, S-shaped back splat is tongue-and-grooved into the underside of the top rail and the back member of the seat frame. The stiles are tenoned into the top rail and like the front posts, pass through the seat to become the legs. The elongated S-shaped arms, mortised and tenoned into the stiles and the posts are supported by round S-shaped braces. There are small cloud-shaped spandrels where the arms meet the posts. The mitred, mortised and tenoned seat frame, with exposed tenons on the short rails was drilled for soft seat construction and has now been restored with old matting. There are two transverse braces underneath. Below the seat is a curvilinear-shaped, beaded-edged apron. The side aprons are similar but the back one is plain and high. The legs are joined by a shaped footrest in front and on the sides, rectangular stretchers, rounded on the outsides, and in the back an oval stretcher. There are plain shaped aprons below the footrest and the side stretchers.

High yoke back armchairs are perhaps the most classic in Ming chair designs and they are also the rarest type in surviving examples.

The members of these chairs are carved from large timber to achieve sweeping curves, and the resultant fluid lines and beautiful shape render these chairs of high artistic value.

Provenance

Grace Wu Bruce, Hong Kong, 1986

Published

Michael Markbreiter, The Grace Wu Bruce Collection of Chinese Furniture, *Arts of Asia*, November – December 1987, Hong Kong, p. 137

黄花梨素南官帽椅（成对）

晚明（1573–1644）

- 长 60 厘米　宽 47.6 厘米
- 高 105.3 厘米

此对椅子的搭脑弯弧有劲，中部削成枕形。后腿穿过椅盘以挖烟袋锅榫连接搭脑，下方材而上圆材且呈曼妙的曲度。素面三弯靠背嵌入搭脑下方及椅盘后大边的槽口。三弯弧形的扶手后端出榫接入后腿上截，中间支以三弯形上细下大的圆材联帮棍，前端与鹅脖也以挖烟袋锅榫连接，鹅脖向下延伸穿过椅盘一木连做成为前腿足，同样由圆形成为方形。椅盘格角攒边，抹头见透榫，四框内缘踩边打眼造软屉，现用旧席是更替品。下有两根托带支承。冰盘沿线脚上舒下敛底压窄边线。座面壸门轮廓券口牙子，周起饱满灯草线，上齐头碰椅盘下，两侧嵌入腿足，底端出榫纳入踏脚枨。左右两面及后方安素面短牙条。前腿间下施一作肩牙子作脚踏，左右两边安方材管脚枨，后方为上下削平椭圆枨子，皆出透榫。脚踏与两侧枨子下各安一素牙子。脚踏枨安黄铜护片。扶手与腿足相接处均装黄铜片加强稳固。

此对南官帽椅与嘉木堂1995年展览"嘉木堂中国家具精萃展"图录编号22中的例子如出一辙，原为四具一堂，展览时被香港退一步斋收纳。退一步斋的一对其后在台北历史博物馆展出（历史博物馆1999，页85）。

明式椅具安脚踏护片有黄铜做，有竹片做，但不常见。究竟脚踏加护片的制法是明式或是较后期加置尚待考。

来源
| 香港嘉木堂 1996

出版
| 从未发表

《圣谕像解》
Shengyu Xiangjie
Imperial Edicts, Annotated and Illustrated

Pair of continuous yoke back armchairs

Huanghuali wood
Late Ming (1573-1644)
Width 60 cm (23 ⅝") Depth 47.6 cm (18 ¾")
Height 105.3 cm (41 ⁷⁄₁₆")

The well-shaped top rail with a headrest is piped-joined to the round stiles which pass through the seat to become the square section legs. The plain S-shaped back splat is tongue-and-grooved into the underside of the headrest and the back member of the seat frame. The elongated S-shaped arms, mortised and tenoned into the stiles and pipe-joined to the posts which like the stiles, pass through the seat to become the front legs, are supported by tapering S-shaped braces of circular sections. The mitred, mortised and tenoned seat frame with exposed tenons on the short sides was drilled for soft seat construction and is now restored with old matting. There are two transverse braces underneath. The edge of the frame moulds downwards and inwards to end in a narrow flat band. Below the seat is a curvilinear apron with a pronounced beaded edge. The side and back aprons are plain and high, made of one piece of wood. The legs are joined by a mitred stretcher in front serving as a footrest, rectangular stretchers on the sides and in the back, an oval one flattened on the top and bottom, all with exposed tenons. There are plain shaped aprons beneath the footrest and side stretchers. *Huangtong* footrest guards are mounted on the footrests. *Huangtong* reinforcement plates are also found on the arm joins.

Provenance

Grace Wu Bruce, Hong Kong, 1996

Published

Never published

香港退一步齋藏品
Take One Step Back Studio collection, Hong Kong

脚踏枨安黄铜护片
Huangtong footrest guards are mounted on the footrests

This pair of chairs is from a set of four. The other pair in the 1995 exhibition in the Grace Wu Bruce gallery, "Ming Furniture", published in the exhibition catalogue, no. 22 was acquired by Take One Step Back Studio, Hong Kong. Subsequently, they were exhibited at the Museum of History, Taipei "Splendor of Style: Classical Furniture from the Ming and Qing Dynasties" (Museum of History, 1999, p. 85).

Very occasionally, footrest guards are found on Ming chairs, sometimes made of bamboo, sometimes *huangtong*. Whether they were a convention contemporary to Ming chair making, or something added subsequently, still need to be researched.

黄花梨高靠背周制南官帽椅 (成对)

晚明 (1573–1644)

- 长 61.9 厘米　宽 47 厘米
- 高 127.6 厘米

此对椅子造型流畅，比例匀称。弯弧优美的搭脑，中部成枕形，两端以挖烟袋锅榫的造法连接后腿上截。搭脑下方打槽装镶嵌有螺钿牛角花鸟吉祥图案的三弯靠背板，下端出榫纳入椅盘后边。三弯弧形的扶手与前腿鹅脖也以挖烟袋锅榫连接，穿过椅盘成为腿足，造法与后腿相同。扶手中间支以三弯圆材联帮棍，插入椅盘边框。椅盘格角攒边框，抹头见透榫。冰盘沿上舒下敛至底压窄边线。椅盘四框内缘踩边打眼造软屉，现用旧席是更替品，下有两根托带支承。座面下安窄平直券口牙子，上齐头碰椅盘下方，两侧嵌入腿足，底端出榫纳入踏脚枨。左右两面也安券口牙子，后方则为短素牙条。前腿间下施一脚踏榫，左右两边安方材管脚枨起混面，后方管脚枨则为椭圆形上下削平，除了前腿，其他部位均出透榫。脚踏与两侧脚枨下安一素牙子。

此对南官帽椅通高127.6厘米，可能是同类最高的椅子。比例匀称，是明朝典型之优秀范例。

传世明代硬木家具饰有填嵌珍贵材料的例子极为稀少。此类家具通称"周制"，自明末扬州工匠周翥手中臻至完美。清初钱泳在《履园丛话》中说及，"填嵌珍贵材料之作法称'周制'……惟扬州有之，明末有周姓者始创此法……其法以金银、宝石、珍珠、珊瑚、碧玉、翡翠、水晶、玛瑙、玳瑁、车渠、青金、绿松、螺钿、象牙、蜜蜡、沉香为之，雕成山水、人物、树木、楼台、花卉、翎毛，嵌于檀梨漆器之上。大而屏风、桌椅、窗、书架，小则笔床、茶具、砚匣、书箱"。

公开发表例子中有一组黄花梨周制南官帽椅，但背板镶嵌均大量修配。此对保存状况良好，几乎全部原配。

来源
香港嘉木堂 1994

出版
从未发表

Pair of inlaid continuous yoke back armchairs

Huanghuali wood
Late Ming (1573-1644)
Width 61.9 cm (24 ⅜")   Depth 47 cm (18 ½")
Height 127.6 cm (50 ¼")

Of flowing lines and elegant proportions, the shaped top rail with a headrest is pipe-joined to the stiles which continue through the seat frame to become the back legs. The S-shaped back splat, inlaid with auspicious motifs of birds, magnolia and plum blossoms made of horn and mother of pearl, is tongue-and-grooved into the top rail and tenoned into the seat frame. The elongated S-shaped arms are pipe-joined to the posts which pass through the seat to become the front legs. There are tapering S-shaped supports of circular section fitted into sockets in the seat frame and the underside of the arms. The seat, of standard mitred, mortised and tenoned construction has a gently moulded edge ending in a narrow band. There are exposed tenons on the short sides of the seat frame. It was drilled for soft seat construction and now has been restored with old matting and there are two transverse braces underneath. Below the seat is a narrow and straight apron butt-joined to the underside of the seat, tongue-and-grooved to the legs and tenoned into the shaped footrail. There are similarly shaped aprons on the sides while the back one is plain and high. The legs are joined by a shaped footrest in front and on the sides, rectangular stretchers rounded on the outside, and on the back an oval one flattened at the top and bottom, all with exposed tenons except not through the front legs. There are plain shaped aprons underneath the footrest and the side stretchers.

These exceptionally tall and well-proportioned chairs are classic examples of Ming chairs. This pair is perhaps the tallest of their type in published examples.

Surviving examples of hardwood furniture inlaid with precious material dated to the Ming are extremely rare. This group of furniture, called *zhouzhi*, was perfected in the late Ming in Yangzhou by Zhou Zhu. The 18th century author Qian Rong in his publication *Li Yuan Cong Hua* noted that the method of "inlaid precious material into hard wood pieces is called *zhouzhi* ... first practiced in Yangzhou in the late Ming by Zhou ... to

Provenance

Grace Wu Bruce, Hong Kong, 1994

Published

Never published

use gold, silver, precious stones, pearls, coral, green jade, emerald, crystal, agate, tortoise shell, sea shell, brass, malachite, mother of pearl, ivory, amber and eagle wood carved into landscape, figures, trees, pavilions, flowers and birds and inlaid into *tanmu* and (*hua*) *limu* and lacquerware. Large as screens, tables and chairs, window partitions, bookshelves; small as brushrests, cup stands, inkstone boxes and book boxes."

There is a group of published examples of *huanghuali* continuous yoke back chairs with inlaid back splats but this pair is the only pair with most of the original inlay intact.

搭脑下方打槽装镶嵌有螺钿牛角花鸟吉祥图案的三弯靠背板

The S-shaped back splat, inlaid with auspicious motifs of birds, magnolia and plum blossoms made of horn and mother of pearl, is tongue-and-grooved into the top rail

黄花梨卡子花靠背玫瑰椅（成对）

晚明至清前期（1600-1700）

- 长 53 厘米　宽 43.5 厘米
- 高 80 厘米

圆材搭脑两端以挖烟袋锅榫与后腿上截连接。圆材扶手后端出飘肩榫纳入后腿上截，前端同样以挖烟袋锅榫与鹅脖连接，鹅脖穿过椅盘成为腿足。靠背上下安圆材横枨将其分成三段，上段装透雕卷草灵芝纹卡子花，中段两侧二直枨将大空间一分为三，中间安沿边起线壶门轮廓券口牙子，两侧嵌入透雕卷龙草纹卡子花。下段的枨子与椅盘间安两根矮老。两扶手下安沿边起线壶门券口牙子，其下横枨与矮老两根。椅盘为标准格角榫攒边，边抹冰盘微隆，抹头可见明榫。四框内缘踩边打眼造软屉，现用旧席是更替品，下装一根弯带支承。座面下安直券口牙子，沿边起线，上齐头碰椅盘下方，两侧嵌入腿足的槽口，左右两边与后方亦然。前方腿足间施踏脚枨，其他三面安圆材赶枨。脚踏下安素牙子。

现例是标准玫瑰椅子造型的变体，靠背加装卡子花。标准玫瑰椅，直接源自后背全敞的宋代模式。玫瑰椅雏形早在宋代画如《十八学士图》等已见，陈置于亭园厅堂，上坐文人雅士。现例添加了壶门牙子，透雕卡子花，有妍秀轻盈、面面生姿之妙。

来源

香港嘉木堂 1992-1994
瑞士　格施塔德　私人藏品 1994-2014
纽约　苏富比 2014 年 3 月 18 日

展览

香港艺术亚洲国际古董艺术博览会 1994

出版

Sotheby's, *Fine Chinese Ceramics and Works of Arts*, New York, 18, March, 2014. 苏富比《中国陶瓷器工艺精品》纽约，2014 年 3 月 18 日，编号 409

Pair of Rose Chairs with Inset Struts and Aprons

Huanghuali wood
Late Ming to early Qing (1600-1700)
Width 53 cm (20 ⅞")   Depth 43.5 cm (17 ⅛")
Height 80 cm (31 12")

The round corner top rail is pipe-joined to the stiles which continue through the seat-frame to become the back legs. The arms, with similar round corners, are mortised, tenoned and half-lapped to the stiles and pipe-joined to the posts which also continue through the seat frame to become the front legs. Two horizontal stretchers divide the chair back into three sections, the top inset with a central open-work strut carved with *lingzhi* scrolls. The large central section is divided by two vertical stretchers and there are exquisitely carved open-work dragon struts on the sides and a shaped beaded-edged apron in the centre. Two pillar-shaped struts are tenoned to the lower horizontal stretcher and the seat frame in the bottom section. Similar stretchers and struts are mortised and tenoned to the stiles, posts and seat below the arms and above them are beaded-edged curvilinear aprons, echoing that in the centre of the chair back. The seat frame of standard mitred, mortised and tenoned construction, with a rounded edge, was drilled for soft seat and now has been restored with old matting. There are exposed tenons on the short rails and one support stretcher underneath. Beneath the seat, the straight, beaded-edged mitred apron is tongue-and-grooved to the legs and butt-joined to the underside of the seat frame. There are similar aprons on the sides and back. A shaped footrest join the front legs and round stretchers the sides and the back. There is a shaped apron below the footrest.

Provenance

Grace Wu Bruce, Hong Kong, 1992 – 1994

Private Collection, Gstaad, Switzerland, 1994-2014

Sotheby's, New York, 18 March 2014

Exhibited

Hong Kong, 1994, Art Asia

Published

Sotheby's, *Fine Chinese Ceramics and Works of Arts*, New York, 18 March 2014, No. 409

靠背上下安圆材横枨将其分成三段，上段装透雕卷草灵芝纹卡子花，中段两侧二直枨将大空间一分为三，中间安沿边起线壸门轮廓券口牙子，两侧嵌入透雕卷龙草纹卡子花；下段的枨子与椅盘间安两根矮老

Two horizontal stretchers divide the chair back into three sections, the top inset with a central open-work strut carved with *lingzhi* scrolls. The large central section is divided by two vertical stretchers and there are exquisitely carved open-work dragon struts on the sides and a shaped beaded-edged apron in the centre. Two pillar-shaped struts are tenoned to the lower horizontal stretcher and the seat frame in the bottom section

上段装透雕卷草灵芝纹卡子花

The top inset with a central open-work strut carved with *lingzhi* scrolls

两侧嵌入透雕卷龙草纹卡子花

There are exquisitely carved open-work dragon struts on the sides

These chairs are variations from the standard rose chairs in that they have additional carved struts. The design origin of the standard form was from the Song dynasty chairs of the same shape with open backs, as depicted in Song paintings like the well-known "Eighteen Scholars", placed in courtyards, pavilions and halls. These Ming examples, with their beautifully shaped aprons and carved decorations are added attractions to the plain form.

黄花梨圈口靠背玫瑰椅四具成堂

晚明至清前期（1600–1700）
- 长 59.5 厘米　宽 45.5 厘米
- 高 81 厘米

圆材搭脑两端以挖烟袋锅榫连接穿过椅盘的后腿上截。圆材直扶手后端出飘肩榫纳入后腿上截，前端以挖烟袋锅榫的造法与鹅脖连接，鹅脖腿足一木连做。靠背内镶嵌沿边起线壸门式圈口牙子。两边扶手下亦装有同式牙子。椅盘为标准格角榫攒边框，下装两根托带支承，抹头可见透榫。四框内缘踩边打眼造软屉，现用旧席是更替品。边抹上下压一窄线，中起混面。座面下安起线洼堂肚券口牙子，上齐头碰椅盘下方，两侧嵌入腿足，底端出榫纳入踏脚枨。左右两面亦有类似券口牙子，后方安短牙条。前方腿足间施踏脚枨，下有一素牙条。其他三面安长方外起棱形管脚枨，皆出透榫。

玫瑰椅款式变化颇多，这堂椅背与扶手皆安装造型优美的圈口牙子，是基本椅型的另一美观典范。

此堂椅子分别两对先后入藏木趣居。首对是 1995 年。二十年后竟拍得到香港奉文堂的另一对，合并成堂。（佳士得2015，编号2812）

来源
>其中一对：香港嘉木堂 1995
>另外一对：香港　奉文堂 1995 – 2015
>　　　　　香港　佳士得 2015 年 6 月 3 日

出版
>其中一对：从未发表
>另外一对：佳士得《奉文堂藏竹雕及家具》香港，
>　　　　　2015 年 6 月 3 日，编号 2812

Set of four rose chairs with inset aprons

Huanghuali wood
Late Ming to early Qing (1600-1700)
Width 59.5 cm (23 7/16")   Depth 45.5 cm (17 15/16")
Height 81 cm (31 7/8")

The round cornered top rail is pipe-joined to the stiles which continue through the seat frame to become the back legs. The arms, with similar round corners, are mortised, tenoned and half-lapped to the stiles and pipe-joined to the posts which also pass through the seat frame to become the front legs. Curvilinear-shaped, beaded-edged aprons are inset into the chair back top rail, posts and seat frame. There are similar aprons below the arms. The seat frame of standard mitre, mortise and tenon construction was drilled for soft seat construction and is now restored with old matting, supported by two transverse stretchers underneath. There are exposed tenons on the short rails. The edge of the frame begins and ends in a raised bead and is curved in the middle. Below the seat, the beaded-edged, very gently curved apron is butt-joined to the underside of the seat frame, tongue-and-grooved to the legs, and tenoned to the footrest. There are similar aprons on the sides while the back one is plain and high. The legs are joined by a shaped footrest in front and on the sides and back, rectangular stretchers, ridge-shaped on the outside, all with exposed tenons. Below the footrest is a plain shaped apron.

Rose chairs come in many designs; this set with elegantly shaped inset aprons on the back and sides, is a beautiful variation to the standard design.

This set of four chairs was acquired on two separate occasions, the first pair in 1995 and the second, completing the set of four, twenty years later, when they came up at auction at the Feng Wen Tang Collection of Bamboo Carvings and Furniture (Christie's 2015, no. 2812)

Provenance

One pair: Grace Wu Bruce, Hong Kong, 1995

The other pair: Feng Wen Tang Collection, Hong Kong, 1995 - 2015

Christie's, Hong Kong, 3 June 2015

Published

One pair never published

The other pair : Christie's, *The Feng Wen Tang Collection of Bamboo Carvings and Furniture*, Hong Kong, 3 June 2015, no. 2812

靠背内镶嵌沿边起线壸门式圈口牙子

Curvilinear-shaped, beaded-edged aprons are inset into the chair back top rail, posts and seat frame

圆材直扶手后端出飘肩榫纳入后腿上截，前端以挖烟袋锅榫的造法与鹅脖连接

The arms with round corners, are mortised, tenoned and half-lapped to the stiles and pipe-joined to the posts

椅盘为标准格角榫攒边框，四框内缘踩边打眼造软屉，现用旧席是更替品，下装两根托带支承

The seat frame of standard mitre, mortise and tenon construction was drilled for soft seat construction and is now restored with old matting, supported by two transverse stretchers underneath

黄花梨圆后背交椅

晚明（1573–1644）

- 长 66.7 厘米　宽 43 厘米
- 高 102.2 厘米

交椅背扶手以楔钉榫五接，两端出头回转收尾成扁圆钮形。一弯独板靠背板出榫纳入扶手和后椅盘，上端两侧锼出托角牙子，背板看似三段攒成，其实是独板雕刻模仿。上段雕起线如意团花张口螭虎盘龙，中段是木纹生动的心板，下雕亮脚。大三弯形的支撑构件向前探伸连接扶手，另一端接合前腿足上截，造型流畅。转弯处安云纹角牙支撑，与扶手相交处也嵌有小角牙。支撑构件转弯接合前腿处与扶手相交处，背板接入椅圈处及扶手接榫处均有铁造叶片包裹加固。扶手下与支撑构件转弯处皆装金属竹节纹支柱。软屉现用绳索编织，穿入座面横材，后方素面横材接入前腿，前方横材雕双龙隔灵芝花纹相对。前后腿足出榫纳入足下横材，前方有脚踏以帽钉固定镂有古钱与杂宝的铁片。轴钉贯穿前后两足，穿铆处垫有护眼钱和菊花瓣形饰件，腿足、座面及足下横材接合处均包菊瓣纹铁片以加固。

家具研究学者多推崇圆后背交椅为中国古典家具最优秀的经典作品，交椅是从最古老的设计之一的交机演变而来。交机的文献记录可以追溯至东汉灵帝（公元168–189年在位），称为胡床，是与其源自番邦有关。

交椅是现代家具收藏家力求的类别，公开发表的明制传世品不超过二十件。

来源
香港嘉木堂 1993

出版
从未发表

Folding horseshoe armchair

Huanghuali wood
Late Ming (1573-1644)
Width 66.7 cm (27") Depth 43 cm (16 15/16")
Height 102.2 cm (40 ¼")

The arm of five sections, joined by overlapping pressure-pegged scarf joints, begins and ends in flattened rounded-knob handgrips. The C-curved back splat, mortised and tenoned into the underside of the arm and the back stretcher of the seat has flanges on the sides made from the same piece of wood. It is carved to simulate a three-section back divided by mitred stretchers, the top section carved with an open-mouth, coiled *chihulong* dragon enclosed in a beaded-edged *ruyi* shaped medallion, the middle a well-figured panel and below a cusped apron. Elongated S-shaped support members join the underside of the arm near the handgrips at one end, and at the other, the top section of the front legs, in a sweeping curve. There are cloud-shaped spandrels below, and another smaller one in front near the handgrip. Iron reinforcing plates and strips are mounted onto this sweeping curve join where the front legs extend to meet the arm-supports, the arm joins as well as where the arm meets the back-splat. There are ribbed metal braces below the arm and another brace at the arm-support-extended leg join for further support. The restored seat is woven into holes drilled into the two rectangular seat stretchers, the plain back one joined to the front legs and the front one well carved with two dragons facing each other with two *lingzhi* fungi in between. The legs are mortised and tenoned into floor stretchers and between the front legs, there is a footrest with an iron mount of openwork antique coin and other treasure symbols, secured by round headed pins. The legs are hinged with metal pins and there are chrysanthemum-shaped cushion plates below the pinheads. Iron plates with chrysanthemum-shaped ends are found at the leg joins where they meet the floor stretchers and the front seat rail for further reinforcement.

The folding horseshoe armchair is considered perhaps the most classic form of Chinese furniture by furniture historians. It is probably evolved from one of the oldest designs, the folding stool, which was recorded as having been used as early as the Han dynasty by emperor Ling di (AD 168 – 189 reign period), and called *huchang*, the barbarian bed, alluding to its foreign origin.

Very sought after by present day collectors, there are fewer than twenty extant examples known to have survived from the Ming dynasty.

Provenance

Grace Wu Bruce, Hong Kong, 1993

Published

Never published

Copyright © 2017 by SDX Joint Publishing Company.
All Rights Reserved.
本作品版权由生活·读书·新知三联书店所有。
未经许可，不得翻印。

图书在版编目（CIP）数据

　　木趣居：家具中的嘉具 / 伍嘉恩著. — 北京：生活·读书·新知三联书店，2017.9 （2017.12 重印）
　　ISBN 978-7-108-06066-2

　　Ⅰ.①木… Ⅱ.①伍… Ⅲ.①木家具- 收藏- 中国- 图录 Ⅳ.① G262.5-64

　　中国版本图书馆 CIP 数据核字 (2017) 第 195466 号

伍 嘉 恩
GRACE WU

木趣居
家具中的嘉具

The Best of The Best
The
MQJ
Collection
of Ming Furniture

下
Vol. 2

生活·讀書·新知 三联书店

杌凳

STOOLS

黄花梨有束腰雕龙纹三弯腿罗锅枨方凳（成对）

清前期（1644-1722）
- 长 52.6 厘米　宽 52.4 厘米
- 高 54.1 厘米

方凳座面为标准格角榫攒边框，抹头可见明榫。边抹冰盘沿向下内缩，中部打洼儿，至底压窄平线。四框内缘踩边打眼造软屉，现用旧席是更替品，下有两根托带支承。束腰和起灯草线锼壸门轮廓的牙条一木连做，以抱肩榫与三弯腿结合。灯草线顺势伸延至腿子，下展为马蹄足。牙条与腿足满雕龙纹、花、草及兽面纹。牙条下安罗锅枨，两端雕张口龙头。马蹄足上也施雕饰。

此对方凳与加州中国古典家具博物馆旧藏一对如出一辙（王、袁 1997，页10-11）。另一例则出版于王世襄《明式家具珍赏》（王世襄1985，图版24）

来源
香港嘉木堂 1993 – 1998

展览
伦敦，1998，嘉木堂开幕展览

巴黎，2003，吉美国立亚洲艺术博物馆"明·中国家具的黄金时期"

出版
Grace Wu Bruce, *On the Kang and Between the Walls : the Ming Furniture Quietly Installed, Hong Kong*, 1998. 嘉木堂《炕上壁间》香港，1998，页 20-21

Musée national des Arts asiatiques – Guimet, *Ming: l'Âge d'or du mobilier chinois, The Golden Age of Chinese Furniture*, Paris, 2003. 吉美国立亚洲艺术博物馆《明·中国家具的黄金时期》巴黎，2003，页 94-95

前加州中国古典家具博物馆旧藏
Formerly in the collection of the Museum of Classical Chinese Furniture

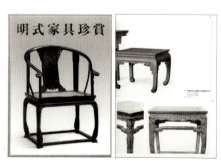

《明式家具珍赏》内另一例
Another example in Classical Chinese Furniture

Pair of carved square stools

Huanghuali wood
Early Qing (1644-1722)
Width 52.6 cm (20 11/16") Depth 52.4 cm (20 5/8")
Height 54.1 cm (21 1/4")

The frame top of standard mitre, mortise and tenon construction with exposed tenons on the short sides of the frame. The edge of the frame moulds downwards and inwards forming a groove in the middle and ends in a narrow flat band. It was drilled for soft seat construction and is now restored with old matting. There are two transverse braces underneath. The recessed waist and the beaded-edged curvilinear-shaped apron, made of one piece of wood, is mitred mortised, tenoned and half-lapped onto the beaded-edged cabriole legs which end in shaped hoof feet. The aprons and legs are profusely carved with stylised dragons, foliage and flowers and animal masks. Below the apron is a hump-back shaped stretcher, carved on the ends with the heads of open mouth dragons. The hoof feet are also decorated with carving.

This pair of stools are identical to the pair illustrated in Wang Shixiang et al, *Masterpieces from the Museum of Classical Chinese Furniture*, 1995, no. 17, and another one illustrated in Wang Shixiang, *Classic Chinese Furniture : Ming and Early Qing Dynasties*, 1986, plate 24.

Provenance

Grace Wu Bruce, Hong Kong, 1993 – 1998

Exhibited

London, 1998, the inaugural exhibition of the Grace Wu Bruce gallery

Paris, 2003, Musée national des Arts asiatiques – Guimet, Ming: l'Âge d'or du mobilier chinois. The Golden Age of Chinese Furniture

Published

Grace Wu Bruce, *On the Kang and Between the Walls : the Ming Furniture Quietly Installed*, Hong Kong, 1998, pp. 20-21

Musée national des Arts asiatiques – Guimet, *Ming: l'Âge d'or du mobilier chinois. The Golden Age of Chinese Furniture*, Paris, 2003, pp. 94-95

方凳座面为标准格角榫攒边框，四框内缘踩边打眼造软屉，现用旧席是更替品，下有两根托带支承

The frame top is of standard mitre, mortise and tenon construction. It was drilled for soft seat construction and is now restored with old matting. There are two transverse braces underneath

黄花梨有束腰马蹄足罗锅枨长方凳（成对）

晚明（1573-1644）

- 长 58 厘米　宽 44 厘米
- 高 50 厘米

长方凳座面格角攒边框，抹头见透榫。凳盘四框内缘踩边打眼造软屉，现用旧席是更替品，下支有两根托带两端出榫纳入边框。冰盘沿上舒下敛至底压平窄边线。束腰与直素牙条一木连做，以抱肩榫与腿足结合，腿子自肩部向下略微兜转，成马蹄足着地，明练而有力。牙条下罗锅枨齐肩膀与腿足相交。

基本式的马蹄足罗锅枨方凳腿子直伸至着地处翻出马蹄足。此对腿子自肩部非常轻微地内弯，至底内翻马蹄足，营造出一种彭腿的视觉效果，十分特殊，有别于基本式之马蹄足设计。传世实例中不多见。

来　源
| 香港嘉木堂 1991

出　版
| 从未发表

Pair of large rectangular stools

Huanghuali wood
Late Ming (1573-1644)
Width 58 cm (22 ¹³⁄₁₆″)   Depth 44 cm (17 ⁵⁄₁₆″)
Height 50 cm (19 １¹⁄₁₆″)

The frame top of standard mitre, mortise and tenon construction with exposed tenons on the short sides of the frame. It was drilled for soft seat construction and is now restored with old matting with two transverse braces tenoned into and half lapped onto the frame underneath. The edge of the frame moulds gently inwards and downwards to end in a narrow flat band. The recessed waist and the apron, made of one piece of wood, is mitred, mortised, tenoned and half-lapped onto the legs which curve very gently inward to end in well drawn hoof feet. Below the apron is a hump-back shaped stretcher.

The standard model of stools with hump-back shaped stretchers and hoof feet have straight legs that end in hoof feet. The legs of this pair curve very gently inwards starting from the shoulder, creating a bulging impression, different from the standard model. Extant examples are rare.

Provenance

Grace Wu Bruce, Hong Kong, 1991

Published

Never published

长方凳座面格角攒边框，凳盘四框内缘踩边打眼造软屉，现用旧席是更替品，下支有两根托带两端出榫纳入边框

The frame top is of standard mitre, mortise and tenon construction
It was drilled for soft seat construction and is now restored with old matting with two transverse braces tenoned into and half lapped onto the frame

黄花梨无束腰直足罗锅枨透雕牙条大方凳（成对）

晚明（1573-1644）

- 长 58.2 厘米　宽 58 厘米
- 高 46.3 厘米

方凳座面为标准格角榫攒边框，抹头可见明榫。四框内缘踩边打眼造软屉，现用椰棕网与旧席是更替品，下有两根托带支承。腿足打洼儿踩委角线，上端以长短榫纳入椅盘边框。牙条沿边起线，两端透镂卷云一朵，后退安入腿足，上方齐头碰椅盘底面。牙条下罗锅枨后退安装入四腿子。

此对方凳造型美观，造工精良。牙条带透雕，洼面腿足踩委角线。杌凳基本式设计为罗锅枨马蹄足，传世明朝实例绝大多数是基本式造型，另类设计的数量十分稀少。

来源
| 香港嘉木堂 1987

出版
| 从未发表

方凳座面为标准格角榫攒边框，四框内缘踩边打眼造软屉，现用椰棕网与旧席是更替品，下有两根托带支承

The top is of standard mitre, mortise and tenon construction. It was drilled for soft seat construction and is now restored with coconut web and old matting supported by two transverse braces underneath

Pair of large square stools

Huanghuali wood
Late Ming (1573-1644)
Width 58.2 cm (22 ⅞") Depth 58 cm (22 ¹³⁄₁₆")
Height 46.3 cm (18 ¼")

The top is of standard mitre, mortise and tenon construction with exposed tenons on the short sides of the frame top. It was drilled for soft seat construction and is now restored with coconut web and old matting supported by two transverse braces underneath. The legs with butterflied *wojiao* moulding corners are thumb-moulded and are double tenoned into the frame top. The beaded-edged, shaped apron with cloud-shaped openings at the ends, is tongue-and-grooved into the legs, slightly set back from the edge, and butt-joined to the underside of the seat frame. Hump-back shaped stretchers are tenoned into the legs, also slightly set back from the legs.

The design of these stools with openwork decorations in the apron and moulded legs is exquisite. The classic design of Ming stools is that of hump-back stretcher with hoof feet. Surviving examples are mostly of the classic form with those of other designs being very rare.

Provenance

Grace Wu Bruce, Hong Kong, 1987

Published

Never published

腿足打洼儿踩委角线，上端以长短榫纳入椅盘边框；牙条沿边起线，两端透镂卷云一朵，后退安入腿足，上方齐头碰椅盘底面；牙条下罗锅枨后退安装入四腿子

The legs with butterflied *wojiao* moulding corners are thumb-moulded and are doubled tenoned into the frame top. The beaded-edged, shaped apron with cloud-shaped openings at the ends, is tongue-and-grooved into the legs, slightly set back from the edge, and butt-joined to the underside of the seat frame. Hump-back shaped stretchers are tenoned into the legs, also slightly set back from the legs

黄花梨无束腰长方凳四张成堂

晚明（1573–1644）

- 长 51.2 厘米　宽 40.6 厘米
- 高 51.2 厘米

长方凳座面以格角榫攒边，抹头可见明榫。凳盘混面压边线。四框内缘踩边打眼造软屉，其中一对现用贴席硬屉，下装两根穿带支承。另一对现用旧席是更替品，但保留原件两根弧形弯带与中间桥形木方连成一体。腿足微带侧脚，外圆内方，交接处起一平线，上端以双榫纳入座面边框。牙条沿边起线，以揣揣榫接牙头，上方齐头踹座面边框底面，两侧嵌入腿足。牙头起小委角。牙条下装椭圆直枨，底部削平，长边一根，短边一双。

这堂长方凳座面经历不同手法复修，是因为它们在中国近代动荡期间曾失散，有幸被重新凑合成堂。同属这套的还有一对，是王世襄先生旧藏（王世襄 1985，页 58），现藏上海博物馆。

来　源

其中一对：香港嘉木堂 1987

另外一对：美国加州中国古典家具博物馆旧藏，
约 1989 – 1996
纽约　佳士得 1996 年 9 月 19 日
新加坡私人收藏，1996 – 1999

出　版

其中一对：从未发表

另外一对：Christie's, *Important Chinese Furniture, Formerly The Museum of Classical Chinese Furniture Collection*, New York, 19 September 1996. 佳士得《中国古典家具博物馆藏珍品》纽约，1996 年 9 月 19 日，编号 15
王世襄　袁荃猷《明式家具萃珍》美国中华艺文基金会 Tenth Union International Inc，芝加哥·旧金山，1997，页 3
王世襄《明式家具研究》生活·读书·新知三联书店，北京，2008，页 407

Set of four rectangular stools

Huanghuali wood
Late Ming (1573-1644)
Width 51.2 cm (20 ⅛") Depth 40.6 cm (15 ¹⁵⁄₁₆")
Height 51.2 cm (20 ⅛")

The frame top is of mitre, mortise and tenon construction with exposed tenons on the short sides. The edge of the frame begins with a raised edge, curves to a convex centre, and ends in a narrow flat band. It was drilled for soft seat construction and one pair now has a recessed hard mat seat supported by two transverse stretchers, while the other pair now has renewed matting, but retained their original two curved transverse braces connected by a bridge-like board in the centre. The gently splayed legs, squared on the insides and rounded on the outsides and edged with a flat band where they meet, are double tenoned to the top. The beaded-edged, mitred, spandrelled apron is tongue-and-grooved to the legs and butt-joined to the underside of the seat frame. The ear-shaped spandrels have indented corners. Below the aprons are oval stretchers, flattened on the underside, one on the long sides and two on the short sides.

This set of stools have seats restored by different methods because they were separated during the period of upheaval in modern China and only fortunately reunited later. Another pair belonging to the set was in the collection of Wang Shixiang, (Wang 1986, p. 58), now in the collection of the Shanghai Museum, China.

Provenance

One pair: Grace Wu Bruce, Hong Kong, 1987

The other pair: Museum of Classical Chinese Furniture, California, approximately 1989 – 1996
Christie's, New York, 19 September 1996
Singapore privation collection, 1996 - 1999

Published

One pair never published

The other pair: Wang Shixiang and Curtis Evarts, *Masterpieces from the Museum of Classical Chinese Furniture*, Chicago and San Francisco, 1995, p. 33

Christie's, *Important Chinese Furniture, Formerly The Museum of Classical Chinese Furniture Collection*, New York, 19 September 1996, no. 15

Wang Shixiang, *Mingshi Jiaju Yanjiu* (Ming Furniture Research), SDX Joint Publishing Company, Beijing, 2008, p. 407

长方凳座面以格角榫攒边，四框内缘踩边打眼造软屉，其中一对现用贴席硬屉，下装两根穿带支承。另一对现用旧席是更替品，但保留原件两根弧形弯带与中间桥形木方连成一体

The frame top of mitre, mortise and tenon construction was drilled for soft seat construction and one pair now has a recessed hard mat seat supported by two transverse stretchers, while the other pair now has renewed matting, but retained their original two curved transverse braces connected by a bridge-like board in the centre

《鲁班经匠家镜》
Lu Ban Jing Jiang Jia Jing
The Classic of Lu Ban and the Craftsman's Mirror

黄花梨四足带托泥圆凳（成对）

晚明至清前期（1600–1700）
- 直径 42.3 厘米
- 高 49.5 厘米

圆凳座面四段弧形弯材用楔钉榫攒边成框，立面沿边起阳线。边框内缘踩边打眼造软屉，现用椰棕和旧席是更替品。软屉编制成后，座面与底的子口均用木条填盖。四根沿边起线的腿足，外彭后回收，以插肩榫与座面边框和托泥结合。托泥也以楔钉榫四接而成。

明代家具软屉的基本造法是在座内缘踩边打眼，编织藤席坐面，然后用窄木条遮盖子口，以销钉固定。如现例般座底也压木条盖藤席孔眼十分罕见。非常讲究。

黄花梨木造圆凳成对，传世实例中极为罕见，虽然在明代绘画中常常见到它们的形象。

来源
香港嘉木堂 1996

出版
从未发表

Pair of round stools

Huanghuali wood
Late Ming to early Qing (1600-1700)
Diameter 42.3 cm (16 ⅝")   Height 49.5 cm (19 ½")

The round top of four beaded-edged curved members joined by exposed pressure-pegged scarf joints. It was drilled for soft seat construction and is now restored with coconut web and old matting. Finishing strips were applied to both the top and the underside concealing the drilled holes. Bulging legs with beaded edges join the top and the base stretchers in "shoulder insertion" *qiajiansun* joins. The base stretcher is also made in four sections, joined by pressure-pegged scarf joints.

Drilling holes on the inside ledge of seats to thread through the supporting web and matting, and then applying finishing strips to conceal the ends, are standard procedures of soft seat construction of Ming chairs, beds and stools. It is extremely rare, however, to find finishing strips applied also to the underside of the seats, as in the present example, a very refined feature.

Round stools made in *huanghuali* wood are very, very rare in surviving examples of Ming furniture although they were often depicted in period paintings and illustrations.

Provenance

Grace Wu Bruce, Hong Kong, 1996

Published

Never published

《御世仁風》
Yushi Renfeng
Tales of Benevolent Emperors

黄花梨有踏床交机

晚明（1573–1644）

- 长 59.7 厘米　宽 40.6 厘米
- 高 53.4 厘米

来源
| 香港嘉木堂 1997

出版
| 从未发表

交机座面横材锼出壶门曲线并沿边起阳线，立面玲珑浮雕缠莲卷草纹。座面原为织物软屉，现以近代绳索编屉代之。圆材机足皆以透榫接入机面与着地横材的卯眼。轴钉贯穿前后两足，穿铆处垫有铁片护眼钱和长方形如意头饰件。踏床下锼壶门轮廓牙子加两小足，以榫卯与前足及着地横材接合。

交机源自古代。早自东汉（公元25 – 220年），已有以"胡床"命名此种腿足相交的机凳。通常视为出游之用。

此具雕饰精美的交机，属体形较大之例。明代画家仇英所绘之《列女传》版画插图可见一名随从扛着交机，跟在主人马后，暗示有协助上下马的用途，或可解释交机俗称为马扎的来源。

《仇画列女传》
Qiuhua Lienu Zhuan
Biography of Women in Ancient China
Illustrated by Qiu Ying

Folding stool

Huanghuali wood
Late Ming (1573-1644)
Width 59.7 cm (23 ½")   Depth seat 40.6 cm (16")
Height 53.4 cm (21")

The seat comprises two top rails of gentle curvilinear shape edged with a raised beading and carved with scrolling lotus flowers in high relief. It was drilled for a woven seat and has now been restored with woven ropes. The round legs are mortised, tenoned and lapped to the seat rails and base stretchers, all with exposed tenons, and are hinged by metal rods passing through openings in their centre secured on both ends by pinheads cushioned with shaped iron plates. There are additional rectangular plates with *ruyi* heads extending beyond these hinge plates. A shaped footrest with small feet and curvilinear-shaped apron is mortised and tenoned to the two front legs and base stretcher.

This folding stool is a descendant of the standard design from ancient time. As early as Eastern Han dynasty (AD 25 – 220), the name *huchuang*, barbarian bed, has been used to refer to folding stools. They were thought to be used for travelling.

This refined example with decorated seat rails is large in size. The woodblock illustration to *Qiuhua Lienu Zhuan*, Biography of Women in Ancient China by the Ming dynasty painter Qiu Ying shows an attendant carrying a folding stool following his master riding on a horse, an allusion to their usage as travelling seats as well as stools for alighting from horsebacks.

Provenance

Grace Wu Bruce, Hong Kong, 1997

Published

Never published

座面原为织物软屉，现以近代绳索编屉代之；圆材杌足皆以透榫接入杌面与着地横材的卯眼

The seat was drilled for a woven seat and has now been restored with woven ropes. The round legs are mortised, tenoned and lapped to the seat rails and base stretchers, all with exposed tenons

黄花梨夹头榫卷云纹牙头带托子二人凳

晚明（1573-1644）
- 长 120.6 厘米　宽 34 厘米
- 高 47.6 厘米

凳面格角攒边打槽平镶木纹华美锼圆角独板面心，下装四根穿带出梢支承。边抹立面平直，自中部向下内缩至底压窄平线，抹头可见明榫。带侧脚长方腿足中部起两柱香线脚，两旁隆起混面，两侧起灯草线。上端开口嵌夹带精工雕饰牙头的起线牙条，出双榫纳入凳面边框。腿子左右的牙头上各透锼卷云一朵，和造出卷叶形装饰。腿足间两根横枨打槽装挖鱼门洞绦环板，其下空档安冬瓜桩圈口。足端落在起线拱桥形托子上。

此二人凳与古斯塔夫·艾克收藏的一对同出一式（艾克1962，图版64）。现为文化部恭王府管理中心收藏。2007年在中国国家博物馆展览《简约·华美：明清家具精粹》展出，载录于展览图录页44 – 45。

来源
| 香港嘉木堂

出版
| 从未发表

带侧脚长方材腿足中部起两柱香线脚，两旁隆起混面，两侧起灯草线；上端开口嵌夹带精工雕饰牙头的起线牙条，出双榫纳入凳面边框；腿子左右的牙头上各透锼卷云一朵，和造出卷叶形装饰

The gently splayed rectangular legs, carved with double beaded *liangzhuxiang* moulding in the middle, curve outwards on both sides to finish with beaded edges. They are cut to house the beautifully worked beaded-edged, spandrelled apron and are double tenoned to the top. The spandrels on either side of the legs are carved with an openwork cloud scroll and below, leave-shaped mouldings

抹头可见明榫；腿足间两根横枨打槽装挖鱼门洞绦环板，其下空档安冬瓜桩圈口；足端落在起线拱桥形托子上

The tenons are exposed on the short sides of the frame top. Between the legs are two horizontal stretchers with an inset panel carved with a *yumendong* opening and below, an inset curved beaded-edged *quankou* apron-frame. The legs extend down to fit into moulded arch-shaped shoe-type feet

Recessed-leg bench

Huanghuali wood
Late Ming (1573-1644)
Width 120.6 cm (47 ½") Depth 34 cm (13 ⅜")
Height 47.6 cm (18 ¾")

The top is of mitre, mortise and tenon frame construction with a round-cornered, single board tongue-and-grooved, flush floating panel supported by four dovetailed transverse stretchers underneath. The edge of the frame is flat and starts to mould inwards and downwards about halfway down its thickness and ends in a narrow flat band. The tenons are exposed on the short sides of the frame top. The gently splayed rectangular legs, carved with double beaded *liangzhuxiang* moulding in the middle, curve outwards on both sides to finish with beaded edges. They are cut to house the beautifully worked beaded-edged, spandrelled apron and are double tenoned to the top. The spandrels on either side of the legs are carved with an openwork cloud scroll and below, leaf-shaped mouldings. Between the legs are two horizontal stretchers with an inset panel carved with a *yumendong* opening and below, an inset curved beaded-edged *quankou* apron-frame. The legs extend down to fit into moulded arch-shaped shoe-type feet.

This bench is identical to the pair that belonged to Gustav Ecke, (Ecke 1962, pl.64) now in the collection of the Prince Gong's Mansion, exhibited in the 2007 exhibition at the National Museum of China, Beijing *Jianyue · Huamei: Mingqing Jiaju Jingcui* (Simplicity · Opulence: Masterpieces of Ming & Qing Dynasty Furniture), and illustrated in the catalogue pp. 44 – 45.

Provenance

Grace Wu Bruce, Hong Kong

Published

Never published

Chinese Domestic Furniture

古斯塔夫·艾克旧藏，现为文化部恭王府管理中心收藏
Previously owned by Gustav Ecke, now in the collection of Prince Gong's Mansion, Beijing

凳面格角攒边打槽平镶木纹华美镂圆角独板面心，下装四根穿带出梢支承

The top is of mitre, mortise and tenon frame construction with a round-cornered, single board tongue-and-grooved, flush floating panel supported by four dovetailed transverse stretchers underneath

脚踏

Footstools

黄花梨有束腰三弯腿石面脚踏

晚明至清前期（1600–1700）
- 长 62.3 厘米　宽 30 厘米
- 高 17.8 厘米

踏面格角榫攒边镶大理石面心，下装三根直带支承，其中两根出透榫。边抹上沿打洼儿后向下内缩，压一窄平线后再向下内缩成束腰。抹头可见明榫。沿边起线的壸门轮廓牙条刻高浮雕卷草纹，以抱肩榫与三弯腿结合。腿足上出双榫纳入踏面边框，下展为外翻马蹄足，上雕三叶纹。

此脚踏结构颇特殊。家具的束腰一般与牙子一木连做，或独立分开做。但现例束腰与踏面框一木连做，十分罕见。透榫的榫头贴上黄花梨木片让较深色的榫头断纹不外露，也不常见。

来源
香港嘉木堂 2002

出版
伍嘉恩《明式家具二十年经眼录》北京，2010，页 172

Footstool

Huanghuali wood and marble
Late Ming to early Qing (1600-1700)
Width 62.3 cm (24 ½")   Depth 30 cm (11 13/16")
Height 17.8 cm (7")

The top is of mitre, mortise and tenon construction with a marble centre supported by three transverse stretchers below, two with exposed tenons. The edge of the frame is carved with a groove and moulds downwards and inwards to a narrow flat band and moulds in again to form a recessed waist. There are exposed tenons on the short sides of the frame. The beaded-edged, curvilinear aprons carved with leaves and scrolling tendrils in high relief are mortised and tenoned into and half-lapped onto the legs, which are double-lock tenoned to the top and terminate in outward flaring feet, carved with three leaves.

This footstool of standard Ming design is constructed in an unusual manner in that the waist is part of the frame, rather than a separate piece or as part of the apron. The exposed tenons of the underneath stretchers are veneered with *huanghuali* strips to conceal the dark end grains of the tenons, also a not often seen feature.

Provenance

Grace Wu Bruce, Hong Kong, 2002

Published

Grace Wu Bruce, *Two Decades of Ming Furniture*, Beijing, 2010, p.172

踏面格角攢邊鑲大理石面心，下裝三根直帶支承

The top of mitre, mortise and tenon construction with a marble centre supported by three transverse stretchers below

黄花梨四面平马蹄足脚踏

晚明（1573–1644）

- 长 68.4 厘米　宽 26 厘米
- 高 9.6 厘米

此脚踏为四面平式结构。格角榫攒边框平镶独板面心，下装两根穿带出梢支承，皆出透榫。边抹立面完全平直，抹头可见明榫。腿足、牙子也全平直与桌面齐平安装。牙子以格肩榫相接腿足，长牙子背面用燕尾形销钉上贯面框底部加固。腿足上以长短榫纳入面框，下展为线条优美的内翻矮马蹄足。

这脚踏比一般椅子长，较适合置于大坐具如禅椅、宝座前用。从传世黄花梨脚踏实例一般长过椅子，或能旁证明代腿踏的使用是配搭大坐具，留给长者与上宾，是有等级、尊卑之分。

来 源
| 香港嘉木堂 1996

出 版
| 从未发表

踏面为格角榫攒边框平镶独板面心，下装两根穿带出梢支承，皆出透榫

The top is of mitre, mortise and tenon frame construction with a single board, flush, tongue-and-grooved floating panel supported by two dovetailed transverse stretchers underneath, both with exposed tenons

Simianping footstool

Huanghuali wood
Late Ming (1573-1644)
Width 68.4 cm (26 15/16")   Depth 26 cm (10 1/4")
Height 9.6 cm (3 13/16")

Of *simianping*, four-sides-flushed construction, the top is of mitre, mortise and tenon frame construction with a single board, flush, tongue-and-grooved floating panel supported by two dovetailed transverse stretchers underneath, both with exposed tenons. The edge of the frame is completely flat and there are exposed tenons on the short sides of the frame top. The aprons and the legs are also flat and they are set flushed to the top. These completely flat aprons are mitred, mortised, tenoned and half-lapped to the legs. Behind each long apron is a wedge-shaped peg further securing it to the top. The legs are double tenoned to the top and terminate in elegant hoof feet below.

This footstool, wider than the width of normal chairs, was probably used in conjunction with a meditation chair or a throne chair. Extant examples of footstools are mostly wider than standard size Ming chairs, perhaps signifying that footrests, like larger seats were reserved for sitters of more exalted status.

Provenance

Grace Wu Bruce, Hong Kong, 1996

Published

Never published

边抹立面完全平直，抹头可见明榫；腿足、牙子也全平直与桌面齐平安装

The edge of the frame is completely flat and there are exposed tenons on the short sides of the frame top. The aprons and the legs are also flat and they are set flushed to the top

脚踏构件榫卯细看
Footstool components joinery details

四面平腿足、牙子与上部结构
Simianping, four-sides-flush, apron-leg-top joinery

腿足上长短榫
Double tenons at the top of the legs

黄花梨有束腰马蹄足脚踏（成对）

晚明（1573–1644）

- 长 69.3 厘米　宽 34.7 厘米
- 高 18 厘米

脚踏边框格角攒边，中一直档做小格肩纳入大边，将边框一分为二。每边四根方材横枨以小格肩接合抹头与直档。边抹立面中部打洼儿后向下内缩至底压一窄平线。抹头可见明榫。一木连做的束腰和沿边起线的直牙条以抱肩榫与腿足结合，腿足上出长短榫纳入边框，下展为刚劲有力的马蹄足。

明代绘画中成对脚踏一般置放罗汉床前。传世成对实例非常稀少。

来 源
| 香港嘉木堂 2001

出 版
| 从未发表

脚踏边框格角攒边，中一直档做小格肩纳入大边，将边框一分为二。每边四根方材横枨以小格肩接合抹头与直档

The top is of mitre, mortise and tenon frame construction, with a stretcher in the middle T-mitred joined to the frame dividing it into two equal sections. In each section, there are four rectangular stretchers, similarly T-mitred joined to the frame and the central stretcher

Pair of footstools

Huanghuali wood
Late Ming (1573-1644)
Width 69.3 cm (27 ¼")   Depth 34.7 cm (13 ⅝")
Height 18 cm (7 1/16")

The top is of mitre, mortise and tenon frame construction, with a stretcher in the middle T-mitred joined to the frame dividing it into two equal sections. In each section, there are four rectangular stretchers, similarly T-mitred joined to the frame and the central stretcher. There are exposed tenons on the short sides of the frame. The edge of the frame has a grooved moulding in the centre and moulds downwards and inwards to end in a narrow flat band. The recessed waist and the beaded-edged, straight apron, made of one piece of wood, is mortised and tenoned into and half-lapped on to the legs, which are double tenoned to the top and terminate in well drawn hoof feet.

Pair of footstools are seen in period paintings placed in front of *luohan* beds but have survived together in very few numbers.

Provenance

Grace Wu Bruce, Hong Kong, 2001

Published

Never published

格角攒边成框出透榫与小格肩榫卯细看图
Mitre, mortise and tenon frame construction and T-mitre join details

抱肩榫与腿子上长短榫细看图
Mortise and tenon, half lap apron-leg join and double tenon leg-top joinery details

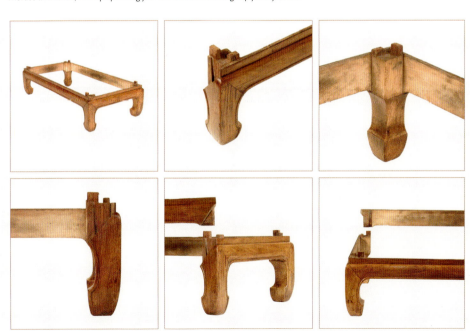

黄花梨案形井字面脚踏

晚明（1573–1644）

- 长 71.3 厘米　宽 29.3 厘米
- 高 19.3 厘米

脚踏腿足内缩安装如案型设计，踏面边框格角攒边，正中安横枨接入抹头两边将边框内空间一分为二，再以横竖短材攒接成井字棂格，全部格肩造。抹头可见明榫。边框四角安灵芝头云纹白铜包角。边抹冰盘沿上部平直，自上中部内缩至底压窄平线。长方腿足中部起两柱香线脚，两旁隆起混面踩边线，上端接入边框，下端出榫与踩两道线脚的托子上的榫眼拍合。腿子两旁装造型美观的两卷相抵圆雕灵芝纹牙头，腿足间镶入透雕大灵芝档板。

脚踏一般腿足安四角，传世品以素身或带些微雕饰为多。此具脚踏腿足内缩成案型，灵芝纹又非常华丽，实属罕见。

来源
| 香港嘉木堂 1998

出版
| 从未发表

边抹冰盘沿上部平直，自上中部内缩至底压窄平线；长方腿足中部起两柱香线脚，两旁隆起混面踩边线，上端接入边框，下端出榫与踩两道线脚的托子上的榫眼拍合；腿子两旁装造型美观的两卷相抵圆雕灵芝纹牙头

The edge of the top is flat and then moulds inwards and downwards from about one third way down to end in a narrow flat band. The rectangular legs, carved with double beaded *liangzhuxiang* moulding in the middle, then curve outwards on both sides to finish on narrow flat edges. They are mortised and tenoned into the top frame the moulded and shaped transverse shoe-type feet below. Exquisitely carved openwork *lingzhi* spandrels are mortised and tenoned to the legs and the underside of the top

Recessed-leg footstool

Huanghuali wood
Late Ming (1573-1644)
Width 71.3 cm (28 ¹⁄₁₆")   Depth 29.3 cm (11 ½")
Height 19.3 cm (7 ⅝")

Of recessed-leg *an* table design, the top is of mitre, mortise and tenon frame construction with a central long stretcher mitred, mortised and tenoned to the shorts sides of the frame dividing the top into two equal halves. Small short mitred members then join the frame, the central long stretcher and each other to form an openwork lattice pattern. There are exposed tenons on the short sides of the frame top. *Lingzhi* shaped *baitong* mounts are surface-mounted on to the four corners. The edge of the top is flat and then moulds inwards and downwards from about one third way down to end in a narrow flat band. The rectangular legs, carved with double beaded *liangzhuxiang* moulding in the middle, then curve outwards on both sides to finish on narrow flat edges. They are mortised and tenoned into the top frame and the moulded and shaped transverse shoe-type feet below. Exquisitely carved openwork *lingzhi* spandrels are mortised and tenoned to the legs and the underside of the top. Between the legs are inset panels carved with an openwork large *lingzhi* in the centre.

Footstools usually have legs at the four corners and are either plain or sparingly decorated. This piece of recessed legs construction is unusual and the *lingzhi* motif is highly glamourous and very rare.

Provenance

Grace Wu Bruce, Hong Kong, 1998

Published

Never published

抹头可见明榫；边抹冰盘沿上部平直，自上中部内缩至底压窄平线；腿足间镶入透雕大灵芝档板

There are exposed tenons on the short sides of the frame top. The edge of the top is flat and then moulds inwards and downwards from about one third way down to end in a narrow flat band. Between the legs are inset panels carved with an openwork large *lingzhi* in the centre

踏面边框格角攒边，正中安横枨接入抹头两边将边框内空间一分为二，再以横竖短材攒接成井字棂格，全部格肩造。边框四角安灵芝头云纹白铜包角

The top is of mitre, mortise and tenon frame construction with a central long stretcher mitred, mortised and tenoned to the shorts sides of the frame dividing the top into two equal halves. Small short mitred members then join the frame, the central long stretcher and each other to form an openwork lattice pattern. *Lingzhi* shaped *baitong* mounts are surface-mounted on to the four corners

黄花梨有束腰马蹄足滚凳脚踏

晚明（1573–1644）

- 长 52.8 厘米　宽 52.8 厘米
- 高 16.8 厘米

滚凳脚踏边框为标准格角攒边造，抹头可见明榫。正中安直枨平镶入大边把边框内空间一分为二，出透榫。每边中部各装横枨两根，中留长条空档，安中间粗两端细的活轴一根。直枨与横枨均以小格肩榫与边抹相互连接。活轴两旁各平镶木纹华美的心板。边抹冰盘沿上舒下敛，线条缓和。束腰与沿边起灯草线的洼堂肚牙条为一木连做，以抱肩榫与腿足和边框结合。牙子上灯草线延伸至腿足，下展为形状美好的马蹄足。边抹外缘包白铜窄条，四角内平镶白铜如意形包角。

脚踏与滚凳一般而言各为独立的家具。15世纪明朝的木匠手册《鲁班经匠家镜》中列有脚踏与滚凳的图例。此具滚凳亦适宜作脚踏用。一器两用，非常特别。

来源
| 香港嘉木堂 1995

展览
| 台北，1999，"风华再现：明清家具收藏展"，历史博物馆

出版
| 历史博物馆《风华再现：明清家具收藏展》台北，1999，页 199

《鲁班经匠家镜》
Lu Ban Jing Jia Jing
The Classic of Lu Ban and the Craftsmen's Mirror

《忠义水浒传》
Zhongyi Shuihu Zhuan
Outlaws of the Marsh

Massage stool & footrest

Huanghuali wood
Late Ming (1573-1644)
Width 52.8 cm (20 ¾")   Depth 52.8 cm (20 ¾")
Height 16.8 cm (6 ⅝")

The top is of standard mitre, mortise and tenon frame construction with exposed tenons on the short sides of the frame. A stretcher in the centre tenoned and set flush to the frame, divides the space inside the frame into two parts. The tenons are exposed. Each part is fitted with two horizontal stretchers, with a gap in between to house an olive-shaped wood-hinged roller. These stretchers meet the frame members and the central stretcher in T-mitre joints. On either sides of the rollers are inset flush, tongue-and-grooved floating panels. The edge of the frame moulds downwards and inwards. The recessed waist and the curved beaded-edged apron, made of one piece of wood, is mitred, mortised, tenoned and half-lapped to the legs which end in well shaped hoof feet. The edges of the frame top are mounted with narrow *baitong* strips and the four corners, inlaid with *ruyi* shaped mounts, also made of *baitong*.

Footrests and massage stools are usually separate pieces of furniture. Refer to the footrests and the massage stool illustrated in the 15th century carpenter's manual, *Lu Ban Jing Jiang Jia Jing*. This unusual piece which combines the functions of a footrest and a massage stool is almost unique.

Provenance

Grace Wu Bruce, Hong Kong, 1995

Exhibited

Taipei, 1999, "Splendor of Style: Classical Furniture from the Ming and Qing Dynasties", Museum of History

Published

Museum of History, *Splendor of Style: Classical Furniture from the Ming and Qing Dynasties*, Taipei, 1999, p. 199

滚凳脚踏边框为标准格角攒边造，正中安直枨平镶入大边把边框内空间一分为二，每边中部各装横枨两根，中留长条空档，安中间粗两端细的活轴一根。直枨与横枨均以小格肩榫与边抹相互连接。活轴两旁各平镶木纹华美心板；边抹外缘包白铜窄条，四角内平镶白铜如意形包角

The top is of standard mitre, mortise and tenon frame construction. A stretcher in the centre tenoned and set flush to the frame, divides the space inside the frame into two parts. Each part is fitted with two horizontal stretchers, with a gap in between to house an olive-shaped wood-hinged roller. These stretchers meet the frame members and the central stretcher in T-mitre joints. On either sides of the rollers are inset flush, tongue-and-grooved floating panels. The edges of the frame top are mounted with narrow *baitong* strips and the four corners, inlaid with *ruyi* shaped mounts, also made of *baitong*

箱 櫥 柜 格

Chests, Shelves & Cabinets

黄花梨衣箱

晚明（1573–1644）

- 长 76.2 厘米　宽 46.3 厘米
- 高 34 厘米

箱盖两拼取自一材，四角锼微弧形接合盖墙，内有两根出梢穿带支承。衣箱身立墙均独板造，底部打槽装底板，下有两根穿带出梢支承。箱身正面平镶莲花瓣形白铜面页，云头形拍子嵌黄铜装饰，开口容纳钮头。两侧安大弧形提环连两枚铜页加一枚护眼钱。背面平镶三只长方形合页，以帽钉固定。所有铜活均白铜制。此箱通体用黄花梨木造，包括盖顶和底板下的穿带，用料讲究。

衣箱为明代家居必备家具。17世纪话本《金瓶梅》版画插图中就多处能见造型与现例相似的衣箱，唯传世衣箱多为柴木造的清后期样品，用珍贵木材如黄花梨造于明末清初的衣箱数量稀少。较细与矮的黄花梨木箱子，传世品中有相当数量，但精致与大型如现例，需要在背面安三只合页支撑开关，实属罕见。

来源
| 香港嘉木堂 1995

出版
| 从未发表

《金瓶梅词话》
Jin Ping Mei Cihua
The Golden Lotus

《鲁班经匠家镜》
Lu Ban Jing Jiang Jia Jing
The Classic of Lu Ban and the Craftsmen's Mirror

Clothes Chest

Huanghuali wood
Late Ming (1573-1644)
Width 76.2 cm (30") Depth 46.3 cm (18 ¼")
Height 34 cm (13 ⅜")

The cover of two boards cut from the same timber, slightly curved at the edges, is tongue-and-grooved to the four sides. There are two transverse dovetailed stretchers on the inside. The body of the chest, made of single boards, has a bottom panel tongue-and-grooved to the sides and supported by two dovetailed transverse braces underneath. The central lotus-shaped *baitong* plate is inlaid flush into the chest. There is a cloud-motif lift-up hasp with *huangtong* inlay decorations and openings to house the lock receptacles. On the sides are two round surface-mounted plates with a large bail handle and a third protective plate below. There are three inlaid rectangular strap hinges on the back, secured by metal pins with rounded tops. The metalware is all made of *baitong*. The chest is made in *huanghuali* wood throughout, including the underneath transverse stretchers.

Clothes chests were an essential part of Ming furnishings as illustrated in the 17th century novel *Jin Ping Mei*, the Golden Lotus, but surviving examples are mostly made of softwood and dated to the Qing with precious *huanghuali* clothes chests being very rare. There is a number of smaller size *huanghuali* wood chests known but few other examples come to mind that are of comparable quality and size as the present piece, requiring three hinges on the back to facilitate the movement of the lid.

Provenance

Grace Wu Bruce, Hong Kong, 1995

Published

Never published

箱身正面平镶莲花瓣形白铜面页，云头形拍子嵌黄铜装饰，开口容纳钮头；两侧安大弧形提环连两枚铜页加一枚护眼钱；背面平镶三只长方形合页，以帽钉固定；所有铜活均白铜制

The central lotus-shaped *baitong* plate is inlaid flush into the chest. There is a cloud-motif lift-up hasp with *huangtong* inlay decorations and openings to house the lock receptacles. On the sides are two round surface-mounted plates with a large bail handle and a third protective plate below. There are three inlaid rectangular strap hinges on the back, secured by metal pins with rounded tops. The metalware is all made of *baitong*

《金瓶梅词话》
Jin Ping Mei Cihua
The Golden Lotus

《仇画列女传》
Qiuhua Lienu Zhuan
Biography of Women in Ancient China
Illustrated by Qiu Ying

《仇画列女传》
Qiuhua Lienu Zhuan
Biography of Women in Ancient China
Illustrated by Qiu Ying

箱盖两拼取自一材,四角锼微弧形接合盖墙,内有两根出梢穿带支承;底部打槽装底板,下有两根穿带出梢支承

The cover of two boards cut from the same timber, slightly curved at the edges, is tongue-and-grooved to the four sides. There are two transverse dovetailed stretchers on the inside. The bottom panel is tongue-and-grooved to the sides and supported by two dovetailed transverse braces underneath

黄花梨大衣箱（成对）

晚明（1573–1644）

- 长 79 厘米　宽 50.8 厘米
- 高 35 厘米

箱盖四立墙打槽嵌装两板相接的盖顶，四角平镶如意云纹白铜饰件，盖墙四角亦平镶白铜护页加固。箱盖内部装两根穿带出梢支承，均出透榫。箱身立墙四角亦平镶铜护页，底部内打槽嵌装底板，下有两根穿带出梢支承，同样出透榫。盖口与箱口接触面上起灯草线，此线不仅是为了装饰，起线加厚子口，有更重要的加固作用。所有铜活皆为白铜制，正面平镶圆形面页，拍子作云头形，开口容纳钮头。两侧各安菊瓣形铜页两枚，弧形提环，其下还加一枚护提环垫铜页。背面平镶两只长方形合页。此箱通体用黄花梨木造，包括盖顶和底板下的穿带，用料讲究。

成对彻黄花梨，即通体以黄花梨造的衣箱，传世品中笔者只知三对，非常难得。

来源

香港嘉木堂 1991

出版

从未发表

Pair of large clothes chests

Huanghuali wood
Late Ming (1573-1644)
Width 79 cm (30 ¼")   Depth 50.8 cm (20")
Height 35 cm (13 ¾")

The two-board top of the lid is tongue-and-grooved to the four sides supported by two transverse dovetailed stretchers underneath, both with exposed tenons. There are *ruyi*-shaped *baitong* mounts set flush at the four corners, and rectangular mounts also set flush at the corners of the walls for reinforcement. The body of the chest, also with *baitong* mounts on all four corners, has a bottom panel tongue-and-grooved to the sides supported by two dovetailed stretchers underneath, also with exposed tenons. There are beaded edges on the lid and the body where they meet, which serve as subtle decoration as well as to improve the durability of the chest by enlarging the area of the surface of contact. The metalware is all made of *baitong*, in front is a round plate inlaid flush into the centre and there is a cloud motif lift-up hasp with openings to house the lock receptacles. On each side are two small chrysanthemum-shaped plates with a wide U-shaped handle and an additional protective plate below. Two rectangular strap hinges are on the back, also inlaid. The chest is made in *huanghuali* wood throughout, including the underneath transverse stretchers.

Among extant examples, there are only three pairs of clothes chests made in *huanghuali* wood throughout known to this author, very rare.

Provenance

Grace Wu Bruce, Hong Kong, 1991

Published

Never published

黄花梨凤纹顶箱柜

晚明（1573–1644）

- 长 58.5 厘米　宽 35 厘米
- 高 42.2 厘米

顶箱柜顶以格角榫攒边框平镶面心板，下装两根穿带出梢支承。抹头可见明榫。方材四足以粽角榫与柜顶边框接合，出一透榫，侧面打槽纳入齐平的心板成柜帮与背板。其下亦以粽角榫与柜底连结。柜底结构与柜顶相同，也装两根穿带出梢支承。柜门可装可卸，用标准格角榫攒边框，平镶起委角灯草线开光内满雕飞凤缠枝牡丹纹心板。背面安一根穿带，出梢装入门框。柜内中央安屉板。柜身之长方形四合页、面页、钮头与寿纹吊牌皆用白铜造。钮头钉在屉板上，面页开口。柜门关后，钮头露出在面页之上，以便穿钉加锁。此具顶箱柜通体用黄花梨制，包括柜顶与底下的穿带，非常考究。

此顶箱柜是四件柜中一组的立柜以上的小柜。柜门高浮雕飞凤，凤身蟠卷两首双向与缠枝牡丹组成图案，非常精美。黄花梨传世品中达到这样雕刻水平的十分罕见。凤纹一般为皇后、公主的标志。这顶箱柜应是宫廷器物。

来　源
| 香港嘉木堂 1998

出　版
| 从未发表

Phoenix-motif cabinet

Huanghuali wood
Late Ming (1573-1644)
Width 58.5 cm (23") Depth 35 cm (13 ¾")
Height 42.2 cm (16 ⅝")

The top of the cabinet is of mitre, mortise and tenon frame construction with a two-board tongue-and-grooved, flush, floating panel supported by two dovetailed transverse stretchers underneath. There are exposed tenons on the short sides of the frame top. The four square uprights, pyramid-joined to the top with one tenon exposed, have *huanghuali* flush, floating panels tongue-and-grooved to them on the sides and back, and are pyramid-joined to the base which is constructed similarly to the top, with two dovetailed transverse stretchers underneath. The two removable doors are also of standard mitre, mortise and tenon frame construction with floating panels beautifully carved in high relief with flying phoenix amidst peonies enclosed in a *wojiao* corner moulded beaded frame. There is a dovetailed transverse stretcher tenoned into the door frame on the inside. Inside the cabinet, a shelf divides the interior into two spaces. The rectangular hinges and the central plates with openings housing the lock receptacles fitted to the edge of the shelf inside, and the stylised *shou*-motif door pulls are all made of *baitong*. The cabinet is made of *huanghuali* wood throughout, including the underneath transverse stretchers.

This cabinet is the top section of a compound cabinet. The doors are exquisitely carved in high relief with flying phoenixes facing each other amidst peonies. It is exceeding rare to find carving of this quality on *huanghuali* wood furniture and the emblem of phoenix, thought to be reserved for the court, would point to an imperial provenance for this piece.

Provenance

Grace Wu Bruce, Hong Kong, 1998

Published

Never published

方材四足以粽角榫与柜顶边框接合，侧面打槽纳入齐平的心板成柜帮与背板。其下亦以粽角榫与柜底连结

The four square uprights, pyramid-joined to the top have *huanghuali* flush, floating panels tongue-and-grooved to them on the sides and back, and are pyramid-joined to the base which is constructed similarly to the top

顶箱柜顶与柜底以格角榫攒边框平镶面心板，下装两根穿带出梢支承

The top and the base of the cabinet is of mitre, mortise and tenon frame construction with a tongue-and-grooved, flush, floating panel supported by two dovetailed transverse stretchers underneath

柜门可装可卸，用标准格角榫攒边框，平镶起委角灯草线开光内满雕飞凤缠枝牡丹纹心板

The two removable doors are also of standard mitre, mortise and tenon frame construction with floating panels beautifully carved in high relief with flying phoenix amidst peonies enclosed in a *wojiao* corner moulded beaded frame

黄花梨扛箱式带抽屉柜

晚明（1573–1644）

- 长 52.7 厘米　宽 38.8 厘米
- 高 64.5 厘米

柜顶与两侧柜帮独板造，用燕尾榫平板接合，插入底座。底座边框锼壸门轮廓打槽装板，下以一根穿带出梢支承。背板四周嵌入柜顶、两侧柜帮和底座的槽口。柜门为格角攒边打槽平镶独板门心，背面安两根穿带出梢装入门框。柜上平镶方形白铜合页，面页作海棠花式，上有钮头与吊牌。两侧安大提环与手掌宽度相合，菊花纹面页，其下加一枚花瓣形护眼钱。柜顶四角镶如意头白铜包角加固，底座包角为长方形。柜内设抽屉四层，总共七具，皆安有菊花纹面页与瓶形拉手。此柜彻黄花梨制，包括抽屉内部，底座心板与其下穿带，非常讲究。

此柜设计近似通常所称的药箱，即内列抽屉的小箱子，通过放大尺寸制造而成。两侧安提环，设底座，似是为便于出行携带。但用通体黄花梨木精制的现例，沉重异常，不方便搬抬上路，更适宜置放书斋或寝室中，用以贮放书籍、文玩和贵重物品。

来源
| 香港嘉木堂 1996

出版
| 从未发表

Carry-type cabinet with drawers

Huanghuali wood
Late Ming (1573-1644)
Width 52.7 cm (20 ¾") Depth 38.8 cm (15 ¼")
Height 64.5 cm (25 ⅜")

The top and the sides of the cabinet are made of dovetailed single board panels and the side panels are inserted into the base, constructed as a stand with curvilinear-shaped stretchers fitted with a floating panel supported by one transverse brace underneath. The back panel is tongue-and-grooved to the top, sides and the base. The two doors of mitred frame construction, have single board, flush tongue-and-grooved floating panels with two dovetailed stretchers tenoned to the door frame on the insides. There are rectangular *baitong* inlaid hinges and begonia-shaped door plates with lock receptacles and shaped door pulls. On the sides are wide U-shaped handles with two chrysanthemum plates and an additional protective plate of floral shape below. There are inlaid *baitong* reinforcement plates ending in *ruyi* head shape at the four corners of the top and rectangular ones at the corners of the base. Inside the cabinet, there are four rows of drawers, seven in all, with *baitong* chrysanthemum-shaped plates and vase-shaped pulls. This cabinet is made in *huanghuali* wood throughout, including the insides of the drawers, the floating panel inside the base and the supporting stretcher underneath.

This cabinet takes its design inspiration from small table top chests, and is a magnified version of a medicine chest, a type of small chest whose interior is fitted with many drawers. This cabinet with handles on the sides and constructed with a base, gives the impression that it was made for easy carriage, and is suitable for travelling. In reality, due to the fact that it is made throughout in precious *huanghuali* wood and is very heavy, it is not easily portable, and is more suitable for usage indoors to store books, antiques and valuables.

Provenance

Grace Wu Bruce, Hong Kong, 1996

Published

Never published

柜顶四角镶如意头白铜包角加固

There are inlaid *baitong* reinforcement plates ending in *ruyi* head shape at the four corners of the top

底座边框锼壸门轮廓打槽装板，下以一根穿带出梢支承

The base, constructed as a stand with curvilinear-shaped stretchers fitted with a floating panel supported by one transverse brace underneath

背板四周嵌入柜顶、两侧柜帮和底座的槽口；底座包铜角加固

The back panel is tongue-and-grooved to the top, sides and the base; Rectangular *baitong* plates at the base corners for reinforcement

两侧安大提环与手掌宽度相合，菊花纹面页，其下加一枚花瓣形护眼钱

On the sides are wide U-shaped handles with two chrysanthemum plates and an additional protective plate of floral shape below

黄花梨两开门扛箱式柜

晚明（1573–1644）
- 长 73.4 厘米　宽 43.8 厘米
- 高 83.1 厘米

柜顶与两侧柜帮均为独板，用燕尾榫平板接合，插入底座。底座攒边打槽装板，下有两根穿带支承。底座大边前后浮雕壸门曲线，四角包铜饰件加固。底座两侧抹头植立柱，用葫芦形站牙抵夹。上与横梁相接。横梁紧贴柜顶。立柱上下均镶铜饰件加固。横梁上安大方角铜环和护页。背板嵌入柜顶、底座、两侧柜帮的槽口。两扇可装可拆的柜门格角攒边装独板心板。独板面心取自一材，木纹对称。背面安两根穿带。方形面页与四合页，均卧槽平镶。柜顶两侧包铜条加固。柜内设隔板两层，底安抽屉三具。铜活皆为黄铜制。此扛箱式柜通体黄花梨造。

此具扛箱造型黄花梨柜，横梁上安大铜环，似供手提或上杠抬行，但此硕大通体黄花梨精工制作的箱柜非常重，立柱上下虽有铜件加固，横梁绝对禁不起抬行，所以与前例相同，它们非实用扛箱，而是室内高级贵重家具。

来源
香港嘉木堂 1998

出版
从未发表

Carry-type cabinet

Huanghuali wood
Late Ming (1573-1644)
Width 73.4 cm (28 ⅞")   Depth 43.8 cm (17 ¼")
Height 83.1 cm (32 ¹¹⁄₁₆")

The top and sides of the cabinet are made of single board panels dovetail-joined together and the side panels are inserted into the base of mitre, mortise and tenon frame construction with a floating panel supported by two stretchers underneath. The front and the back stretchers of the base are carved in relief with curvilinear shapes and there are inlaid metal plates for reinforcement at the corners. On the sides of the base are two uprights joined to a handle at the top, which sits tightly on the top panel of the cabinet. Gourd-shaped spandrels are fitted to the uprights on both sides. Metal plates are applied to where the uprights meet the base and the handle on top for reinforcement. A large square metal handle with a protective plate is fitted to the centre of the handle. The back panel is tongue-and-grooved into the sides, the top and the base. The removable doors, made of mitred frame construction, have two matched, single board panels tongue-and-grooved into the frame with two dovetailed stretchers on the insides. They are fitted with inlaid rectangular plates and lock receptacles. The four hinges are also inlaid. Inside the cabinet, there are two shelves, and three drawers at the bottom. The metalware is all made of *huangtong*. The entire piece is made in *huanghuali* wood throughout.

This cabinet with its fitted large metal handle suitable for slotting a pole through, appears to be made for carriage, for travelling. However, this finely crafted piece made in precious *huanghuali* wood throughout is extremely heavy, and although the upright joins have reinforcement metal plates, they are not strong enough to support the cabinet if lifted. Like the last example, they are not actual carry chests but are fine cabinets meant for indoor use after the design of carry chests.

Provenance

Grace Wu Bruce, Hong Kong, 1998

Published

Never published

《仇画列女传》
Qiuhua Lienu Zhuan
Biography of Women in Ancient China
Illustrated by Qiu Ying

底座两侧抹头植立柱，用葫芦形站牙抵夹；上与横梁相接；横梁紧贴柜顶；立柱上下均镶铜饰件加固；横梁上安大方角铜环和护页

On the sides of the base are two uprights joined to a handle at the top, which sits tightly on the top panel of the cabinet. Gourd-shaped spandrels are fitted to the uprights on both sides. Metal plates are applied to where the uprights meet the base and the handle on top for reinforcement. A large square metal handle with a protective plate is fitted to the centre of the handle

背板嵌入柜顶、底座、两侧柜帮的槽口；底座大边前后浮雕壸门曲线，四角包铜饰件加固

The back panel is tongue-and-grooved into the sides, the top and the base. The front and the back stretchers of the base are carved in relief with curvilinear shapes and there are inlaid metal plates for reinforcement at the corners

横梁紧贴柜顶；横梁上安大方角铜环和护页

The handle at the top, which sits tightly on the top panel of the cabinet
Metal plates are applied to the handle on top for reinforcement. A large square metal handle with a protective plate is fitted to the centre of the handle

底座攒边打槽装板，下有两根穿带支承

The base is of mitre, mortise and tenon frame construction with a floating panel supported by two stretchers underneath

黄花梨三层全敞带抽屉大架格

晚明（1573–1644）

- 长 110.7 厘米　宽 41.1 厘米
- 高 188.1 厘米

大架格方材注面，顶端为格角榫攒边平镶独板面心，下装两根出梢穿带。四腿足以粽角榫与架格顶边框接合，出一透榫。近架格顶部施横枨，顺枨作小格肩与腿足相接，中镶心板，前方装三具抽屉，用矮老两根分隔。两侧及后方落堂装板。架格设三层隔板，中层下亦安三具抽屉，与顶端抽屉结构相同，唯体型较大。横顺枨均用小格肩榫与腿足连接。隔板下都装两根出梢穿带。下层前后方安镂云纹角牙，左右装曲线弧形起灯草线牙子。抽屉脸上均装白铜面页、拉手、圆筒型鼻纽和活动锁片，纳入顺枨底部槽口。此架格通体黄花梨木造。

此件架格内外用纹理细密华美的上等黄花梨木制。每层隔板上空间上小下大渐进。中层抽屉也比上层一组厚，是一件考究平衡比例至极点的作品。而在近1.9米的顶端加设一组抽屉，抽屉脸还安锁销及锁鼻，正是呼应中部抽屉的手段。十分特别。

台北陈启德先生收藏一件大架格（历史博物馆 1999，页164），设计与现例相同，只是尺码微有分别，及前牙条形状不同。

来源
| 香港嘉木堂 1989

出版
| 从未发表

陈启德先生藏品
Chen Chite collection

Large bookcase

Huanghuali wood
Late Ming (1573-1644)
Width 110.7 cm (43 ⁹⁄₁₆″) Depth 41.1 cm (16 ³⁄₁₆″)
Height 188.1 cm (74 ¹⁄₁₆″)

This bookcase is of square thumb-moulded members. The top is of mitre, mortise and tenon construction with a single-board, flush, tongue-and-grooved floating panel supported by two dovetailed transverse stretchers underneath. Four uprights are pyramid-joined to the top, with one tenon exposed. Horizontal stretchers are T-mitred, mortised and tenoned to the uprights near the top with a tongue-and-grooved floating panel to enclose a space to house three drawers, separated by pillar-shaped struts. Single-board panels are fitted to the sides and back. Below are three shelves, the middle one are also fitted with three drawers that are slightly larger than the top ones. All the horizontal stretchers meet the uprights in T-mitre joints and below each shelf, are two transverse dovetailed stretchers for support. Cloud-shaped spandrels are fitted underneath the bottom shelf in front and back and there are beaded-edged curvilinear aprons on the sides. On each drawer front are a *baitong* plate and pull, round tubular lock receptacles and a sliding lock plate which fits into an opening on the underside of the horizontal stretcher above. The entire piece is made of *huanghuali* wood throughout.

This bookcase is made of well-figured, tight grain *huanghuali* wood of fine quality. The spacing between each shelf is smaller at the top, gradually becoming larger at the bottom, and the sets of drawers also vary in size, the top ones less thick than the middle ones. This bookcase is designed and constructed with balance and proportions very much in mind, resulting in the unusual feature of drawers with locks at the height of nearly 1 metre 90 centimetres high, to balance the central ones.

A very similar piece is in the Chen Chite collection, Taipei (Museum of History, 1999, p. 164), differing only slightly in its size and the shape of the low apron.

Provenance

Grace Wu Bruce, Hong Kong, 1989

Published

Never published

下层前后方安镂云纹角牙

Cloud-shaped spandrels are fitted underneath the bottom shelf in front and back

黄花梨大方角柜（成对）

晚明（1573-1644）

- 长 105 厘米　宽 62.6 厘米
- 高 187 厘米

此对方角柜体形硕大，选料考究。柜顶以格角榫攒边框镶板心，下装两根出梢穿带支承。抹头可见明榫。四根方材柜腿足上以棕角榫与顶边框接合，出一透榫。内沿压混面接窄平边线。柜顶边框内沿亦起同样线脚。柜门上方直枨中部隆起刻皮条线，两旁起混面接窄平线，作肩接入柜足，其上落堂装板。活动式闩杆两旁可装可卸的柜门为标准格角榫攒边框，背面各安两根出梢穿带。门框内沿同样起混面连窄平边线。门下两根直枨作肩纳入柜足，两根枨子间落堂装板。板后柜内空间成为柜膛。柜下安壶门轮廓沿边起线牙子。柜内设隔板，下安抽屉两具。柜膛上盖板两块以木轴启闭。抽屉脸与膛板上安拉手与菊花瓣面页。柜背两扇可装可卸，用栽榫与柜身连结。长方形平镶合页、面页、锁钮与拉手俱为白铜。此柜内外所有构件包括柜顶心板、穿带等通体用黄花梨造。

此对大方角柜保存状况极佳。通体黄花梨造。大方角柜外形方正，线条明确利落。虽全身光素，但线脚装饰细腻，壶门式牙条弧线柔和悦目，刚劲中含柔婉，简约明快中见精致。

来源

香港嘉木堂

香港攻玉山房藏品 1991-2002

纽约 佳士得 2002 年 9 月 20 日

展览

香港，1991，香港中文大学文物馆

新加坡，1997-1999，亚洲文明博物馆

伦敦，1999 年 11 月，当代艺术中心

出版

Grace Wu Bruce, *Dreams of Chu Tan Chamber and the Romance with Huanghuali Wood: The Dr. S. Y. Yip Collection of Classic Chinese Furniture*, Hong Kong, 1991. 伍嘉恩《攻玉山房藏明式黄花梨家具：楮檀室梦旅》香港、1991、页 117

Christie's, *The Dr S. Y. Yip Collection of Fine and Important Classical Chinese Furniture*, New York, 20 September 2002. 佳士得《攻玉山房藏中国古典家具精萃》纽约，2002 年 9 月 20 日，编号 41

Pair of square-corner cabinets

Huanghuali wood
Late Ming (1573-1644)
Width 105 cm (41 ⅜") Depth 62.6 cm (24 ⅝")
Height 187 cm (73 ⅝")

Of imposing size and excellent material, the top of the cabinet is of mitre, mortise and tenon frame construction with a tongue-and-grooved, floating panel supported by two dovetailed transverse stretchers underneath. There are exposed tenons on the short sides of the frame. The four square uprights, pyramid-joined to the top, each with one long tenon exposed, are edged with line mouldings ending in a narrow flat band, where they meet the side, back panels and the doors. The top frame members are similarly moulded. In front near the top, a stretcher with a central raised flat band and similar line mouldings on both sides, is mitred, mortised, and tenoned to the uprights above the doors, and above it is inset a recessed panel. The removable doors, on either side of the removable central stile, are of standard mitred, mortised, and tenoned frame single board, floating panel construction, with two transverse dovetailed stretchers tenoned into the door frame on the insides. The door frame members are similarly edged with line mouldings where they meet the recessed door panels. Below the doors are two mitred stretchers, similarly decorated as the stretcher above the doors. A tongue-and-grooved recessed panel is inset between them, forming a cabinet cavity behind. Below is a beautifully shaped, beaded-edged, curvilinear apron. There are similar aprons on the sides and back. Inside the cabinet, there is a central section which constitutes a shelf and two drawers with *baitong* plates and pulls. Below there are two wood-hinged covers for the cabinet cavity, with *baitong* plates and ring pulls. The two back panels are removable. The rectangular *baitong* door hinges are inlaid. The central plates, also rectangular and inlaid, have three lock receptacles and shaped door pulls. Every member of these cabinets, including the top panels, inside stretchers, and back panels, is made of *huanghuali* wood.

This example is in an excellent state of preservation. Made of *huanghuali* throughout, these large cabinets of square shapes with strict, clean lines are subtly decorated with line mouldings and unexpected cusped aprons. These features make them at once powerful and alluring, simple yet refined.

Provenance

Grace Wu Bruce, Hong Kong

Dr S Y Yip Collection, Hong Kong, 1991 – 2002

Christie's, New York, 20 September 2002

Exhibited

Hong Kong, 1991, Art Gallery, The Chinese University of Hong Kong

Singapore, 1997 – 1999, National Heritage Board, Asian Civilisations Museum

London, November 1999, Institute of Contemporary Arts

Published

Grace Wu Bruce, *Dreams of Chu Tan Chamber and the Romance with Huanghuali Wood: The Dr. S. Y. Yip Collection of Classic Chinese Furniture*, Hong Kong, 1991, p. 117

Christie's, *The Dr S Y Yip Collection of Fine and Important Classical Chinese Furniture*, New York, 20 September 2002, no. 41

柜膛上盖板两块以木轴启闭

Two wood-hinged covers for the cabinet cavity

此柜内外所有构件包括柜顶心版、穿带等通体用黄花梨造

Every member of these cabinets, including the top panels, inside stretchers, and back panels, is made of *huanghuali* wood

黄花梨瘿木木轴门圆角柜（成对）

晚明（1573–1644）

- 长 74 厘米　宽 43.8 厘米
- 高 126.4 厘米

柜顶为标准格角攒边打槽镶面心板，下装两根穿带出梢支承。抹头可见明榫。冰盘沿起混面上下压窄边线。四根外圆内方起窄边线的柜腿微向外倾，上以长短榫纳入柜帽边框。活动式闩杆两旁的柜门为标准格角攒边打槽装板，门框三边起混面压边线，外侧起双混面，两头伸出门轴，纳入柜帽与门下前腿足间底枨的白窝。柜门板心使用花纹细密瑰丽的独板楠木瘿子，背面安两根穿带出梢装入门框。柜内有活动隔板两层。门下底枨之下安带耳形牙头牙条，两端嵌入柜脚，上以齐头碰底枨。两侧及后背牙子相类。弧面白铜面页紧贴混面闩杆与门框。吊牌与方形钮头亦为白铜制。独板楠木瘿柜门满布细密葡萄纹。四块独板柜帮纹理相接对称，取自一材。柜内与柜背板上原来的漆灰、糊织物与漆裹保存近乎完整。

圆角木轴门柜是中国传统家具最精巧优美的设计之一。四足自喷面的柜帽下展出。这种下舒上敛的设计赋予此柜集精致优雅亦兼具平衡稳固的优点于一身。柜门门轴纳入柜身的白窝，以为轴门旋转开启，令柜身无须附加铜合页，整体线条利落清爽，一气呵成。

柜门及闩杆上安装长方形白铜面页、吊牌与钮头的用途是为上锁、开启柜门及垫护木门框不被拉手损坏。而铜活安位得宜，又点缀了全身光素的柜子成为装饰。

此对木轴门圆角柜镶楠木瘿心板。多年所见，黄花梨造楠木瘿心板家具均为上品。唯瘿木质软，旋转的纹理多，容易沿着纹理爆裂，所以传世瘿木心板多破裂残缺。保存完好如现例的比率较黄花梨硬木心板面的例子低很多。倍觉珍稀。

来源
| 香港嘉木堂 1996

出版
| 从未发表

Pair of sloping-stile wood-hinged cabinets

Huanghuali and burl wood
Late Ming (1573-1644)
Width 74 cm (29 ⅛") Depth 43.8 cm (17 ¼")
Height 126.4 cm (49 ⅜")

The top is of standard mitre, mortise and tenon, tongue-and-grooved floating panel construction with two dovetailed supporting transverse braces below. The edge of the frame members is rounded with very narrow beaded edges. There are exposed tenons on the short sides of the frame top. The gently splayed main stiles, double tenoned into the top, are rounded on the outside, squared on the inside and beaded where they meet the side panels and the doors. The doors, on either side of the removable central stile, are of standard mitred frame, tongue-and-grooved floating panel construction with beaded edges except for the outside stiles which are double moulded and finish on extended dowels which fit into sockets in the underside of the frame top and the horizontal stretcher below the doors. The single board door panels are made of highly figured burl wood, the burl of *nanmu*, and there are two dovetailed transverse braces tenoned into the door frame. Inside the cabinet there are two removable shelves. Beneath the shaped stretcher below the doors is a shaped apron tongue-and-grooved into the legs and butt-joined to the underside of the stretcher. There are similar aprons on the sides and back. *Baitong* plates are curved to fit the door frame members and the central stile. There are square lock receptacles and shaped door pulls, also made of *baitong*. The door panels are made of single board burl wood of tightly grained grape seed pattern and the four *huanghuali* single board side panels are all matching grain, cut from the same piece of wood. The original clay, ramie and lacquer coating on the insides and the back of the cabinets are almost completely intact.

Provenance

Grace Wu Bruce, Hong Kong, 1996

Published

Never published

冰盘沿起混面上下压窄边线；门框三边起混面压边线，外侧起双混面，两头伸出门轴，纳入柜帽与门下前腿足间底枨的白窝

The edge of the frame members is rounded with very narrow beaded edges. The door frame members are with beaded edges except for the outside stiles which are double moulded and finish on extended dowels which fit into sockets in the underside of the frame top and the horizontal stretcher below the doors

柜背板上原来的漆灰、糊织物与漆裹保存近乎完整

The original clay, ramie and lacquer coating on the insides and the back of the cabinets are almost completely intact.

柜门背面安两根穿带出梢装入门框；柜内有活动隔板两层

The door panels have two dovetailed transverse braces tenoned into the door frame. Inside the cabinet there are two removable shelves

One of the most ingenious and beautiful designs of classic Chinese furniture is the sloping-stile, wood-hinged cabinet. The four main stiles are recessed from the corner of the top and slope gently outward in a subtle, almost imperceptible splay. This simple design feature gives the cabinet its refined elegance and a sense of balance and stability.

The doors, with extended dowels on both ends, fit into sockets in the cabinet frame members and act as hinges. Free from the necessity of applied hinges, the clean lines of the cabinet are not interfered with. The rectangular metal plates with their lock receptacles and door pulls not only serve a practical function, but are also judiciously placed as decoration for the otherwise completely plain piece.

This pair of sloping-stile wood-hinged cabinets has an inset *nanmu* burl panel. *Huanghuali* furniture made with *nanmu* burl wood panels seen by this author has all been exceptionally refined. However, as burl wood is relatively soft by nature and their whirling pattern renders them easily breakable along the grain, many examples encountered were badly damaged with large losses. Hence, the survival rate of burl wood panel pieces is much lower than those made with *huanghuali* panels, making them rarer and more precious.

黄花梨甜瓜棱木轴门圆角柜

晚明（1573–1644）

- 长 93.3 厘米　宽 52 厘米
- 高 184.2 厘米

柜顶为标准格角榫攒边打槽装面心板，抹头可见明榫，下装一根穿带出梢支承。边抹立面起双混面压窄平线。四腿足开甜瓜棱线脚，上端以长短榫纳入柜顶边框，出一透榫。活动式闩杆两旁的柜门，以标准格角榫攒边打槽装独板，门框外侧两头伸出木轴，纳入柜帽与门下前腿足间底枨的白窝。柜门板心整板对开，花纹对称。背面安四根穿带出梢装入门框。柜内有活动屉板一层置于柜帮穿带上，中央一层装两具抽屉，带白铜面页与白铜镶红铜拉手。门下底枨之下安起线牙条格角接合叶形牙头，两端嵌入柜脚，上方齐头碰底枨。两侧亦安类似牙子。弧面长方形白铜面页紧贴双混面闩杆与门框。方形白铜钮头嵌红铜圆框，内镂花纹。白铜吊牌嵌红铜黄铜太极图。柜门门框、柜帮边枨、闩杆和门下底枨皆起双混面。柜内与柜背板部分区域原来的漆灰、糊织物与漆裹保存近乎完整。

甜瓜棱线脚圆角柜属传世木轴门柜中最稀少的种类。黄花梨桌案也不多见腿足起棱分瓣线脚的例子。从多年实例观察，开甜瓜棱线脚的黄花梨家具，一般制作特别精致，选料特别讲究。这具黄花梨甜瓜棱木轴门柜精工细做，比例近乎完美，铜活制作又特别讲究。而木纹对称、纹理飞扬的黄花梨柜门，展示出最上乘黄花梨木材的面貌。

来源

香港嘉木堂 1994

出版

Grace Wu Bruce, "Sculptures To Use", *First Under Heaven: The Art of Asia*, London, 1997. 伍嘉恩《实用雕塑》，《天下第一：亚洲艺术》伦敦，1997，页 78

伍嘉恩《明式家具二十年经眼录》紫禁城出版社，北京，2010，页 220

Sloping-stile wood-hinged cabinet

Huanghuali wood
Late Ming (1573-1644)
Width 93.3 cm (36 ¾") Depth 52 cm (20 ½")
Height 184.2 cm (72 ⁷⁄₁₆")

The top of the cabinet is of standard mitre, mortise and tenon, tongue-and-grooved floating panel construction with exposed tenons on the short sides and a dovetailed supporting transverse brace underneath. The edge of the frame begins and ends in a narrow flat band and is decorated with lobe-shaped mouldings. The four main stiles, double tenoned into the top with one tenon exposed, are lobe-shaped with *tiangualeng* ridges in between. The doors, on either side of the removable central stile, are of standard mitred frame construction and the outside stiles finish on extended dowels which fit into sockets in the underside of the frame top and the horizontal stretcher below the doors. The single board floating panels, with matching grain, has four dovetailed transverse braces tenoned into the door frame. Inside the cabinet, there is one removable shelf which rests on the dovetailed transverse braces of the side panels as well as one lower section which constitutes a shelf and two drawers with *baitong* plates and *baitong* with inlaid *hongtong* pulls. Beneath the shaped stretcher below the doors is a beaded-edged apron with leaf-shaped mitred spandrels. Similarly shaped aprons are on the sides. Rectangular *baitong* plates are curved to fit the door frame members and the central stile. There are *baitong* square lock receptacles and shaped door pulls with inlaid *hongtong* and *huangtong* motifs. All the door frame, side frame stretchers as well as the central stile and the stretcher below the door are decorated with lobe-shaped mouldings. The original clay, ramie and lacquer coating is almost completely intact on the inside and part of the back of the cabinet.

Cabinets with *tiangualeng* lobe-shaped moulded stiles are perhaps the rarest type in surviving examples of Ming sloping-stile cabinets. Tables with lobe-shaped mouldings are also rare. Extant examples of classical furniture made in *huanghuali* wood with these mouldings are often especially refined with superlative choice of timber. The present example with beautifully fashioned mouldings and exquisite metalware is of almost perfect proportions, and its matching door panels of highly figured wood demonstrate *huanghuali* wood at its best.

Provenance

Grace Wu Bruce, Hong Kong, 1994

Published

Grace Wu Bruce, "Sculptures To Use", *First Under Heaven: The Art of Asia*, London, 1997, p. 78

Grace Wu Bruce, *Two Decades of Ming Furniture*, The Forbidden City Publishing House, Beijing, 2010, p. 220

弧面长方形白铜面页紧贴双混面闩杆与门框；方形白铜钮头嵌红铜圆框，内镂花纹；白铜吊牌嵌红铜黄铜太极图

Rectangular *baitong* plates are curved to fit the door frame members and the central stile. There are *baitong* square lock receptacles and shaped door pulls with inlaid *hongtong* and *huangtong* motifs

边抹立面起双混面压窄平线；四腿足开甜瓜棱线脚

The edge of the frame begins and ends in a narrow flat band and is decorated with lobe-shaped mouldings. The cabinet stiles are lobe-shaped with *tiangualeng* ridges in between

柜内有活动屉板一层置于柜帮穿带上，中央一层装两具抽屉，带白铜面页与白铜镶红铜拉手

Inside the cabinet, there is one removable shelf which rests on the dovetailed transverse braces of the side panels as well as one lower section which constitutes a shelf and two drawers with *baitong* plates and *baitong* with inlaid *hongtong* pulls

黄花梨有柜膛方材大木轴门柜（成对）

晚明（1573–1644）

- 长 91.5 厘米　宽 47 厘米
- 高 204.5 厘米

柜顶为标准格角攒边打槽镶板，抹头可见明榫，下装两根穿带出梢支承。四根方材注面柜腿，上以长短榫纳入柜顶边框出一透榫。活动式闩杆两旁的柜门为标准格角攒边打槽装板，门框三边注面，外侧打洼儿后隆起混面，两头伸出门轴，纳入造于柜帽与门下前腿足间横枨的白窝。四块柜门板心皆为整板对开，纹理对称，背面安三根穿带出梢装入门框。柜内有屉板一层和安有两具抽屉的抽屉架。柜帮三面为独板，一为两板拼接。门下横枨打槽嵌入柜膛立墙，下加底枨格肩纳入腿足，底枨下安带牙头的牙条，两端嵌入柜脚，上齐头碰底枨。两侧亦安类似牙子。柜门及闩杆安装长方形白铜面页、吊牌与钮头。此对柜的所有构件均为注面。柜内与背板上原来的漆灰、糊织物与漆裹皆保留完好。

此对方材木轴门柜特别高大，气魄非凡。四块整板对开的柜门心板色泽温润，质地细密，涡状木纹生动瑰丽，将黄花梨木特色展现得淋漓尽致。四柜帮同样纹理细密生动华美呈涡状，与四块门心板取自一材，非常难得。

此对柜也有别于一般使用圆材的木轴门柜，属于较少见的方材类型，其传世件数远少于圆材类型。方材制作，更见平整简洁、干净利落。不愧为超越时空的永恒之作。

来源
| 香港嘉木堂 1991

出版
| 从未发表

Pair of large sloping-stile wood-hinged cabinets

Huanghuali wood
Late Ming (1573-1644)
Width 91.5 cm (36") Depth 47 cm (18 ½")
Height 204.5 cm (80 ½")

The top is of standard mitre, mortise and tenon frame, tongue-and-grooved floating panel construction with exposed tenons on the short sides and two dovetailed supporting transverse braces underneath. The four main stiles, double tenoned into the top with one tenon exposed, are square in section and thumb-moulded. The doors, on either side of the removable central stile, are of standard mitred frame construction and the outside stiles finish on extended dowels which fit into sockets in the underside of the frame top and the horizontal shaped stretcher below the doors. The single board floating panels, all four doors matching, have three dovetailed transverse braces tenoned into the door frame. Inside the cabinet there is a shelf and a central section which constitutes a shelf and two drawers. Three of the side panels are single boards and one is of two-board, but all cut from the same plank. Beneath the shaped stretcher below the doors is a tongue-and-grooved panel, then a mitred stretcher and then a plain shaped apron with spandrels. Similarly shaped aprons are on the sides. There are rectangular *baitong* plates on the door frame members and the central stile with lock receptacles and door pulls. The members of the cabinets are gently thumb-moulded throughout. The original clay, ramie and lacquer coating remain almost completely intact on the inside as well as the back of the cabinets.

This pair of sloping-stile wood-hinge cabinets is extraordinarily tall and imposing. Their single-board doors, with their magnificent colour and tight-grain whirling pattern, all matching and from the same plank of wood, demonstrate *huanghuali* wood at its best. They also belong to a small group of sloping-stile wood-hinged cabinets which are made with square stiles rather than round ones and they are much rarer in extant examples than those of round stiles. The resultant clean strict lines render them almost contemporary in aesthetics, they are timeless classic.

Provenance

Grace Wu Bruce, Hong Kong, 1991

Published

Never published

床榻

BEDS

黄花梨高束腰外翻马蹄足翘头榻

晚明（1573–1644）

- 长 201.2 厘米　宽 84.5 厘米
- 高 48.6 厘米

榻面格角攒边造，两端高起的小翘头与抹头一木连做。边抹冰盘沿平直，自中部打宽洼儿再内缩收尾。四框内缘踩边打眼造软屉，现用旧席是更替品。下有一双弯带出榫纳入大边，另外四根对角出榫纳入边抹加固。高束腰嵌入外露的腿足上部及座面下和直牙条上的槽口，牙条作肩与腿足结合，下展为造型优美的外翻马蹄足。牙条内用穿销贯过高束腰达座面边框加固，短边一枚，长边一双。牙条下沿微向外翻成碗口线，其势延顺至腿足。

翘头案腿足内缩安装，是明式家具标准类别之一。但四角安腿足之桌，带翘头则属稀少品种，几桌腿足以外翻马蹄结束的也十分罕见。此具黄花梨高束腰外翻马蹄足翘头榻，线条柔和悦目，形象清新，造型协调，又集以上两种稀有设计于一身。在公开发表明代家具例子中至今似是孤例。

来　源
  香港嘉木堂 1996

出　版
  从未发表

两端高起的小翘头与抹头一木连做；边抹冰盘沿平直，自中部打宽洼儿再内缩收尾

The small everted flanges on the short sides are carved from the same piece of wood as the short frame members. The edge of the frame is flat and moulds downwards from about half way down to form a groove and moulds downwards and inwards again

高束腰嵌入外露的腿足上部及座面下和直牙条上的槽口，牙条作肩与腿足结合

The recessed high waist is tongue-and-grooved to the exposed top portions of the legs, the underside of the seat frame and the straight apron which is mitred, mortised, tenoned and half-lapped to the legs

High waist daybed with everted ends

Huanghuali wood
Late Ming (1573-1644)
Width 201.2 cm (79 ¼") Depth 84.5 cm (33 ¼")
Height 48.6 cm (19 ⅛")

The daybed is of mitre, mortise and tenon frame construction with small everted flanges on the short sides which are carved from the same piece of wood as the short frame members. The edge of the frame is flat and moulds downwards from about half way down to form a groove and moulds downwards and inwards again. It was drilled for soft seat construction and has now been restored with old matting. There are two curved transverse braces underneath and two straight ones diagonally at the corners on each end. The recessed high waist is tongue-and-grooved to the exposed top portions of the legs, the underside of the seat frame and the straight apron which is mitred, mortised, tenoned and half-lapped to the legs which terminate in exquisitely shaped gently outward flared hoof feet. Wedge-shaped pegs further secure the apron, high waist to the top, two on the long sides and one on the short sides. The edge of the aprons finishes in a subtle, slightly everted edge which continuous down the legs.

Everted ends, often seen in *qiaotouan* tables where the legs are recessed, are rare in corner-legs table design. Outward flaring feet are also very rare in table and stand constructions, with only a few published examples known. This exquisitely shaped daybed of gentle flowing lines and elegant proportions, embodying these rare features, seems to date unique amongst published examples.

Provenance
Grace Wu Bruce, Hong Kong, 1996

Published
Never published

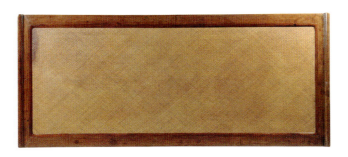

四框内缘踩边打眼造软屉，现用旧席是更替品；下有一双弯带出榫纳入大边，另外四根对角出榫纳入边框两端

It was drilled for soft seat construction and has now been restored with old matting. There are two curved transverse braces underneath and two straight ones diagonally at the corners on each end

黄花梨有束腰马蹄足螭纹榻

晚明（1573–1644）

- 长 207.5 厘米　宽 120.8 厘米
- 高 49 厘米

体型大但比例匀称，床座格角攒边框，边抹冰盘沿上舒下敛至底压一窄边线。抹头可见透榫。四框内缘踩边打眼造软屉，仍保留旧席，下有四根弧形托带支承，另有两短帐出榫装入抹头与尽端托带加强稳固。壸门轮廓牙条沿边起线，其势延续至腿足。牙子正面浮雕草龙隔卷草相对，背面雕卷草纹，另外三面雕圆转自如的卷草纹，与束腰以抱肩榫与腿足结合。腿足上端出长短榫纳入边框，下展为刚劲有力的马蹄足。腿足肩部浮雕花叶纹。

传世黄花梨榻一般长而窄，如现例这般宽的不多见。一向只从唐宋以来的古画中见到，从而知有此古制。

此榻前牙子浮雕形态生动，两草龙隔卷草相对，图纹较其他三边雕草花纹丰富，陈放此榻似有前后之分。参阅《金瓶梅》第九十七回插图版画，宽阔的榻放入用屏风间隔成的小房子内，单边进出。此具正面牙子含较丰富雕饰的榻，就非常适合这种格局。

来 源
| 香港嘉木堂 1988

出 版
| 从未发表

Daybed

Huanghuali wood
Late Ming (1573-1644)
Width 207.5 cm (81 ¾")   Depth 120.8 cm (47 9/16")
Height 49 cm (19 ¼")

Of substantial size yet elegant proportions, the daybed is of mitre, mortise and tenon frame construction, the edge moulding gently downwards and inwards ending in a narrow flat band. There are exposed tenons on the short sides of the frame. It was drilled for soft seat construction and retained an old matting. There are four curved transverse braces underneath and two additional stretchers tenoned to the short sides of the frame and the transverse stretchers at the ends for further support. The recessed waist and the beaded-edged curvilinear aprons carved with hornless facing dragons and scrolling tendrils in front, and scrolling tendrils at the back, and similar tendrils on the sides and back, are mitred, mortised, tenoned and half-lapped to the legs which are double-lock tenoned to the seat frame and end in strong hoof feet. The shoulders of the legs are carved with leaf motifs.

Extant examples of *huanghuali* daybeds are mostly long and narrow with few examples of depth like the present piece. Wide and deep daybeds are however often depicted in paintings from the Tang, Song, Yuan and Ming periods, so one can surmise they are ancient forms.

This daybed with one long apron richly carved with lively dragons amidst tendrils and the other three sides with only tendrils would indicate the piece to have a front and back side. Regard the woodblock illustration to the Ming novel The Golden Lotus, where just such a bed is placed inside a "room" fashioned by surrounding screens with only one entrance making complete sense of a daybed with a front and back.

Provenance

Grace Wu Bruce, Hong Kong, 1988

Published

Never published

《金瓶梅詞話》
Jin Ping Mei Cihua
The Golden Lotus

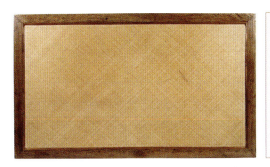 

四框内缘踩边打眼造软屉，仍保留旧席，下有四根弧形托带支承，另有两短枨出榫装入抹头与尽端托带加强稳固

It was drilled for soft seat construction and retained an old matting. There are four curved transverse braces underneath and two additional stretchers tenoned to the short sides of the frame and the transverse stretchers at the ends for further support

壸门轮廓牙条沿边起线，其势延续至腿足；牙子正面浮雕草龙隔草相对，背面雕卷草纹，与束腰以抱肩榫与腿足结合；腿足肩部浮雕花叶纹

The recessed waist and the beaded-edged curvilinear aprons carved with hornless facing dragons and scrolling tendrils in front, and scrolling tendrils at the back, are mitred, mortised, tenoned and half-lapped to the legs. The shoulders of the legs are carved with leaf motifs

黄花梨五屏风攒边装理石围子罗汉床

晚明（1573–1644）

- 长 198.5 厘米　宽 90 厘米
- 高 98.7 厘米　座高 49 厘米

床面格角榫攒边，四框内缘踩边打眼造软屉，下装三根弯带支承，现用旧席是更替品。边抹冰盘沿自中上部上舒下敛，抹头可见明榫。高束腰与直素牙条一木连做，与腿足连结。腿足上端收窄凹入接合束腰，出榫纳入床面边框底部，向下至着地处成三道线脚的方形足垫作结束。牙条内安穿销上贯床座边框底部加强稳固，长边一双，短边一枚。床围子可装可卸，均镶嵌大理石心板，优美的天然纹理如云雾间的山峦。后背板由三片组成。边框上角内外踩线条柔婉的委角。下雕别致舒缓的壸门轮廓牙子。两侧围子构造相同，前端加添造型精致的抱鼓墩形站牙，用走马梢与后围子接合。

传世品中镶嵌石板的黄花梨家具，无论是桌案、椅凳或床榻，都相对稀少。此具罗汉床，其围子边框内外踩柔婉委角，下端典雅别致壸门牙子，前端添加抱鼓墩式站牙等，异常考究，从这样在一般家具难得一见的造法，颇能推断晚明时代黄花梨家具大盛时，镶嵌石板的家具是上乘类别，享有崇高的身价。

来　源
香港嘉木堂 2007

出　版
伍嘉恩《明式家具二十年经眼录》紫禁城出版社、北京、2010, 页 238 – 239

腿足着地处成三道线脚的方形足垫作结束

The legs extend down to end in moulded pad feet

Couch bed *luohan chuang* with marble panels

Huanghuali wood and *dalishi* marble
Late Ming (1573-1644)
Width 198.5 cm (78 ⅛")   Depth 90 cm (35 ⁷⁄₁₆")
Height 98.7 cm (38 ⅞")   Seat height 49 cm (19 ⁵⁄₁₆")

The bed is of mitre, mortise and tenon frame construction supported by three curved transverse braces underneath. It was drilled for soft seat construction and is now restored with old matting. The edge of the frame moulds downwards and inwards from about one third way down and there are exposed tenons on the short sides. The high waist and the plain straight apron, made of one piece of wood, is half-lapped onto and mortised and tenoned to the legs, the upper portion of which indents to appear as part of the waist, and extend down to end in moulded pad feet. There are wedge-shaped dovetailed pegs on the backs of the aprons for further support, two on the long sides and one on the short sides. The back and arms, inset with marble panels of beautiful natural pattern that appear as scenes of misty mountains, are removable. The back is of three framed marble panels, each with butterflied corners and beautifully shaped base aprons. The two arms, similarly constructed with an additional spandrel exquisitely carved with a drum-shaped base, are slide-joined to the back.

There are not many surviving examples of classical furniture made in *huanghuali* wood with inset marble panels, be they tables, chairs or beds. This *luohan* bed with refined features of butterflied corners, beautifully-shaped base aprons and front spandrels rarely seen on other pieces would seem to indicate that *huanghuali* furniture with inset marble panels was an exalted type and highly valued at the time.

Provenance

Grace Wu Bruce, Hong Kong, 2007

Published

Grace Wu Bruce, *Two Decades of Ming Furniture*, The Forbidden City Publishing House, Beijing, 2010, pp. 238 – 239

后背板由三片组成；边框上角内外踩线条柔婉的委角；下雕别致舒缓的壸门轮廓牙子
The back is of three framed marble panels, each with butterflied corners and beautifully shaped base aprons

两侧围子同样边框上角内外踩线条柔婉的委角；下雕别致舒缓的壸门轮廓牙子；前端加添造型精致的抱鼓墩形站牙，用走马梢与后围子接合
The two arms similarly constructed with butterflied corners and beautifully shaped base aprons with an additional spandrel exquisitely carved with a drum-shaped base, are slide-joined to the back

黄花梨三屏风攒接正卍字式围子卷球足罗汉床

晚明（1573-1644）
- 长 202.5 厘米　宽 92.5 厘米
- 高 80 厘米　座高 49 厘米

床座为标准格角榫攒边框，下有一根弯带两端出榫纳入大边支承。两端再各装直带一双对角纳入边框加强支承。四框内缘踩边打眼造软屉，现用椰棕网与旧席是更替品。边抹立面自上中部上舒下敛，中部打洼儿再内缩至底端压一窄边线。抹头可见透榫。前方及两侧直牙子与束腰一木连作，与边框及三弯腿足格肩接合。腿足上端收窄缩入连接束腰。后方牙子则不锼出束腰，直接齐头碰座面边框下部。牙条内有穿销，长边一双，短边一枚，贯上床座边框用以加固。前牙条沿边起线，两侧及后牙子则全素。三弯腿足端卷转成球，下留方足垫作结束，造型优美。床围子可装可卸。攒接透空围子在四框内用横竖短材组成洼面正万字卍纹。

卷球足、卷珠足都悦目美观，黄花梨家具腿足以其结束者不常见，只偶尔出现于香几或炕几。于床榻，属非常罕见。

多年观察研究黄花梨家具发现，罗汉床攒接围子两侧的图案必然比后背的图案细小。比如这罗汉床的正万字卍纹，后背的万字卍就比两侧大。而三边围子内的图案尺码相同，只会在架子床上出现。明此，当架子床围被改装成罗汉床就一目了然。

来源
香港嘉木堂 1991

出版
从未发表

Couch bed *luohan chuang*

Huanghuali wood
Late Ming (1573-1644)
Width 202.5 cm (79 ¾") Depth 92.5 cm (36 ⅜")
Height 80 cm (31 ½") Seat height 49 cm (19 ⁵⁄₁₆")

The bed frame is of standard mitre, mortise and tenon construction supported by one transverse brace underneath. There are four additional corner braces mortised and tenoned to the frames diagonally at the corners for further support. The seat was drilled for soft seat construction and has now been restored with coconut webbing and old matting. The edge of the seat frame moulds inwards and downwards from about one third way down to form a groove and then again to end in a narrow banded edge. There are exposed tenons on the short sides of the seat frame. In front and on the sides, the recessed waist and the straight apron, made of one piece of wood, is mitred, mortised and tenoned and half-lapped to the cabriole-shaped legs, the upper portion of which is recessed to appear as part of the waist. The back apron is not cut with a waist and joins directly to the underside of the seat. There are wedge-shaped pegs on the backs of the aprons joining them to the frame top to provide further support, two on the long sides and one on the short sides. The apron in front is finished with a beaded edge while those on the sides and back are plain. The cabriole legs extend downwards to finish in beautifully shaped ball feet supported on square pads. The removable back and arm railings are made of small members double mitred and mortised together to form the *wan* 卍 patterns, all very gently thumb-moulded.

Huanghuali furniture pieces terminating with beautifully rendered ball-shaped feet, small or large, are quite rare, occasionally seen on incense stands and *kang* tables, but almost not known on beds.

Years of study yielded the conclusion that the pattern made of small members joined together to form the arms on couch beds are smaller in size than those on the back. This means in the present bed, the *wan* 卍 patterns on the back are larger in size than those of the arms. The patterns of the railings on all three sides of canopy beds are, however, of the same size. With this knowledge, the adaptation of canopy bed railings to *luohan* beds can easily be detected.

Provenance

Grace Wu Bruce, Hong Kong, 1991

Published

Never published

三弯腿足端卷转成球，下留方足垫作结束，造型优美

The cabriole legs extend downwards to finish in beautifully shaped ball feet supported on square pads

床围子可装可卸；攒接透空围子在四框内用横竖短材组成洼面正万字卍纹

The removable back and arm railings are made of small members double mitred and mortised together to form the *wan* 卍 patterns, all very gently thumb-moulded

黄花梨四柱海棠十字纹架子床

晚明（1573–1644）

- 长 216 厘米　宽 127 厘米
- 高 213.5 厘米　座高 50.8 厘米

床座为格角攒边结构，边抹冰盘沿自中部向下内敛，抹头见明榫。一木连做的束腰与直牙条以抱肩榫接合腿足。前方与两侧牙子沿边起灯草线，延续伸展至腿足。后方牙子全素。腿足上端以双榫纳入床座边框底部，下展为矮马蹄足。腿足内侧中央挖空，工匠称之为挖缺造。床座边框内缘踩边打眼造软屉，现用椰棕网与旧席是更替品。下有一双弯带出榫装入大边，另四根对角出榫纳入边抹加固。四角立柱八角形，做榫扣合床座边框四角上的凿眼，上承顶架。顶架子攒边造，安横竖枨子分格。床前两立柱下带外撇分瓣的柱础托子。床顶下与角柱间安格角攒边框挂檐，用短柱作肩栽入分格，嵌入用板片透锼成海棠十字图案的绦环板，长边五块，短边三块。挂檐以双榫与角柱接合。床围子用短材攒接成海棠图案以十字连结，做工精湛，造型优美。床座上部结构均可拆卸。

此具四柱海棠十字纹架子床设计端庄大方。挂檐、角柱、直腿足、直牙条的轮廓线条简洁利落。海棠十字纹围子图案工整美观，与挂檐绦环板内微形海棠十字纹一致，视觉统一谐调。整体选用色泽柔和、纹理细密黄花梨木材造。

床围子以圆润饱满的构件攒接而成，用料特别肥厚。海棠形外沿弧线圆转流畅，内沿角位出尖，优美非常。角柱削八角形，二前柱下托分瓣柱础。腿足下展为不常见的矮马蹄足，内侧更以挖缺造。总括来说，每部分都是十分精致、讲究的制作。传世黄花梨架子床，以六柱居多，四柱架子床难得一见。

来　源

香港嘉木堂 1988

出　版

从未发表

Four-post canopy bed

Huanghuali wood
Late Ming (1573-1644)
Width 216 cm (85")   Depth 127 cm (50")
Height 213.5 cm (84")   Seat Height 50.8 cm (20")

The bed frame is of mitre, mortise and tenon construction, the edge moulding downwards and inwards from about half way down, with exposed tenons on the short sides of the frame. The recessed waist and the straight apron, made of one piece of wood, is mitred, mortised and tenoned into and half-lapped onto the legs which are double-lock tenoned to the underside of the mitred frame and end in well-drawn low hoof feet with the inside centre hollowed out, called *waque* in Chinese cabinetry term. The front and side aprons end with beaded edges while the back one is plain. The bed frame was drilled for soft seat construction and has now been restored with coconut webbing and old matting. Underneath there are two curved transverse braces, and four additional braces are tenoned into the frame diagonally at each corner for further support. Four structural upright members, octagonal in shape, the two front ones with everted base caps also with eight facets, rise to support the canopy of the bed of frame construction, with stretchers dividing it into sections. Below the canopy and between the structural uprights are *guayan*, "eave hangings" inset with open work panels of begonia and crosses pattern, five on the long sides and three on the short sides, interphased with mitred struts. These eave hangings are double tenoned into the uprights. Above the seat frame and tenoned to the uprights are railings also with begonia and crosses designs, created by exquisitely shaped mitred members mortised and tenoned together. The entire superstructure can be dismantled.

This four-post canopy bed of formal design, the silhouette of the posts, legs, aprons and canopy are of pure, clean lines. The pattern of begonia shapes and crosses, large ones on the bed railings and miniature ones below the canopy in perfect harmony with each other, is exquisite. The tightly grained *huanghuali* timber a warm rich tone.

The bed railings are made of thick, well-rounded members joined together, the outside corners of the begonia shapes fluidly curvaceous while the insides finish in exquisite points; the four posts are faceted and the front two end in a flared support, also faceted; the straight legs with the inside section cut out in refined *waque* manner end in rarely seen low hoof feet, all special features well crafted to the highest degree.

Extant examples of *huanghuali* wood canopy beds are mostly of six posts with four-post ones being very rare.

Provenance

Grace Wu Bruce, Hong Kong, 1988

Published

Never published

床围子用短材攒接成海棠图案以十字连结，做工精湛，造型优美

Railings with begonia and crosses designs, created by exquisitely shaped mitred members mortised and tenoned together

四角立柱八角形，下带托子，外撇分瓣如柱础

Upright members are octagonal in shape, the two front ones with everted base caps are also with eight facets

腿足内侧中央挖空，工匠称之为挖缺造

Feet with the inside centre hollowed out, called *waque* in Chinese cabinetry term

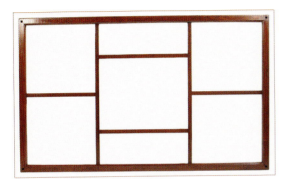

顶架子攒边造，安横竖帐子分格

The canopy of the bed of frame construction, with stretchers dividing it into sections

床座边框内缘踩边打眼造软屉，现用椰棕网与旧席是更替品

The bed frame was drilled for soft seat construction and has now been restored with coconut webbing and old matting

黄花梨六柱透雕攒斗瑞兽凤鸟螭纹架子床

晚明（1573–1644）

- 长 239 厘米　宽 168.5 厘米
- 高 238.5 厘米　座高 54.2 厘米

床座为格角攒边框，抹头可见透榫。边抹冰盘沿线脚上舒下敛，自上中部向下内缩至底压一窄平线。高束腰四角植竹节形短柱，长边加一双，短边加一根。中间以绦环板。前方及两侧绦环板高浮雕螭纹，后方则雕几何图案，分段嵌装入短柱、床座边框下与托腮间。壶门式牙条沿边起饱满灯草线，高浮雕卷草纹，作肩与腿足接合。腿肩雕仿金属片纹。牙条沿阳线延续至三弯腿足，以形状优美卷云纹足着地。床座边框内缘踩边打眼造软屉，现用椰棕网与旧席是更替品。下有四根托带支承，二直二弧形，出榫装入大边，抹头每边加安两根短枨加强支撑。大床四角柱踩甜瓜棱线腿，下端拍合床座边框上凿的榫眼，上承用横顺枨分为十二个卍字纹方格的顶架。顶架下装格角攒边框的挂檐，以短柱作肩分段嵌装绦环板，前后各三块，两侧各二。门楣子透雕凤鹤戏云图，两侧以及后面几何图案，用短料攒接。正面挂檐下加螭雀云纹牙条，再支以门柱，下端出榫拍入床沿。挂檐边框踩甜瓜棱线脚与立柱互相呼应，四角安长尾龙形角牙。角柱与门柱间装罗锅枨。床围子设计华美，下截以四簇云纹蟠螭环组成细密图案。上截长窄空格安圆形蟠螭纹卡子花。门围子卜截安卡子花一朵，贯彻三边长围子设计。下截在肥厚菱形出尖开光内透雕异兽瑞鸟、山石灵芝松竹，组配成图。床座上部结构均可拆卸。

架子床围子以及挂檐可分三大类造法：用板片锼镂雕刻图纹而成为其一；还有是用短材攒接组成各式样几何形图案，如前例四柱海棠十字纹架子床；第三种是将锼镂的花片，裁销把它们连接斗拢成图案花纹，称为斗簇的造法。传世架子床中，第一种造法最常见，多为透雕螭纹。攒接与斗簇围子的较罕见。

现例架子床集三种制法于一身。门围子与门楣子透雕瑞兽、灵芝山石松竹凤鸟仙鹤，祥云瑞日；大长围子四簇云纹围蟠螭卡子花，组成细密繁缛但有规律匀称的图案。挂檐攒斗几何形图案。床身高浮雕生动螭虎龙吉祥草。其高度装饰，豪华秾丽。顶架上出图案花纹，似是传世品中绝无仅有。

来 源
| 香港嘉木堂 1996

出 版
| 从未发表

Six-post canopy bed

Huanghuali wood
Late Ming (1573-1644)
Width 239 cm (94 ⁱ⁶⁄₁₆") Depth 168.5 cm (66 ⁵⁄₁₆")
Height 238.5 cm (93 ⁷⁄₈") Bed Height 54.2 cm (21 ⁵⁄₁₆")

The bed frame is of mitre, mortise and tenon construction with exposed tenons on the short sides. The edge of the frame moulds downwards and inwards from about one third way down and again to end in a narrow flat band. The recessed high waist comprises of bamboo shaped struts at the corners and two more on the long sides and one on the short sides, with *taohuan* panels carved with lively dragons in front and on the sides in high relief, and geometric patterns on the back. These panels are inset into the struts, the underside of the seat frame and the *tuosai* ridge below. The beaded-edged curvilinear apron carved with scrolling tendrils in high relief, is mitred, mortised and tenoned into and half-lapped onto the legs carved at the shoulders to simulate metal mounts. They extend downwards to flare outwards into beautifully shaped feet decorated with cloud scrolls. The seat was drilled for soft seat construction and has now been restored with palm fibre webbing and old matting. Underneath there are two curved and two straight transverse braces and two additional short braces, tenoned into the short sides of the bed frame and the transverse brace at the ends for further support. Four structural uprights, round with grooved mouldings, rise at the corners of the bed to support the canopy of frame construction with transverse and longitudinal braces dividing it into twelve squares, each inset with a *wan* 卍 pattern. Below the canopy and between the structural uprights are eave hangings on all four sides, comprising frameworks inset with openwork panels outlined with beaded edges separated by short mitred stretchers, three on the long sides and two on the short sides. The front panels are carved with phoenixes, cranes and swallows amidst clouds, while the side and back ones are geometric patterns formed by short mitred members joined together. These frameworks are double tenoned into the uprights and the canopy. The front one with an additional apron below beautifully carved with dragons, birds and clouds, and is further supported by two upright members, tenoned to the seat frame of the bed below. These eave frame members are all carved with mouldings echoing those on the uprights. Spandrels carved in the shape of stylised dragons with long scrolling tails are at each corner on the sides and back. There are hump-back shaped stretchers between the uprights. Above the seat frame and tenoned to the uprights are railings of beautiful design. The side and back ones with a tightly knit pattern formed by four pointed cloud shapes enclosing a coiled dragon roundel on the lower section, the upper part a narrow open space inset with coiled dragon roundels. The upper part of the front panels is similar to the sides and back while the lower sections are carved with mythical birds and beasts amidst *lingzhi*, rocks, bamboos and pines contained within a wide double banded rhombus with pointed sides. The entire superstructure can be dismantled.

There are three types of canopy beds: those with railings of openwork carving, and those with railings made of mitred short members forming geometric patterns like the previous four-post canopy bed, and a third type with carved ele-

大床四角柱上承用横顺枨分为十二个卍字纹方格的顶架

Four structural uprights rise at the corners of the bed to support the canopy of frame construction with transverse and longitudinal braces dividing it into twelve squares, each inset with a *wan* 卍 pattern

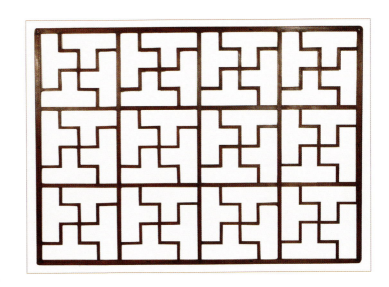

Provenance

Grace Wu Bruce, Hong Kong, 1996

Published

Never published

ments joined together to form usually a tightly knit pattern. There are quite a number of canopy beds made with carved railings, usually dragons. The two other types are much rarer.

The present example utilizes all three methods in its making. The front railings and eaves panels are richly carved with mythical beasts, amidst *lingzhi,* rocks, pines and bamboos, phoenixes and cranes amidst clouds; the side and back railings comprise carved cloud-shaped elements enclosing coiled dragon roundels joined by pegs to form a tight, rich pattern, while the eave panels on the sides and back are of geometric patterns formed by small members joined together. The bed base is carved with lively dragons and scrolling tendrils in high relief. These elaborate decorations combine to give the bed a rich luxurious glamour. The ceiling is with a perfectly preserved lattice pattern, a rare feature almost unknown in surviving examples.

门围子上截安卡子花一朵，贯彻三边长围子设计；下截在肥厚菱形出尖开光内透雕异兽瑞鸟、山石灵芝松竹，组配成图

The upper part of the front panels is similar to the sides and back while the lower sections are carved with mythical birds and beasts amidst *lingzhi*, rocks, bamboos and pines contained within a wide double banded rhombus with pointed sides

黄花梨拔步床

晚明（1573-1644）

- 长 222 厘米　宽 242 厘米
- 高 238 厘米

床座格角攒边，边抹冰盘沿上部平直，自中上部打洼儿成凹槽，下部内缩成束腰，一木连造。素直牙条以抱肩榫与腿足结合，腿足上端出双榫纳入床座边框底部，下展为强而有力的矮马蹄足。床座边框内缘踩边打眼造软屉，现用棕榈纤维织网与旧席是更替品。下有四根弯带出榫装入大边。床座四角立柱下端做榫拍合边框上凿的卯眼，上承黄花梨框、四拼榉木板面心造的床顶。床围以椭圆形帐子攒接而成。床顶挂檐如是。床前地平两角植入立柱，与连接的栏杆在床前围出空间造成床廊，上盖顶架。廊顶架边框以及四拼的板心，皆黄花梨造。廊顶三面安椭圆帐子挂檐。拔步床底部地平两块造，以榫卯连结。黄花梨木攒边安榉木心板，下支以小马蹄腿足，腿足间安直素牙条。

拔步床造型雄伟壮丽。四柱床前围栏杆设床廊。正中入口。整件安放在地平上，以小马蹄腿足升起离地。全件盖顶架。此拔步床选材及施工精巧绝伦，令人惊叹。床顶、廊顶和原件地平底部下的漆面、糊织物与漆裹保存近乎完整。

此床之设计、比例、工艺均臻至完美，是明式家具神品。

自20世纪，堪萨斯市纳尔逊-阿特金斯艺术博物馆藏拔步床是传世明朝黄花梨拔步床孤例，其体型较现例细，床顶及地平为柴木所制。这两件拔步床是至今公开传世品仅有的二例（Ellsworth 1971, 图32；Handler 2001, 页156）。

美国堪萨斯市纳尔逊 - 阿特金斯艺术博物馆藏品
Nelson-Atkins Museum of Art collection, Kansas City

来　源
| 香港嘉木堂 1989

出　版
| 从未发表

Alcove bed

Huanghuali wood
Late Ming (1573-1644)
Width 222 cm (87 ⅜") Depth 242 cm (95 ¼")
Height 238 cm (93 ¹¹⁄₁₆")

The seat of the bed is of mitre, mortise and tenon frame construction, the edge of the frame is flat and moulds from about one third way down to form a groove and moulds in again to become the recessed waist. The plain straight aprons are mitred, mortised and tenoned into and half-lapped onto the legs which are double-lock tenoned to the underside of the bed frame and extend down to terminate in strong low hoof feet. The bed was drilled for soft seat construction and has now been restored with palm fibre webbing and old matting. Underneath there are four curved transverse braces tenoned into the frame. Four upright members, rise at corners to support a canopy made of *huanghuali* frame inset with a four-board *jumu* panel. Above the bed are railings made of oval stretchers joined together within a frame. The eaves, *guayan*, "hanging railings" below the canopy are similarly constructed. In front of the bed at the corners of the platform are two structural uprights. Railings also made of oval stretchers are joined to them to surround a space in front of the bed, and capped with a canopy above, form an alcove, giving the bed its name. This canopy, its frame and the four-board floating panel, are made of *huanghuali* wood. Hanging railings, *guayan* are also on the sides and front of the alcove. At the base is the platform, which comprises two parts, each made with a *huanghuali* mitred frame inset with *jimu* panels, raised on small low hoof feet and inset with straight aprons.

This magnificent alcove bed comprises a four-post bed and an alcove section in front with railing surrounds and a central opening, set on two joined platforms raised on small hoof-shaped feet. The entire superstructure is covered with a canopy made in two parts, one for the alcove section, and one for the bed. The exceptional quality of timber chosen and the exquisite craftsmanship of each member of this piece is astounding. The lacquer surfaces of the canopy top and the underside of the original platform are almost completely intact.

The design, proportion, and workmanship of this alcove bed is near perfection, a masterpiece of the joiners' art.

Until the appearance of this piece, the only known alcove bed made of *huanghuali* wood dated to the Ming is the example in the Nelson-Atkins Museum of Art, Kansas City. (Ellsworth 1971, pl 32; Handler 2001, p. 156). Compared to the present example, the Nelson-Atkins bed is smaller, with the canopy as well as the platform being made of softwood. These two alcove beds are the only surviving examples known to date.

Provenance

Grace Wu Bruce, 1989

Published

Never published

其他

OTHERS

黄花梨六足高面盆架

晚明（1573–1644）

- 长 46.4 厘米　宽 40.4 厘米
- 高 149.5 厘米

面盆架两后足向上伸展，以飘肩榫与搭脑相接，搭脑两端雕抽象龙头纹。中牌子两根横枨间嵌入透雕灵芝纹花板，下装壶门轮廓沿边起线的亮脚牙子。六足间轮辐枨为三根直材于中段剔燕尾榫相交拍拢，端末出榫接入六腿足上的卯眼，均出透榫。四根前腿顶端雕莲苞莲叶纹。

虽然面盆架只是一般的日常用品，但此例造工精巧，雕饰生动细致。再看下文同样是日常用物的灯台、火盆架和琴架等造型之美，制作水平之高，颇能令人体会晚明时代士工商贾的生活风格是何等精致。

来源

香港嘉木堂 2000

出版

从未发表

《二刻拍案惊奇》 Erke Paian Jingqi, Amazing Tales – Second Series

Tall basin stand

Huanghuali wood
Late Ming (1573-1644)
Width 46.4 cm (18 ¼")   Depth 40.4 cm (15 ⅞")
Height 149.5 cm (58 ⅞")

The top rail ends in two carved stylised shapes, perhaps that depicting dragon heads. Two round long uprights mitred, mortised and tenoned into and half-lapped to the top rail serve as the hind legs of the stand. Between two horizontal stretchers, the central section is inset with a tongue-and-grooved panel carved with beautiful openwork *lingzhi* fungus. There is a curvilinear-shaped beaded-edged apron below. Between the legs, is the wheel-like structure with spokes made of three straight members dovetail-joined together intersecting in the middle spot, all with exposed tenons. The four front legs are carved with lotus bud finials.

Although this basin stand is only for mundane use, it is of excellent proportions and expertly crafted with fine carving. The lamp stand, brazier stand and music stand in the following pages are also exquisitely modelled and ingenuously made, attesting to the refined and elegant living of the literati and wealthy merchants of the late Ming.

Provenance

Grace Wu Bruce, Hong Kong, 2000

Published

Never published

搭脑两端雕抽象龙头纹

The top rail ending in two carved stylised shapes, perhaps that depicting dragon heads

中牌子两根横枨间嵌入透雕灵芝纹花板,下装壸门轮廓沿边起线的亮脚牙子

Between two horizontal stretchers, the central section is inset with a tongue-and-grooved panel carved with beautiful openwork *lingzhi* fungus. There is a curvilinear-shaped beaded-edged apron below

六足间轮辐枨为三根直材于中段剔燕尾榫相交拍拢,端末出榫接入六腿足上的卯眼

Between the legs, is the wheel-like structure with spokes made of three straight members dovetail-joined together intersecting in the middle spot

黄花梨灵芝纹衣架

晚明（1573–1644）

- 长 141.5 厘米　宽 33.5 厘米
- 高 162 厘米

灵芝纹棂格中牌子黄花梨衣架，尺寸不大，骤看不大起眼，细味就能领悟到匠师的意匠经营。高盆架搭脑翘头两端颇常见的灵芝纹，在这衣架上有不同手法的演绎，别具风韵。中牌子由仰俯山字变化的棂格组成，下部两根横枨中嵌开孔的绦环板，上虚下实，比重恰到好处。中牌子以下牙子又用同样是别类的灵芝纹牙头，与搭脑翘头相呼应。而两个墩子上立柱旁的站牙，用灵芝蟠错成纹，设计妙绝，前所未见，甚具创意。

查究明代书籍版画插图，见衣架放置处多为内室，架子床旁靠墙的一边，而衣衫就搭于其上，而不是挂起，故衣架一律无挂钩装置。亦见其上系以丝绸帐子，使整幢起屏风的作用。黄花梨木制明代衣架，可能是明式家具传世品中最稀少的一类，实例屈指可数。

来源

香港嘉木堂 1987-1990

香港攻玉山房藏品 1990-2002

纽约佳士得 2002 年 9 月 20 日

香港嘉木堂 2002-2003

香港攻玉山房藏品 2003-2015

展览

香港，1991，香港中文大学文物馆

新加坡，1997-1999，亚洲文明博物馆

出版

Grace Wu Bruce, *Dreams of Chu Tan Chamber and the Romance with Huanghuali wood: The Dr S. Y. Yip Collection of Classic Chinese Furniture*, Hong Kong, 1991. 伍嘉恩《攻玉山房藏明式黄花梨家具：楮檀室梦旅》香港，1991，页 138 – 139

Wang Shixiang, "Additional Examples of Classical Chinese Furniture" *Orientations*, January 1992, Hong Kong. 王世襄〈古典中国家具其他例子〉，《东方艺术》1992 年 1 月，香港，页 48

国家文物局《亚洲文明博物馆之中国文物收藏》新加坡，1997，图版 122

Christie's, *The Dr S Y Yip Collection of Fine and Important Classical Chinese Furniture*, New York, 20 September 2002. 佳士得《攻玉山房藏中国古典家具精萃》纽约，2002 年 9 月 20 日，编号 23

王世襄《明式家具研究》生活·读书·新知三联书店，北京，2007，页 391

伍嘉恩《明式家具二十年经眼录》紫禁城出版社，北京，2010，页 252 - 253

衣架上搭衣服
《醒世恒言》
Clothes being "thrown over" and not hung
Xingshi Hengyan
Lasting Words to awaken the World

衣架上搭衣服
《仙媛纪事》
Clothes being "thrown over" and not hung
Xianyuan Jishi
Chronicles of Immortal Beauties

衣架系以帐子作屏风
《苏门啸》
Clothes rack mounted with textiles being used as a screen
Sumen Xiao
Howling at Sumen Mountain

Clothes rack

Huanghuali wood
Late Ming (1573 – 1644)
Width 141.5 cm (55 ⁵⁄₁₆″)   Depth 33.5 cm (13 ³⁄₁₆″)
Height 162 cm (63 ¾″)

This clothes rack of *lingzhi* fungus motif and lattice panel is not large and imposing, but careful observations reveal the carpenter's art. The everted ends of the top rail, like that often seen on tall basin stands, are carved *lingzhi* shapes, but here they are rendered in a different manner, unusual and tasteful. The central lattice panel is light and airy, while the inset panels at the bottom between the two horizontal stretchers are more solid, seemingly to anchor the piece at the base, creating a perfect balance. The spandrels of the apron below the lattice panel are also unusual *lingzhi* shapes, echoing those of the top rail. And those on either sides of the uprights, above the solid plank feet, are fantastic intertwisted *lingzhi* shapes, artistic and unique.

Woodblock illustrations to Ming period publications often showed clothes racks being placed against the wall besides canopy beds, and clothes were mostly "thrown over" them and not being "hung up" as in modern times. Textiles mounted on clothes racks rendering the structure as a screen can also be seen. Clothes racks made of *huanghuali* wood are perhaps the rarest type of extant Ming furniture, with but a handful of genuine surviving examples.

Provenance

Grace Wu Bruce, Hong Kong, 1987-1990

Dr S Y Yip Collection, Hong Kong, 1990-2002

Christie's, New York, 20 September 2002

Grace Wu Bruce, Hong Kong, 2002-2003

Dr S Y Yip Collection, Hong Kong, 2003-2015

Exhibited

Hong Kong, 1991, Art Gallery, The Chinese University of Hong Kong

Singapore, 1997 – 1999, National Heritage Board, Asian Civilisations Museum

Published

Grace Wu Bruce, *Dreams of Chu Tan Chamber and the Romance with Huanghuali wood: The Dr S. Y. Yip Collection of Classic Chinese Furniture*, Hong Kong, 1991, pp. 138 – 139

Wang Shixiang, 'Additional Examples of Classical Chinese Furniture' *Orientations*, January 1992, Hong Kong p. 48

National Heritage Board, *Asian Civilisations Museum: The Chinese Collection*, Singapore, 1997, plate 122

Christie's, *The Dr S Y Yip Collection of Fine and Important Classical Chinese Furniture*, New York, 20 September 2002, no. 23

Wang Shixiang, *Mingshi Jiaju Yanjiu* (Ming Furniture Research), SDX Joint Publishing Company, Beijing, 2007, p. 391

Grace Wu Bruce, *Two Decades of Ming Furniture*, The Forbidden City Publishing House, Beijing, 2010, pp. 252 – 253

高盆架搭脑翘头两端颇常见的灵芝纹，在这衣架上有不同手法的演绎，别具风韵

The everted ends of the top rail, like that often seen on tall basin stands, are carved *lingzhi* shapes, but here they are rendered in a different manner, unusual and tasteful

中牌子以下牙子又用同样是别类的灵芝纹牙头，与搭脑翘头相呼应

The spandrels of the apron below the lattice panel are also unusual *lingzhi* shapes, echoing those of the top rail

两个墩子上立柱旁的站牙，用灵芝蟠错成纹，设计妙绝，前所未见，甚具创意

Those on either sides of the uprights, above the solid plank feet, are fantastic intertwisted *lingzhi* shapes, artistic and unique

附

这件灵芝纹衣架的归属,多次来回于嘉木堂与攻玉山房之间,纵横交错似甚复杂,背后的故事也颇有趣。

"[收藏故事]这件高格调的黄花梨衣架,笔者得自1987年。因为衣架属明式家具传世品中最稀少的种类,当时没有打算从速卖出,直至三年后才出让给香港收藏家叶承耀医生,成全他追求较有代表性一系统明式家具结集出版收藏专册的意愿。2002年叶医生整理藏品,将部分明式家具在纽约佳士得上拍,包括现例衣架,被笔者成功竞得。叶氏虽然已拥有另一具雕工十分精美的黄花梨衣架,但对此件还是念念不忘,于是再从笔者手中购回。一买一卖,一卖一买,再卖再买,竟然是同样两个人的来回交易! 可见灵芝棂格黄花梨衣架如何扣人心弦。"

录自 伍嘉恩《明式家具二十年经眼录》页253

[故事后续]

以上的收藏故事,是2002年的事情了。2015年叶氏再次整理藏品,求笔者策划并执行。笔者与香港苏富比合作,举办展览、媒体活动等,令其后的秋季专拍取得空前佳绩。为了成全收藏整理,令笔者应允后续策划工作,叶医生同意出让灵芝纹衣架,其后辗转归木趣居。

Addendum

The criss-cross nature of ownership of this piece between the Grace Wu Bruce gallery and Dr S Y Yip is very unusual and behind it lies an intriguing series of event.

"Collecting History: This superb *huanghuali* clothes rack was purchased by the author for Grace Wu Bruce gallery in 1987. Clothes racks dated to the Ming period are extremely rare and my intention was not to let it go in a hurry. So it was not until three years later that we sold the piece to the Hong Kong collector Dr S Y Yip, to enrich his collection for the publication of his collection of Ming furniture in 1991. Ten years later, Dr Yip put part of his collection up for sale at auction in Christie's New York, including the clothes rack, and I fought off other bidders and successfully bought it back. Alas, Dr Yip was not to forget the clothes rack and subsequently repurchased it from the Grace Wu Bruce gallery again! "

Translated from an excerpt from Grace Wu Bruce, *Two Decades of Ming Furniture*, p. 253

Collecting history continued:

The above record stopped at 2002. In 2015 Dr S Y Yip asked the author to plan and execute the sale of part of his collection of Ming furniture. The Grace Wu Bruce gallery masterminded the programme of exhibitions, media campaign, special events and in cooperation with Sotheby's Hong Kong, the subsequent auction was an unprecedented success. In order to secure the author's agreement to manage his collection, Dr Yip agreed to let go of his clothes rack and the piece eventually entered this collection.

黄花梨升降式灯台（成对）

晚明至清前期（1600–1700）

- 长 31.5 厘米　宽 31.5 厘米
- 高 131.5 厘米　伸长高 174.6 厘米

可升降的灯杆头顶承接六角型平台，高度可调节。下安三块透雕卷草叶纹挂牙。灯杆插入底座墩子正中树立的空心柱。柱洞内上部设开口扣紧灯杆上安的凸榫，结构如安灯泡。座墩用两块厚板造出如意云头刻弧线十字相交，上植下方上圆的空心柱。透雕花卉卷草纹站牙从四面抵夹，降低了灯台重心。灯柱方段上部凿孔设木楔。要调节灯台的高度，转动灯杆使其下滑停在木楔上。抽出木楔，灯杆直抵座撤，方便储藏。

明刊本《鲁班经匠家镜》内的灯台与现例颇相似 (*Ruitenbeek 1993*, 页 32)。传世实物异常罕见，屈指可数，非常珍贵。

来源

其中一件：北京／纽约 金瓯卜家族藏品 2003 年前

另外一件：北京中国嘉德 2015 年 11 月 14 日

出版

其中一件：从未发表

另外一件：中国嘉德《逸居 — 文案清供》北京，2015 年 11 月 14 日，编号 4383

《鲁班经匠家镜》
Lu Ban Jing Jiang Jia Jing
The Classic of Lu Ban and the Craftsmen's Mirror

Pair of lampstands

Huanghuali wood
Late Ming to early Qing (1600-1700)
Width 31.5 cm (12 ⅜")   Depth 31.5 cm (12 ⅜")
Height 131.5 cm (51 ¾")   Extended height 174.6 cm (68 ¾")

The lamp pole supports a hexagonal lamp rest at the top and three spandrels carved with openwork stylised leaves are fitted below. The pole, inserted into the central opening of the lampstand post, is adjustable. A notch cut inside the post grips the tenon fitted to the pole, similar to the fitting of a light bulb. The lamp post is in turn anchored to the cross-shaped base below, made of two thick solid planks fitted together. The feet are carved with cloud scrolls. Four large openwork spandrels *zhanya*, are at the base effectively stabilizing the lampstand by lowering the centre of gravity. An opening in the post between the *zhanya* spandrels houses a removable peg. To adjust the height of the lampstand, just turn the pole to release it from the notch, and it will slide down to rest on the peg. Remove the peg, the pole slides further down to rest on the base for easy storage.

The Ming carpenters' manual *Luban Jing Jiang Jia Jing* illustrates a very similar lampstand (Ruitenbeek 1993, p. 32). Surviving examples are very very rare, only a handful of published examples is known.

Provenance

One stand: Jin Oubu family collection, New York and Beijing, before 2003

The other: China Guardian, Beijing, 14 November 2015

Published

One stand never published

The other, China Guardian, *House of Leisure – Scholar's Studio Objects*, Beijing, November 14, 2015, no. 4383

座墩用两块厚板造出如意云头刻弧线十字相交，上植下方上圆的空心柱；透雕花卉卷草纹站牙从四面抵夹，降低了灯台重心；灯柱方段上部凿孔设木楔

The cross-shaped base is made of two thick solid planks fitted together. The feet are carved with cloud scrolls. An opening in the post between the *zhanya* spandrels houses a removable peg

可升降的灯杆头顶承接六角型平台，高度可调节；下安三块透雕卷草叶纹挂牙

The lamp pole supports a hexagonal lamp rest at the top and three spandrels carved with openwork stylised leaves are fitted below

黄花梨折叠式琴架

晚明（1573–1644）

- 长 90 厘米　宽 32.5 厘米
- 高 81 厘米（展开）　125.5 厘米（折叠）

琴架为折叠式结构，由两组相同构件结合组成。搭脑两端出头成圆钮形并顺势刻有一弧线以强调其转折。腿足两端以榫卯纳入搭脑与足下着地横材，交接处镶嵌如意头黄铜饰件，上下各一横梁。两组构件以金属轴钉贯穿腿足中部相互衔接，出卯处垫有黄铜圆形护眼钱。近上端的横梁装有铜片与环圈，可挂拆卸式的带钩金属细杆，用以平衡维持琴架高度。

乐器承架可见于明朝话本与戏曲的插图及绘画中。但传世实例非常罕见。公开发表的只有香港攻玉山房藏一具十分相似，曾于台北历史博物馆"风华再现：明清家具收藏展"中展出（历史博物馆 1999，页 134）。

来源
香港嘉木堂 1994

出版
Grace Wu Bruce Co Ltd, *Ming Furniture*, Hong Kong, 1995. 嘉木堂《中国家具精萃展》香港，1995，页 62-63

攻玉山房藏品
Dr S Y Yip collection

Musical instrument stand

Huanghuali wood
Late Ming (1573-1644)
Width 90 cm (35 ⁷⁄₁₆″) Depth 32.5 cm (12 ¹³⁄₁₆″)
Height 81 cm (31 ⁷⁄₈″) (extended) 125.5 cm (49 ⅜″) (folded)

The stand is of folding construction and comprises two identical parts. Each part has a rounded top rail which begins and ends in flattened round knobs, engraved with a curl to accentuate the turn of the ends. The two legs are mortised, tenoned and lapped to the top rail and the base feet stretcher. There are inlaid *ruyi*-head *huangtong* mounts where they meet. Near the upper and the lower ends are two horizontal stretchers. The two identical parts are joined by metal rods passing through openings in the middle of their legs, serving as hinges and cushioned with round *huangtong* plates on both ends. Metal rings cushioned with plates are fitted to the higher level horizontal stretchers to allow a detachable metal rod ending with a hook on each end to constrain the stand to an appropriate height.

Musical instrument stands are seen in woodblock illustrations to Ming publications as well as paintings but few actual examples have come to light. The only piece known is the very similar example in the Dr S Y Yip collection exhibited at the "Splendor of Style" exhibition in the Museum of History, Taipei. (Museum of History, 1999, p. 134)

Provenance

Grace Wu Bruce, Hong Kong, 1994

Published

Grace Wu Bruce Co Ltd, *Ming Furniture*, Hong Kong, 1995, pp.62 – 63

《征播奏捷传》Zhengbo Zoujie Zhuan
Putting Down the Rebellion at Bozhou

《灵宝刀》Ling Bao Dao
The renown knife Lingbao

黄花梨有束腰马蹄足矮火盆架

晚明(1573–1644)
- 长 55.5 厘米　宽 37.8 厘米
- 高 16 厘米

边框为标准格角榫攒边造,抹头可见明榫。边抹冰盘沿平直,自上中部下敛,至底压窄平线。束腰与形状优美沿边起线的壸门式牙条以抱肩榫与腿足和桌面结合。四足内翻马蹄,造型低扁,劲峭有力。

火盆架为古代中国家居中必备家具之一,严寒时室内用以烧炭取暖,木刻版画与绘画中皆多见。唯黄花梨木制传世品异常稀少。火盆架既为日常用品,而使用时又近火源易被炭火烧灼,理当用一般柴木制作,珍贵木材如黄花梨的实例不多也就不足为奇。

来　源
| 香港嘉木堂 1995

出　版
| 伍嘉恩《明式家具二十年经眼录》北京,2010,页 260

Low brazier stand

Huanghuali wood
Late Ming (1573-1644)
Width 55.5 cm (21 ⅞") Depth 37.8 cm (15 ¼")
Height 16 cm (6 ¼")

The top is of standard mitred, mortised and tenoned frame construction with exposed tenons on the short sides of the frame top. The edge of the frame is flat and moulds inwards and downwards from about a third way down to end in a narrow band. The recessed waist and the deep curvilinear, beaded-edged apron are mortised and tenoned and half-lapped to the straight legs ending in elegantly shaped hoof feet.

Brazier stands were an essential type of furniture for warming up the cold interiors in old China as depicted in many woodblock prints and paintings although extant examples in *huanghuali* wood are very rare. As they were mundane articles for everyday use and their function to support a brazier with burning charcoal made them susceptible to damage by fire, it stands to reason that most were made of inexpensive soft wood and few were ever made of the precious and durable *huanghuali*.

Provenance

Grace Wu Bruce, Hong Kong, 1995

Published

Grace Wu Bruce, *Two Decades of Ming Furniture*, Beijing, 2010, p. 260

《南宋杂传》
Nansong Zhuzhuan
Historical Tales of the Southern Song

束腰与形状优美沿边起线的壶门式牙条以抱肩榫与腿足和桌面结合；四足内翻马蹄，造型低扁，劲峭有力

The recessed waist and the deep curvilinear, beaded-edged apron are mortised and tenoned and half-lapped to the straight legs ending in elegantly shaped hoof feet

黄花梨嵌寿山石人物瑞兽图十二扇围屏

清前期（1644-1722）

- 每扇长 56.2 厘米　通长 677 厘米
- 宽 3 厘米　高 314 厘米

围屏中部十扇，每扇两根立材与五根横枨组成框架镶入花板。立材横枨均内沿压窄边线。每扇可分为三部分，上部装外刷槽落堂踩鼓委角长方框，内套花卉形开光绦环板，镶嵌寿山石精工雕八仙及罗汉图。四角浮雕以旋卷多姿的螭龙。中部为屏心，用斗簇法构成各种形的透空图案。下部又分三段：上为绦环板，与屏顶相同，花朵开光内嵌八仙罗汉图。中段为裙板，造法相似，但踩委角方框内再套委角方开光，镶嵌寿山石雕瑞兽图。四周用螭龙纹填满。下段亮脚剜出曲线，起阳线并雕两螭隔卷草相对。左右尽端两扇上下与其余十扇相同，只是增加立柱将屏心一分为二，内半部也安透空图案心。外侧则栽入横枨两根，镶绦环板三块，长方形框套海棠开光内嵌人像，上下由螭纹组成，尾部衍为卷草，卷卷相转。十二扇屏之间各用三组黄铜钩环连结，腿足包黄铜套。围屏背面绦环板镶嵌人像位置浮雕博古纹。裙板雕螭纹团寿图。

此套围屏造工精湛，镶嵌精雕寿山石八仙、罗汉及瑞兽图，每扇形态各异，生动传神。弥足珍贵的是大部分为原配，只尽端两扇缺镶嵌石，其余只有少部分脱落。而屏心透空图案保留甚佳，也十分难得。

至停笔为止，笔者未见亦未闻黄花梨木造十二扇围屏传世品中有明代的。都损破、失传了？还是此类别当时不存在？尚待考。

来 源
| 香港嘉木堂 2002

出 版
| 从未发表

Twelve-leaf folding screen

Huanghuali wood
Early Qing (1644-1722)
Width each panel 56.2 cm (22 ⅛")   Overall 677cm (266 ½")
Depth 3 cm (1 3/16")   Height 314 cm (123 ⅝")

The ten leaves in the centre are each constructed with two long uprights and five horizontal stretchers, edged on the insides with a narrow moulding, forming a framework to house the carved panels. Each leaf comprises three parts: The top is an inset panel with a beaded-edged, butterflied cornered rectangle enclosing a floral-shaped medallion inlaid with soapstone figures of *lohans* and immortals. The four corners are carved with lively *chi*-dragons with curling tails. The centre is an opening housing frameworks of various open shapes made by small members joined together. The lower part also comprises three sections: The top is similarly with an inset panel, floral-shaped medallion inlaid with soapstone figures. The centre is also inset with a panel, but of butterflied cornered squares enclosing a smaller square medallion, again inlaid with soapstone carvings, but here of mythical animals. The surrounds are carved with eight *chi*-dragons. Below is a curvilinear beaded-edged apron carved with dragons amidst scrolls in relief. The two end leaves are similarly constructed at the top and bottom as the others while the central space has an additional section formed by an upright dividing it into two halves. The inside half is filled with frameworks of open shapes. Two short mitred stretchers divide the outside half into three sections, each inset with a panel with a beaded-edged rectangle enclosing a begonia-shaped medallion, again inlaid with soapstone figures. Lively *chi*-dragons with scrolling tails are carved above and below. The twelve removal panels are connected to each other by three sets of *huangtong* hinges and their feet capped, also in *huangtong*. The back of the folding screens are similarly decorated as the front, but with carved antique treasures and *shou* character pattern at the place of the stone inlays.

This twelve-leaf folding screen is beautifully crafted with superb carved inlays of *lohans*, immortals and mythical animals, all vividly portrayed and different on every panel. In excellent state of preservation, except for the two end leaves where the inlays were missing, there were only minor losses on the central panels, now

Provenance

Grace Wu Bruce, Hong Kong, 2002

Published

Never published

expertly restored. It is also rare to find the openwork frames in the central section in such good condition.

To date, no twelve-leaf folding screen made in *huanghuali* wood dated to the Ming has come to the attention of this author. Whether they were all damaged and vanished or this type did not exist then need further research.

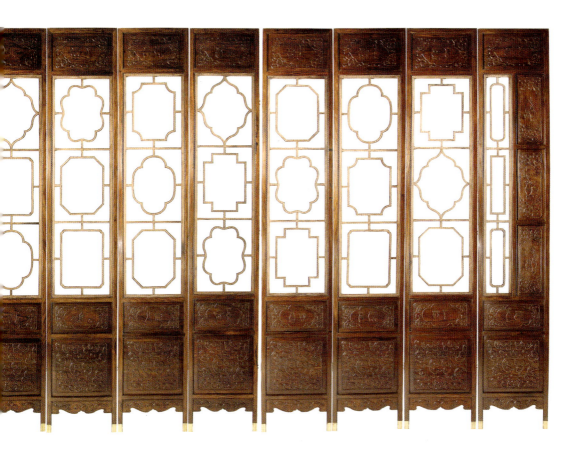

上层八仙罗汉图绦环板

Lohans and immortals panels at the top

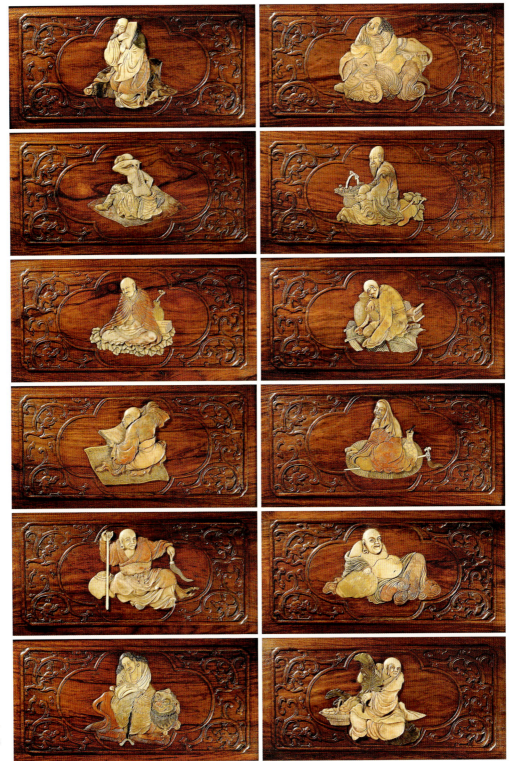

瑞兽图裙板

Mystical animals panels below

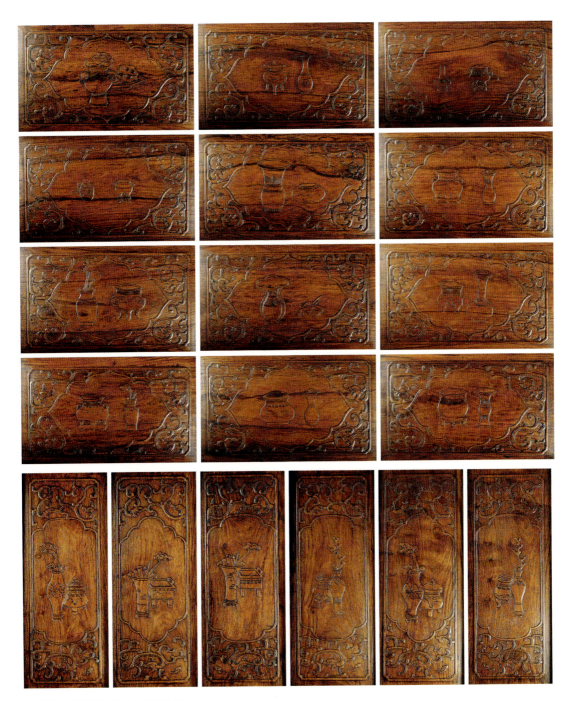

围屏背面绦环板镶嵌人像位置浮雕博古纹

The back of the folding screens are similarly decorated as the front, but with carved antique treasures and *shou* character pattern at the place of the stone inlays

案头家具

TABLE TOP
FURNITURE

笔筒

Brushpots

《画中人》
Huazhongren
Beauty from the Hanging Scroll

《郁轮袍》
Yulun Pao
The Tale of a Pipa Song

笔筒的主要功能是承载各种类的笔，因而得名。硬木制的笔筒多为圆形素身，最能呈现黄花梨、紫檀等珍贵木材天然生动有致的纹理。圆形素笔筒腔壁多直，也有微敛，口沿外撇，或些微束腰，上下添线脚。其他形状的笔筒如方形、葵瓣形、随形等均为少见的品种。这类笔筒或沿口起阔扁平线，底座加雕饰，或在筒壁凿出瘿节，又有嵌银嵌宝装饰。硬木制笔筒浮雕花卉纹等则属十分罕见的类别。

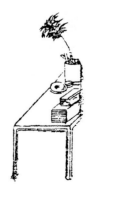

《西湖二集》
Xihu Erji
Two Collections of Stories of the West Lake

The function of brushpots is to hold brushes, hence the name. Brushpots made of hardwoods are usually round and plain, which best reveal the natural, lively grains of precious hardwoods such as *huanghuali* and *zitan*. The walls of plain round brushpots are usually straight, but there are occasional examples with very gently flaring mouths or almost imperceptibly recessed waist, and some have mouldings at the mouth rim and the base. Other shapes like square, lobe-shaped and naturalistic shapes are all rare examples. These types sometimes have wide mouldings at the rim, decorations at the base, or carved nodules on its walls, even silver or precious stones inlays. Carved brushpots with motifs like flowers and foliages belong to one of the rarest types.

黄花梨雕花卉笔筒

十七至十八世纪
- 直径 21.4 厘米
- 高 19.4 厘米

HUANGHUALI CARVED BRUSHPOT
17th to 18th century
Diameter 21.4 cm (8 7⁄16") Height 19.4 cm (7 5⁄8")

黄花梨葵瓣式笔筒

十七至十八世纪
- 直径 17.5 厘米
- 高 19.2 厘米

HUANGHUALI LOBE-SHAPED BRUSHPOT
17ᵗʰ to 18ᵗʰ century
Diameter 17.5 cm (6 ⅞") Height 19.2 cm (7 %16")

黄花梨素笔筒

十七至十八世纪
- 直径 20.4 厘米
- 高 17.8 厘米

H̲UANGHUALI͟ ͟P͟L͟A͟I͟N͟ ͟B͟R͟U͟S͟H͟P͟O͟T͟
17th to 18th century
Diameter 20.4 cm (8″) Height 17.8 cm (7″)

紫檀葵瓣式嵌银笔筒

十七至十八世纪
- 长 13 厘米　宽 12.2 厘米
- 高 18 厘米

ZITAN LOBE-SHAPED BRUSHPOT WITH SILVER INLAY
17th to 18th century
Width 13 cm (5 ⅛")　Depth 12.2 cm (4 ¾")　Height 18 cm (7 1/16")

紫檀方形嵌银笔筒

十七至十八世纪
- 长 11.5 厘米　宽 11.5 厘米
- 高 15.5 厘米

ZITAN SQUARE BRUSHPOT WITH SILVER INLAY
17th to 18th century
Width 11.5 cm (4 ½")　Depth 11.5 cm (4 ½")　Height 15.5 cm (6 ⅛")

紫檀雕花卉笔筒

十七至十八世纪
- 直径 16.2 厘米
- 高 16.2 厘米

Zitan carved brushpot
17th to 18th century
Diameter 16.2 cm (6 ⅜")　Height 16.2 cm (6 ⅜")

紫檀方形笔筒

十七至十八世纪
- 长 13.9 厘米　宽 13.9 厘米
- 高 16.2 厘米

ZITAN SQUARE BRUSHPOT
17th to 18th century
Width 13.9 cm (5 7/16")　Depth 13.9 cm (5 7/16")
Height 16.2 cm (6 3/8")

瘿木笔筒

十七至十八世纪
- 直径 20.6 厘米
- 高 19.5 厘米

Burlwood brushpot
17th to 18th century
Diameter 20.6 cm (8 ⅛″)   Height 19.5 cm (7 11/16″)

黄花梨微型翘头案

十七至十八世纪
- 长 51 厘米　宽 18.8 厘米
- 高 16 厘米

独板微型翘头案，形象与大型家具无异，但结构有别。应该不是近人传为明代工场作坊供人订购家具的模型。云纹牙头牙条一木连做，大型翘头案多分开制作。牙头两旁出尖，俏丽异常，大型家具罕见。托子上嵌厚板，成为板足，凿开口钳夹牙条，镂大云头。大型翘头案多为脚足间嵌档板结构。小案独板纹理细密生动，有斑眼花纹。

此类小型家具，可以摆在大条案上陈置文玩或独立鉴赏，当是古代文人书斋内的案头珍玩。

H*UANGHUALI* MINIATURE *QIAOTOUAN* TABLE

17th to 18th century
Width 51 cm (20 1/16")   Depth 18.8 cm (7 3/8")
Height 16 cm (6 5/16")

This miniature *qiaotouan* table looks similar to its large size counterpart but is in fact constructed differently. So miniatures were unlikely to be workshop models of the Ming for patrons to order furniture as claimed by some present day scholars. The cloud-spandrelled apron is made of one piece of wood, unusual in large size *qiaotouan* tables. The spandrels end in delicate, attractive points rarely seen in large scale *qiaotouan* tables. In addition, thick planks inset into the shoe feet carved with a large cloud shape serve as legs. Regular *qiaotouan* tables are constructed with two legs and an inset panel in between. The single plank top is tightly grained with attractive whirling pattern and "eyes".

Miniature tables like the present piece may be placed on painting tables, desks serving as stands for treasured antiques, or as an independent object to be admired in the studios of the literati in old times.

黄花梨围棋子盒（成对）

十七至十八世纪
- 肩径 12.7 厘米
- 高 8.3 厘米

盒作瓜棱式，整挖而成。腔壁向内微弯，木纹毕现。鬼脸、狸斑纹纷然入目。穹顶盖子刻尖角八瓣花卉纹。

《唐书志传》
Tangshu Zhizhuan
Romance of the Tang dynasty

Huanghuali pair of *weiqi* counter containers

17th to 18th century
Diameter 12.7 cm (5")   Height 8.3 cm (3 ¼")

These *weiqi* containers are fashioned in the shape of a melon, rounded with high shoulders, the lobe segments divided by a groove. Formed and carved from a single piece of wood, the walls slope in gently revealing the *guilian* "ghost faced" pattern of *huanghuali* wood. The gently domed covers are carved with a pointed eight-petalled flower.

黄花梨折叠棋盘

十七至十八世纪

- 长 46.5 厘米　宽 46.5 厘米
- 高 1.6 厘米

此精制棋盘由两块攒边框心板，中间阔直绦，用铜轴钉连接组成。可折叠，方便携带及储存。黄花梨心板纹理生动醒目，咫尺间有风起云涌之势。天然纹理之美，叹为观止。心板嵌银丝一面格出象棋盘，背面围棋盘。围棋与象棋虽然自古代至今为人喜爱，但传世珍贵硬木晚明清初棋盘却十分罕见。

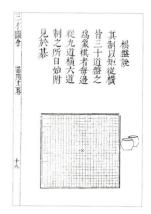

《三才图会》
Sancai Tuhui
Pictoral Encyclopedia of Heaven, Earth and Man

Huanghuali Folding Game Board

17th to 18th century
Width 46.5 cm (18 5⁄16″)   Depth 46.5 cm (18 5⁄16″)
Height 1.6 cm (5⁄8″)

This well crafted game board comprises two halves joined to the middle wide band by metal pivots allowing it to be folded for easy transportation and storage. Each half is with a framed floating panel of tightly grained, highly figured *huanghuali* wood conjuring up swirling cloud patterns. The natural grain of the wood is exquisite, a sight to behold. These panels are inlaid with silver wire in a grid pattern creating a *xiangqi* chess board on one side and a *weiqi* board on the reverse. In spite of the popularity of these games from ancient times to the present day, hardwood *weiqi* and chess boards datable to the Ming and early Qing are relatively rare.

多撞提盒

Tiered carry boxes

多撞提盒设计源自食格类器物。为了便于携带,食格多用竹或较轻的柴木制成。明代画作及小说版画插图也常有描绘出游时侍从挑食格的情景。

制作精良、用木质细密坚实的珍贵硬木黄花梨与紫檀木造的提盒,设计如一般食格,但其用途已演变为储存珍贵物品。这类提盒都设特别装置把盒盖与提梁立柱锁紧,确保每撞内所存物品安全。此装置颇能引证此类提盒用途为储存珍贵物品。

The design of tiered carry boxes originated from food boxes, made mostly of bamboo and lightweight woods for easy carriage. Attendants carrying them on outings were frequently depicted in Ming period paintings and woodblock illustrations to Ming novels.

Refined examples made in heavy and dense precious hardwoods *huanghuali* and *zitan* are likely derived from the common food boxes and used to contain valuables. This assumption is reinforced by the presence of a lock mechanism securing the lid to the sides of the handles, rendering the box trays inaccessible.

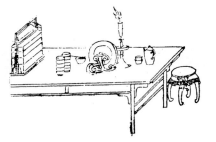

《西湖二集》
Xihu Erji
Two Collections of Stories of the West Lake

《诗赋盟》
Shifu Meng
Alliance sworn with Poetry

《金瓶梅词话》
Jin Ping Mei Cihua
The Golden Lotus

《望湖亭》
Wanghu Ting
Lake View Pagoda

黄花梨三撞提盒

晚明至清前期（1600–1700）

- 长 34.3 厘米　宽 19.1 厘米
- 高 22 厘米

此提盒底座长方框用两根托带连接，在短边上竖立柱，两旁有站牙抵夹。上接横梁，两端拱起。构件相交处均嵌镶铜页加固。上一撞口内设平盘。盒盖与每撞沿口均起灯草线，加厚子口。盒盖两侧立墙正中打眼，立柱与此眼相对处也打眼，用铜条贯穿。由于下撞盒底坐入底座槽口中，每层又均有子口衔扣，铜条贯穿后提盒就被固定。铜条端小孔上如再加铜锁，整件三撞提盒就被锁上，不能开启。

Huanghuali three-tier carry box
Late Ming to early Qing (1600-1700)
Width 34.3 cm (13 ½")   Depth 19.1 cm (7 ½")
Height 22 cm (8 ⅝")

The base of the carry box comprises a rectangular frame connected by two transverse stretchers. An upright, with spandrels on either sides, rises from the short sides of the base frame to meet the arch-shaped handle. Inlaid metal plates are fitted where each two members meet for reinforcement. Inside the top tier, resting on its lip edge is a shallow tray. There is a beaded edge on the cover and the mouth of each tier, to increase the size of the surface where they meet. There is an opening in the centre of the cover on each short side aligned with the opening on the uprights at the same position to house a long metal rod passing through. As the bottom tier box is fitted inside the ledge of the base frame and each tier as well as the cover are interlocked by their ledges, the placement of the metal rod secures the whole carry box in its base. If a lock is fitted to the opening at one end of the metal rod, the whole structure is locked, rendering the box trays inaccessible.

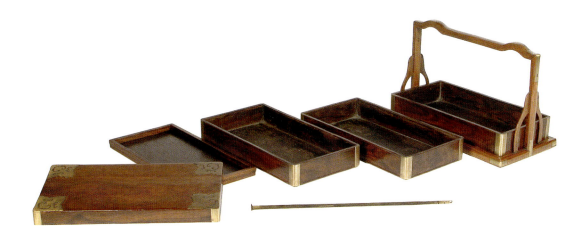

紫檀四撞提盒

晚明至清前期（1600–1700）
- 长 43.8 厘米　宽 25.5 厘米
- 高 37 厘米

这紫檀四撞提盒，与前例黄花梨三撞提盒结构无异，只是体型更大，亦多一撞。四撞提盒传世品有相当数目，但硕大如此十分罕见，特别是紫檀木制的。

此提盒选料讲究。其天然纹理之美，颇能说明明代鉴赏紫檀木，也以纹理生动醒目为上。

ZITAN FOUR-TIER CARRY BOX

Late Ming to early Qing (1600-1700)
Width 43.8 cm (17 ¼")   Depth 25.5 cm (10 ¹⁄₁₆")
Height 37 cm (14 ⁹⁄₁₆")

This four-tier carry box made in *zitan* wood is constructed in a similar manner as the previous *huanghuali* piece, only much larger and with an additional tier. There are a number of four-tier boxes but large size ones such as this example is very rare, especially in *zitan* wood.

The timber used has beautiful natural figuring demonstrating that in the Ming, the connoisseurship of *zitan* pieces included appreciating their highly figured pattern.

镜架

Mirror stands

镜架是状如帖架的一种梳妆用具，多作折叠式，宋代已流行。苏州博物馆藏元代出土的折合式银镜架（见图），就是明代折叠式镜架的华丽前身。

宝座式镜台是宋代扶手椅式镜台的进一步发展。台北故宫藏宋画《绣栊晓镜图》中可以看到一具扶手椅式镜台的形象，是木趣居宝座式镜台（页468）的雏形。

五屏风式镜台如《鲁班经匠家镜》内一具（见图），是三种中出现较晚的，传世实物也以此式为多，所以没有收入木趣居。

元　银镜架
Silver Mirror stand, Yuan dynasty

Mirror stands are pieces of small furniture like book stands, placed on dressing tables for supporting a mirror. Popularly in use at least by Song, most examples are foldable. The folding mirror stand made in silver, in the Suzhou Museum, excavated from a Yuan period tomb (see picture), is a glamorous predecessor of the Ming folding mirror stands.

Throne-form mirror stands is a development from the Song type that is shaped like an armchair. Such a piece can be seen in the Song period painting Xiu Long Xiao Jing Tu which depicts an elegant lady looking at herself in a mirror. The mirror stand is the prototype of the throne-form piece in this collection. (p.468)

Mirror stands with inset five-panel screens like the piece illustrated in *Lu Ban Jing Jiang Jia Jing*, The Classic of Lu Ban and the Craftsmen's Mirror (see picture) are a further development from the above, with the most extant examples and therefore not included in this collection.

《琵琶记》
Pipa Ji
Story of the Lute

《双鱼记》
Shuang Yu Ji
A Pair of Fishes

《占花魁》
Zhan Huakui
Tale of the Popular Courtesan

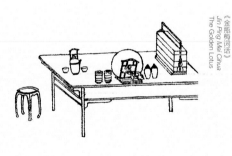

《金瓶梅词话》
Jin Ping Mei Cihua
The Golden Lotus

《鲁班经匠家镜》
Lu Ban Jing Jiang Jia Jing
The Classic of Lu Ban and the Craftsmen's Mirror

黄花梨螭龙云纹折叠式镜架

晚明至清前期（1600–1700）
- 长 31.4 厘米　宽 31.4 厘米
- 支起高 26 厘米　放平高 7.5 厘米

黄花梨镜架，在妆台上承放镜子的用具。折叠式，可支起承镜，不用时放平。支架铜镜的背板攒框造成。四角安两卷相抵云纹角牙，正中大圆透雕螭龙，龙身蟠转，组成图案。四周斗四簇云纹。下部正中安荷叶式托子承镜。镜架座安装壶门轮廓牙子，小马蹄足劲俏可人。

Huanghuali carved *chi*-dragon folding mirror stand

Late Ming to early Qing (1600-1700)
Width 31.4 cm (12 ⅜")   Depth 31.4 cm (12 ⅜")
Height when set up 26 cm (10 ¼")   Height when folded 7.5 cm (2 ¹⁵⁄₁₆")

Mirror stands are small pieces of furniture on the dressing table for supporting a mirror. This folding example may be set up to support a mirror or folded flat when not in use. The mirror support panel comprises a frame inset with corner spandrels of C-scroll design, and in the centre, a large roundel with openwork carving of a coiled *chi*-dragon flanked by four double cloud scrolls. A lotus leaf-shaped support where the mirror would rest is fitted in the centre below. The base is with curvilinear-shaped aprons and beautifully modelled low hoof feet.

黄花梨折叠式镜架

晚明至清前期（1600–1700）

- 长 38 厘米　宽 42 厘米
- 支起高 35.5 厘米　放平高 4 厘米

这大镜架结构与前例基本相同，只是承托铜镜的支架不嵌透雕花片，而用两根直材分格。框与直材起双混面，沿边起线，中踩带洼儿皮条线。支架四周与架座都安黄铜包角加固。铜片镂如意头纹，正中荷叶式镜托子也安铜如意纹饰件。

Huanghuali folding mirror stand

Late Ming to early Qing (1600-1700)
Width 38 cm (14 15/16")   Depth 42 cm (16 9/16")
Height when set up 35.5 cm (14")   Height when folded 4 cm (1 3/4")

This large mirror stand is similarly constructed as the previous piece except the mirror support framework is divided into sections by two stretchers and not inset with carved elements. The frame and the stretchers have moulded edges, a double convex surface with a grooved wide band in the centre. The four corners are reinforced with *huangtong* metal mounts as are the four corners of the base, all crafted with *ruyi* pattern. The lotus leaf-shaped support in the centre is also decorated with *ruyi*-shaped metal mounts.

紫檀龙纹折叠式镜架

清前期（1644-1722）

- 长 56 厘米　宽 56.5 厘米
- 支起高 54 厘米　放平高 5 厘米

此具紫檀木制镜架特别大，结构与前两具镜架基本相同，只是铜镜支架用不同长短的直材横材分格成长方空隔，拱形搭脑两端出头，精雕立体写实龙头，华丽美观。正中安素身荷叶式托子。

出 版

Grace Wu Bruce, "Classic Chinese Furniture in Tzu-Tan Wood", *Arts of Asia*, November-December 1991, Hong Kong. 伍嘉恩《紫檀木造古典中国家具》，《亚洲艺术》1991 年 11-12 月，香港，页 147

伍嘉恩《中国古典紫檀家具—几件明及清初实例及其纵横探讨》，《中国古典家具研究会会刊》十二，1992 年 11 月，北京，页 47

伍嘉恩《从几件实例探讨中国古典紫檀家具》，《文物天地》第 213 期，中国文物报社，北京，2009 年 3 月，页 91

Zitan CARVED DRAGON FOLDING MIRROR STAND

Early Qing (1644-1722)
Width 56 cm (22 1/16")   Depth 56.5 cm (22 1/4")
Height when set up   54 cm (21 1/4")   Height when folded   5 cm (2")

This very large *zitan* wood folding mirror stand is similarly constructed as the two previous pieces, the mirror support structure a lattice panel created by round stretchers of various sizes joined together, the arched top rail ending in protruding carved heads of dragon realistically modelled, and a lotus leaf-shaped rest set in the centre.

Published

Grace Wu Bruce, Classic Chinese Furniture in Tzu-Tan Wood, *Arts of Asia*, November-December 1991, Hong Kong, p. 147

Grace Wu Bruce, *Zhongguo Gudian Zitan Jiaju - Jijian Ming ji Qing Chu Shili jiqi Zongheng Tantao* (Chinese Classic Furniture in *Zitan* - Some Ming and Early Qing Examples and Their exploration), *Zhongguo Gudian Jiaju Yanjiuhui Huikan* (Journal of the Association of Chinese Classical Furniture), No. 12, November 1992, Beijing, p.47

Grace Wu Bruce, *Cong Jijian Shili Tantao Zhongguo Gudian Zitan Jiaju* (Some Examples of Chinese Classic Furniture in *Zitan* Wood and Their study), *Cultural Relics World*, issue 213, Zhongguo Wenwu Baoshe, Beijing, March 2009, p. 91

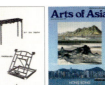

黄花梨宝座式镜台

晚明（1573-1644）

- 长 45.5 厘米　宽 32 厘米
- 高 60 厘米

Huanghuali throne-form mirror stand
Late Ming (1573-1644)
Width 45.5 cm (17 15/16″)　Depth 32 cm (12 5/8″)
Height 60 cm (23 5/8″)

台座设抽屉三具，抽屉面浮雕折枝花卉。台座上后背安山字式屏风，正中高出，左右递减。搭脑均远跳出头，雕造卷叶纹。两侧安螭龙角牙，中扇嵌三块透雕仙鹤麒麟瑞兽云纹绦环板，左右用不同长短的横竖材攒成卍纹。台座两侧和前方设有望柱的栏杆，中间开敞。栏杆框内装透雕花卉绦环板。望柱上蹲狮子。台面正中原有装置，为支架铜镜而设，已失落。形状可参照15世纪明朝的木匠手册《鲁班经匠家镜》内版画插图。

传世各种形状的镜台，以宝座式最为罕见。

The mirror stand is of a type resembling a throne with two arms and a tall back. The back is in three sections, high in the centre flanked by two lower panels, each with extended protruding top rails that end in carved scroll leaves shapes. On the sides are hung two pierced dragon spandrels. The central section is inset with three openwork carved panels of stork, *qilin* and auspicious animal amidst clouds and waves. The two sides are each inset with 卍 pattern lattice formed by short mitred members joined together. There are railings on the sides and in front, the centre left open. Openwork carved panels of flowers and foliage are inset into the railings, and lions squat on top of the short pillars. In the centre of the stand was placed a support for a mirror, now lost. For a similar fitment, refer to the woodblock illustration to the 15th century carpenter's manual, *Lu Ban JingJiang JiaJing*.

Of all types of surviving examples of mirror stands of *huanghuali* wood, throne-form pieces are the rarest.

紫檀官皮箱

晚明至清前期（1600–1700）
- 长 40 厘米　宽 32.5 厘米
- 高 35.5 厘米

官皮箱传世实物颇多，形制尺寸差别不大，应是平常人家常备之物，而不是衙门官府的专门用具，因此"官皮箱"之名的由来尚待考证。

此类官皮箱男女皆适用来存放梳妆用品、珠宝首饰以及其他贵重物件。也可以置于书桌上，便于收纳文房书写用具以及印玺。《西厢记》"妆台窥简"一回，各版本插图中皆见官皮箱。

紫檀官皮箱，平顶，箱盖掀开是一个平屉，两扇小门后设抽屉两层，上二下一共三具。门上缘留子口，顶盖关好后，扣住子口，两门就不能开启。箱盖四角用长方以及如意云头形白铜片加固，箱身与箱盖背后安长方形合页。正面莲瓣形面页，云头形拍子开口容纳钮头，其下安拉手连长方面页。两侧有提环。底座锼出壸门式轮廓，雕卷草叶纹。

出 版

Grace Wu Bruce, "Small Portable Treasures, Examples of Classic Chinese Furniture: (V)", *Oriental Art*, Autumn 1993, London. 伍嘉恩《经典明朝家具之五：轻巧袖珍宝》，《东方艺术》，1993 年秋季刊，伦敦，页 50

伍嘉恩《明式家具二十年经眼录》北京，2010，页 270

《西厢记》妆台窥简
Xi Xiang Ji, The West Chamber

《西厢记》玉台窥简
Xi Xiang Ji, The West Chamber

Zitan table cabinet

Late Ming to early Qing (1600-1700)
Width 40 cm (15 ¾")   Depth 32.5 cm (12 13/16")
Height 35.5 cm (14")

These table cabinets were used as dressing cases by both men and women to store toiletries, jewellery and other valuables. They were also used on desks for the storage of stationery, writing implements and seals. Woodblock illustrations to the popular drama *Xi Xiang Ji*, The West Chamber show these table cabinets in use in all its various editions.

The top of the lid is flat and it opens to reveal a tray-like compartment. The doors are cut with ledges on their upper edges so that when the lid is closed, these ledges fit behind the lid, preventing the doors from being opened. Behind the two doors are three drawers. The corners of the lid are fitted with rectangular and *ruyi*-shaped *baitong* plates for reinforcement. Rectangular strap hinges of the lid and the doors, and in front, the lotus-shaped plate with a hasp and lock receptacles, small plates with door pulls below, and handles on both sides are all made of *baitong*. The curvilinear-shaped base is carved with scrolling tendrils.

Published

Grace Wu Bruce, "Small Portable Treasures, Examples of Classic Chinese Furniture: (V)", *Oriental Art*, Autumn 1993, London, p. 50

Grace Wu Bruce, *Two Decades of Ming Furniture*, Beijing, 2010, p. 270

黄花梨茶壶桶

晚明至清前期（1600–1700）

- 长 20.6 厘米　宽 17.2 厘米
- 高 25.5 厘米

茶壶桶传世品众多，多为晚清、民国旧物。柴木制，也有髹漆的。属晚明以珍贵黄花梨木造者十分罕见。

桶身刻多瓣纹，盖周亦然。壶嘴开口处镶如意形白铜护片。两侧把手用菊瓣白铜钉固定。提把镶抽象龙凤纹白铜饰件。桶底透雕古钱纹。整件造型装饰，华丽美观。

Huanghuali teapot holder

Late Ming to early Qing (1600-1700)
Width 20.6 cm (8 ⅛")   Depth 17.2 cm (6 ¾")
Height 25.5 cm (10 1/16")

There are plenty of surviving examples of teapot holders, mainly from the late Qing and Republic period. Almost all are made of miscellaneous soft woods, some lacquered. Those made of precious *huanghuali* and dated to the Ming are very rare.

The container is carved like a fluted column, the edge of the cover similarly carved. A *ruyi*-shaped *baitong* plate is mounted to the opening where the teapot sprout protrudes. The wing-like handles are secured by chrysanthemum-shaped pins and stylised dragons and phoenix plates are applied to the central handle, the metal all of *baitong*, the base carved with an openwork cash coin. Beautifully modelled and attractively decorated, the container is a glamorous piece.

黄花梨四足三弯腿圆盘几

晚明（1573–1644）
- 直径 39.5 厘米
- 高 17 厘米

明式家具中无论是标准着地家具或案头家具，圆形的都属罕见。传世实例中之圆香几、圆凳、二件并接成圆形的月牙桌，都如凤毛麟角般难得一见。而案头家具中圆形盒也比长方形小箱子稀少得多。此具四足三弯腿圆盘几在传世种类中颇为独特。除了中国国家博物馆藏有一件十分相似几乎如出一辙的例子（吕章申 2014, 页96），似别无他例。

圆盘边框四接造，平屉下单穿带承托。三弯腿足外翻马蹄，与线条柔婉和束腰一木连做的壶门轮廓牙子配合恰到好处。沿边隆起肥厚灯草线赋予圆盘稳重更能承托盘内物的观感。

中国国家博物馆藏品
National Museum of China collection

Huanghuali Cabriole-leg round tray
Late Ming (1573-1644)
Diameter 39.5cm (15 ⁹⁄₁₆")   Height 17cm (6 ¹¹⁄₁₆")

In surviving examples of Ming furniture, be those resting at ground level or table top pieces, round examples are rare. Round incense stands, round stools, half-moon tables which when paired become round are all exceedingly rare. Even round boxes are much less frequently encountered than rectangular ones. This cabriole-leg round tray is a very unusual type. Except for the almost identical example in the collection of the National Museum of China, Beijing (Lu 2014, p.96), there seems to be no other similar piece known.

The round frame comprises four parts joined together and the tray is supported by a single stretcher underneath. The graceful curvilinear-shaped aprons with a recessed waist made from the same piece of wood, are joined by beautifully shaped cabriole legs ending in outward hoof feet. The wide beaded edges add steadiness to the form, giving the impression of balance to what the tray might hold.

黄花梨螺钿花盆

晚明（1573–1644）
- 长 48.5 厘米　宽 34.2 厘米
- 高 23.5 厘米

花盆结构简单，四壁以纹理生动黄花梨厚板明榫结合，板厚逾两厘米，内敛斜度显著，下接四扁足承托，盆口沿微隆。正面嵌镶螺钿组成蜻蜓蝴蝶牡丹图，两侧缠枝花卉。

明代绘画及书籍版画插图均常见户外庭园陈置大小花盆，内植花卉，但都似陶瓷制作，不像木器。此珍贵螺钿黄花梨木大花盆似不宜直接种植花卉，推测其用途为承载植有花卉的花盆，在户内陈设。

Huanghuali mother-of-pearl inlaid flowerpot

Late Ming (1573-1644)
Width 48.5 cm (19 1/16") Depth 34.2 cm (13 7/16")
Height 23.5 cm (9 1/4")

This flowerpots of simple construction with thick plank walls joined to each other with exposed tenons. The wall panels with gently curved lips, exceed two centimetres in thickness and slant downwards, and there are four small flat feet at the base. Thick mother-of-pearl pieces are inlaid to the walls, peonies, dragonflies and butterflies in front and flowers and foliage on the sides.

Ming paintings and woodblock illustrations to Ming publications often depict potted plants of various sizes being placed in gardens, with the flowerpots appearing to be made of pottery or porcelain rather than wood. This large inlaid flowerpot made of precious *huanghuali* wood seems not suitable to be used directly for planting. Perhaps it is used to contain outdoor potted plants for placement indoors.

《金瓶梅词话》
Jin Ping Mei Cihua
The Golden Lotus

《二刻拍案惊奇》
Erke Paian Jingqi
Amazing Tales – Second Series

《杜骗新书》《鼓掌绝尘》
Du Pian Xin Shu; Gu Zhang Jue Chen

黄花梨鹌鹑笼箱

晚明至清前期（1600–1700）
- 长 40 厘米　宽 25.1 厘米
- 高 30.7 厘米

此具箱子四墙上段及顶盖用短材攒接出卍字纹，都打洼。下段嵌海棠形沿边起线开光绦环板，下装窄牙条。四角柱，四边两根横枨与顶框都沿边起灯草线。长边横枨在箱的内部宽出作子口，承接顶盖下放时把箱子内空间一分为二。底板亦是黄花梨木做。

斗鹌鹑，据说源自唐玄宗时代。原是民间游戏，后成为宫中、官宦富豪、纨绔子弟清闲取乐和赌博的活动。故宫博物院藏《明人绘宣德帝斗鹌鹑图轴》，描绘明宣德皇帝朱瞻基与随从八人，围着似是特制带圆围墙方桌在园内斗鹌鹑的情景。宣德皇帝也喜欢斗蟋蟀，传世有宣德款青花蟋蟀罐。鹌鹑箱笼一般用柴木做，此具黄花梨木精制鹌鹑笼箱，为笔者多年仅见之孤例。

《明人绘宣德帝斗鹌鹑图轴》
Mingren Hui Xuande Di Dou Anchun Tuzhou

Huanghuali quail cage
Late Ming to early Qing (1600-1700)
Width 40 cm (15 ¾")   Depth 25.1 cm (9 ⅞")
Height 30.7 cm (12 ¹⁄₁₆")

The upper portion of the cage walls and the cover are made with thumb-moulded short members mitred and mortised together, forming the 卍 pattern. The lower part is inset with panels decorated with begonia shapes with moulded edges, and below are small, narrow aprons. The four posts, the horizontal stretchers as well as the top frame are edged with raised beadings. On the long sides of the cage, the horizontal stretchers are made with a ledge on the insides to receive the cover when placed at this lower level, dividing the interior space into two parts. The bottom panel is also made of *huanghuali* wood.

Quail fighting reportedly originated in eighth century Tang Dynasty. It was at first a game of leisure by the populace, then it became popular at court, amongst high officials and the wealthy as a pastime and also for gambling. In the Palace Museum, Beijing, the painting "Mingren Hui Xuande Di Dou Anchun Tuzhou" depicts the Ming emperor Xuande with eight attendants watching quails fighting in what appears to be a specially made table with a circular enclosure in a garden scene. The emperor Xuande is also known to be fond of cricket fighting and there are extant examples of blue and white porcelain cricket cages with Xuande mark. Quail cages are usually made of softwoods, this *huanghuali* example is the only one this author has encountered over these years.

小箱子

SMALL BOXES

珍贵硬木制造的小箱子实物传世不少，多为长方形约40厘米长，小于或大过此尺码的都不多。用材以黄花梨木制居多，紫檀次之，其他木制较少。小箱子基本形式全身光素，大多数在盖口及箱口起两道灯草线，也有平整无线的。正面铜面页多为圆形，方形与荷花瓣形则较少。拍子云头形。常见立墙四角用铜页包裹，以及盖顶四角镶钉云纹或如意头纹饰件。此等小箱子的结构，与典型的大衣箱无异。

有称此类箱子为文件箱，但实际用途应该较为广泛，包括存放文件、印玺、贵重物品如珠宝、现钞以及银两等。值得一提的是此等小箱子都含锁鼻，可以加锁。而且通常都在两侧设提环，显示其经常被移动携带使用。《忠义水浒传》"梁山泊分金大买市"一回插图，描绘各路英雄拆伙分金时的情景中，可见多件大小箱子。

经手过眼箱子无数，发现制作讲究的黄花梨箱子都全彻作，即底板、穿带都用黄花梨木做。而讲究的紫檀木箱内部则只用紫檀木或黄花梨木，而不取他材。除了标准器页484紫檀小箱，以下收集了特别少见、非常独特的其他例子。部分更是多年所遇的孤品，也包括一个不多见的大圆盒。

《忠义水浒传》梁山泊分金大买市 Zhongyi Shuihu Zhuan (Outlaws of the Marsh)

《清夜钟》 Qing Ye Zhong Alarm Bell on a Still Night

《仇画列女传》 Qiuhua Lienu Zhuan Biography of Women in Ancient China Illustrated by Qiu Ying

There are numerous surviving examples of small boxes made in precious hardwoods, mostly made of *huanghuali* wood, some of *zitan* wood, with those made of other woods being quite rare. Rectangular ones measuring about forty centimetres long are the most common. Larger or smaller size ones are rarer. The standard design is completely plain with only beadings on the edge of the cover and the body where they meet. There are also examples with no beadings. The metal plate in front is usually round. Square or lotus-shaped ones are also found but less frequently. The hasp is almost always cloud-shaped and on the walls, there may be metal plates mounted to wrap round the corners. The top of the cover may also have corner metal mounts, usually shaped like *ruyi* heads. The design and construction of these small boxes are similar to their large scale counterparts, clothes chests.

In spite of being called document boxes, these boxes actually can be used to store a large variety of items, ranging from documents and seals to valuables like jewellery, cash and silver. It is interesting to note that boxes as small as these were all fitted with openings to house locks, allowing them to be locked. In addition, on the sides there are often handles, indicating their association with frequent carriage. In the woodblock illustration to the historical novel *Zhongyi Shuihu Zhuan,* Outlaws of the Marsh, the rebel heroes at Liang Shan Bo are seen dividing their spoils, gold and other valuables after they decided to disband, using numerous boxes of the standard design.

Having handled a large body of these boxes, this author finds that fine *huanghuali* examples were made with the same wood throughout including the base panels and support stretchers while fine *zitan* examples have either *zitan* or *huanghuali* base panels and support stretchers, but not any other woods. In addition to the classic example of a *zitan* small box on page 484, included here are very rare and unusual pieces, some unique among all boxes encountered throughout these years. A large round box, a rare type, is also included.

紫檀小箱

晚明至清前期（1600–1700）
- 长 43.5 厘米　宽 24.5 厘米
- 高 20 厘米

此箱为传世晚明小箱子的基本式。盖口与箱口起两度灯草线，起加固作用。正面荷花瓣形面页，立墙四角用铜页包裹，顶盖镶钉云纹如意头形饰件。两侧安提环，并设护眼钱。铜活均白铜做。此箱子选材讲究，充分呈现紫檀天然紧密回旋的纹理。

Zitan small box

Late Ming to early Qing (1600-1700)
Width 43.5 cm (17 ⅛") Depth 24.5 cm (10 ¹⁄₁₆")
Height 20 cm (7 ⅞")

This box of classical design is a standard example of its type in surviving examples of the late Ming. It is completely plain but for the beadings on the edges of the cover and the body. The *baitong* metalware includes the lotus-shaped plate in front, the rectangular corner mounts on the walls and the inlaid *ruyi*-shaped mounts at the four corners of the lid. There are also bale handles on the sides with protective plates. The box is made of choice *zitan* wood with tight grains and whirling patterns.

黄花梨小箱

晚明至清前期（1600–1700）

- 长 39.3 厘米　宽 22.4 厘米
- 高 18.5 厘米

与前例同是小箱，但采用大面积的方铜面页，覆盖整个箱子立面的高度，所有角位无论是平面、立面都包镶铜片，观感与上例就很不一样。加上铜页全用厚片、方形手提环，更觉小箱子厚重。厚片铜活亦能起较强的加固作用，以承载重物。箱子彻黄花梨木制。

来源

香港嘉木堂

Nicolas Berggruen 藏品 1994 – 2011

纽约 佳士得 2011 - 2016

出版

Christie's, *Fine Chinese Ceramics and Works of Art Part I*, New York, 24 March 2011. 佳士得《中国陶瓷与工艺精品》纽约，2011 年 3 月 24 日，编号 1375

Christie's, *Fine Chinese Ceramics and Works of Art*, New York, 16 September 2016. 佳士得《中国陶瓷与工艺精品》纽约，2016 年 9 月 16 日，编号 1216

Huanghuali small box
Late Ming to early Qing (1600-1700)
Width 39.3 cm (15 ½")   Depth 22.4 cm (8 ¾")
Height 18.5 cm (7 ¼")

Although similar in construction to the last example, the application of a large *huangtong* metal plate covering the entire height of the front wall, metal strips at every corner on all horizontal and vertical planes, changes the appearance of this box completely. The thick *huangtong* plates employed provide additional reinforcement and together with the rectangular shaped handles allow this box to support more heavy objects. This box is made of *huanghuali* wood throughout.

Provenance
Grace Wu Bruce, Hong Kong

Nicolas Berggruen collection, 1994- 2011

Christie's, New York, 2011-2016

Published
Christie's, *Fine Chinese Ceramics and Works of Art Part I*, New York, 24 March 2011, no. 1375

Christie's, *Fine Chinese Ceramics and Works of Art*, New York, 16 September 2016, no. 1216

黄花梨方箱

十七至十八世纪
- 长 40 厘米　宽 39.4 厘米
- 高 17 厘米

此箱近方形,又带座,是稀有的种类。白铜面页也不是一般圆形而是长方形,两侧提环亦成长方。箱子彻黄花梨木制,包括箱内底板。

Huanghuali square box

17th to 18th century
Width 40 cm (15 ¾")   Depth 39.4 cm (15 ½")
Height 17 cm (6 11/16")

This nearly square box with a base is a rare type. The *baitong* metalware with its rectangular front plate and handles on the sides is also less common than the round ones. This box is made of *huanghuali* wood throughout, including the base panel.

黄花梨带抽屉箱

十七至十八世纪

- 长 52 厘米　宽 30.5 厘米
- 高 33 厘米

此箱比一般长方箱高、大，但外形与基本式相同。盖与箱口起两度阳线，全身光素，设白铜圆面页。背面安较少见的圆形合页。其特别之处为内部两端各设两抽屉，在传世箱子中无论大少都属罕见。采用纹理活泼生动的黄花梨木全彻制，包括箱底板、盖内穿带以及四抽屉内里。

Huanghuali box with drawers

17th to 18th century
Width 52 cm (20 ½")   Depth 30.5 cm (12")
Height 33 cm (13")

This box is larger than standard examples but its appearance is similar. It is completely plain but for the beaded edges on the cover and the body. It has an inlaid *baitong* round front plate, and the back inset with the more unusual round hinge plates. What is unusual is that there is a pair of drawers installed on each end of its interior, a feature rarely seen in surviving examples. It is made of actively grained *huanghuali* wood throughout, including the base panel, the support stretchers of the cover and the interiors of all four drawers.

黄花梨长箱

十七至十八世纪
- 长 82 厘米 宽 26 厘米
- 高 22.5 厘米

传世品中如此长的黄花梨木箱子十分罕见。此箱结构与基本式无异，盖口箱口踩灯口线，平镶白铜面页，云头拍子，立墙四角用铜页包裹，顶盖四角镶钉云纹铜饰件。两侧设提环。只是因其长度背面加装合页一对成三对，又在盖与箱长边上下前后各嵌装三对如意头纹铜饰件加固。短边也上下安一双。此箱选料精良，全彻制，包括穿带及内底板。

Huanghuali long box
17th to 18th century
Width 82 cm (31 ⅞") Depth 26 cm (10 ¼")
Height 22.5 cm (8 ⅞")

It is very rare to find such a long box made of *huanghuali* wood in surviving examples dated to the classical period. It is similarly constructed as standard pieces with beadings on the edge of the cover and the body. Inlaid metalware made in *baitong* comprises the front plate, hasp, corner mounts, *ruyi*-shaped mounts on the cover and handles on both sides. The only difference is an additional pair of hinges on the back and three sets of *ruyi*-shaped inlaid mounts on the long sides of the box at the top and bottom, and in the front and back. An additional set on the short sides. This box is made of choice timber, *huanghuali* wood throughout including the support stretchers and interior base panel.

黄花梨画箱

十七至十八世纪
- 长 140.7 厘米　宽 13.5 厘米
- 高 10.5 厘米

此黄花梨木箱长近一米半，盖上挖凿两个近方形圆角槽口，各安白铜提环。提环两半组成，放平卧藏入槽口时与盖面齐平，竖立时方便人用双手提起颇沉的黄花梨木箱盖。盖与箱踩子口上下扣合。立墙四角镶钉厚铜页包角。顶盖四角厚铜饰件同类型。此箱用材极致精美，黄花梨木色泽浓华，纹理细密生动，取自一材。此箱子用途似放画轴，如此制作是笔者多年所见的孤例。

Huanghuali scroll box
17th to 18th century
Width 140.7 cm (57")   Depth 13.5 cm (5 5/16")
Height 10.5 cm (4 1/8")

This box measuring nearly one and a half metres long has carved on its cover two square shape grooves with round corners housing a *baitong* handle each. Comprising two halves, the handles are flush with the cover when folded flat, and when raised they facilitate the lifting of the heavy *huanghuali* wood cover. The cover and the box are rabbeted on the edges to slot in to fit together. Thick metal mounts are on the four corners of the box and the lid. This long box is made of the choicest timber *huanghuali*, of rich colour and tight active grain, cut from the same tree. This box was likely made for the storage of a painting scroll and is the only example like it this author has come across.

黄花梨圆盒

十七至十八世纪

- 直径 23.7 厘米
- 高 8 厘米

此盒独木为之，看似至简，而所需工至繁，艺至高。盖口及箱口起两道阳线，盖与箱踩子口上下扣合。正面镶莲瓣形白铜面页，拍子作云头形，开口容纳钮头，背面安长方形白铜合页。传世品中黄花梨木制圆盒不多，属珍稀种类。这个从整木挖凿而成的圆盒非常精致。取材自木纹华美的黄花梨独木，盒盖与盒身上的纹理连接，如行云流水。

Huanghuali round box

17th to 18th century
Diameter 23.7 cm (9 5/16") Height 8 cm (3 1/8")

This simple round box carved from a solid piece of wood appears easy to make but in fact requires a high degree of skill and craftsmanship. The edge of the cover and the box are beaded on the outsides and rabbeted on the insides for a tight fit. There is a *baitong* lobe-shaped plate inlaid into the front, and a cloud-shaped lift-up hasp with opening for the lock receptacle. The back has a rectangular strap hinge, also made of *baitong*. Round boxes made in *huanghuali* wood are very rare. This exquisite round box is fashioned from one solid piece of beautifully grained *huanghuali* wood, with both the cover and the body of the box showing flowing patterns like clouds and rivers.

紫檀轿箱

晚明（1573–1644）
- 长 76.3 厘米　宽 19.7 厘米
- 高 14 厘米

轿箱是古代在轿子上使用的箱具，形状像是一个长方箱盒将底部两端各切除一个方块，这样箱子才可架搭在轿子的两根轿杠上。古代乘轿者多为官绅，故有说轿箱为官吏专门用具。

此轿箱全身光素，正面安长方形白铜面页，拍子作云头形，开口容纳钮头，背面安两只长方形合页，俱为白铜制。打开盖子，中间活动式浅屉，两端各安高低两层小侧室，室盖嵌入箱身槽口，打横推动启闭。平盘下是深且长的储物空间。

Zitan sedan chair box
Late Ming (1573-1644)
Width 76.3 cm (30")   Depth 19.7 cm (7 ¾")
Height 14 cm (5 ½")

The shape of a sedan chair box is a long rectangle with a square section cut out from both ends at the bottom. This extraordinary feature is to enable the box to be placed on the poles of a sedan chair. In Ancient China, sedans were used mainly by officials, hence these boxes were considered to be exclusively for the use of officials.

This box is completely plain, with a rectangular *baitong* plate in front, a *ruyi*-shaped hasp with openings to house the lock receptacles and two rectangular strap hinges in the back, also made of *baitong*. The lid opens to reveal a removable tray in the centre, with two small hidden compartments at each end with sliding covers and a deep storage section in the centre below the tray.

黄花梨天平架

晚明（1573–1644）

- 长 62.5 厘米　宽 22 厘米
- 高 75.5 厘米

天平是称银两等用的小秤，在以白银为主要货币的时代，天平是常用的衡具，天平架就是应运而生的案头家具。明代家居及商铺同样使用天平架。

天平架底箱以两块木板横放嵌入两厚板足构成，中设抽屉两具。两根方材立柱下端出榫纳入板足，上接横梁，横梁下安横枨，全部沿边起线。立柱两侧精雕螭纹抵夹站牙。立柱上下端卧镶黄铜饰件与横梁和底箱相连，起加固作用。板足与箱面板接合处也卧镶腰码形铜片加固。抽屉脸安铜面页，上设锁销锁鼻，使抽屉能上锁。

Huanghuali balance stand

Late Ming (1573-1644)
Width 62.5 cm (24 ⅝") Depth 22 cm (8 ⅝")
Height 75.5 cm (29 ¾")

Balances are small scales used to weigh silver pieces etc, which were widely used as measures when silver was the common currency, and balance stands were the accessory furniture to hang the balance scales.

The base section comprises two solid planks feet and two horizontal boards, housing a couple of drawers in between. Two uprights rise from the plank feet and are joined by a top rail, below is a horizontal stretcher, all with beaded-edges. There are well-carved *chi*-dragon spandrels on either side of the uprights. *Huangtong* metal plates are set flush to the uprights at the top and below where they meet the base section for further support. There are also metal plates of waisted weights shape where the base meets the plank feet. A rectangular central plate is inlaid to the drawers front, with sliding lock plate and receptacles.

《三才圖會》
Sancai Tuhui
Pictorial Encyclopedia of Heaven, Earth and Man

《水滸傳》
Zhongyi Shuihu Zhuan
Outlaws of the Marsh

《二刻拍案驚奇》
Erke Paian Jingqi
Amazing Tales – Second Series

黄花梨神龛

晚明至清前期（1600-1700）

- 长 24.4 厘米　宽 23.6 厘米
- 高 44 厘米

神龛是传统家居供奉神明的用具，传世品似多为紫檀、红木或漆木制作，黄花梨木造不多见。

门楼式神龛，以三块独板插入如地平的下座，加板盖成龛室。地平下座四边镂出壸门式亮脚。室前立柱两根，用栏杆围出前廊，中间开敞，栏杆嵌装螭纹花卉纹绦环板。廊顶三面均设绦环板挂檐，透雕花卉、寿字和古钱纹图案。内室安券口牙子，下垂短柱雕莲苞莲叶。

出 版

伍嘉恩《明式家具经眼录》故宫出版社，北京，2015，页 289

Huanghuali shrine

Late Ming to early Qing (1600 - 1700)
Width 24.4 cm (9 ⅝")   Depth 23.6 cm (9 ⁵⁄₁₆")
Height 44 cm (15 ¾")

Traditional households often have shrines to house deities for worship. Most surviving examples are made of *zitan* wood, *hongmu* or lacquered softwood with *huanghuali* pieces being quite rare.

This shrine is shaped like a gatehouse. Three single boards are inserted into the base, and one on top creating the shrine cavity. The base stretchers are carved with curvilinear silhouettes and two uprights rise from the corners in front with low railings, encircling an anteroom-like space in front of the shrine cavity, the central part left open. Openwork carved panels of *chi*-dragons are inset into the railings. On top of the anteroom are eaves, *guayan*, on all three sides, inset with openwork panels of floral, *shou* character and antique coin pattern. The shrine cavity has long aprons on the sides while the one on top is fitted with short columns carved with lotus buds and leaves.

Published

Grace Wu Bruce, *Ming Furniture Through My Eyes*, The Forbidden City Publishing House, Beijing, 2015, p. 289

黄花梨理石大案屏

晚明（1573–1644）

- 长 72 厘米　宽 28 厘米
- 高 59.7 厘米

案屏除了体积较小，适合放置于桌案上之外，与大型座屏的构造没有两样。此具大理石案屏，就正如常见于明代绘画与书籍插图版画内大座屏的缩影。

这具插屏式案屏格角攒边框嵌装大理石板，纹理如同泼墨山水画般呈现山峦隐现在云雾间，淡素清雅。二墩子上植立柱，柱顶刻仰俯莲纹，两边抵夹锼卷草纹站牙。墩柱间石板下装入两块透雕灵芝纹绦环板，下安披水牙子，中部刻分心花，两侧翻出卷草。

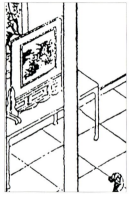

《金瓶梅词话》 Jin Ping Mei Cihua The Golden Lotus

《金瓶梅词话》 Jin Ping Mei Cihua The Golden Lotus

Huanghuali dali-marble table screen
Late Ming (1573-1644)
Width 72 cm (28 ⅜")   Depth 28 cm (11")
Height 59.7 cm (23 ½")

Table screens are contracted versions of large floor screens. Their method of making is often identical to their large counterparts. This piece is a smaller version of the large floor screens often depicted in Ming paintings, woodblock illustrations to contemporary publications.

This piece with a removable panel comprises a mitred frame inset with *dalishi* marble, evocative of a misty ink landscape. Uprights with carved lotus finials are planted into the thick, shaped bases and carved scroll-leaf spandrels are on either sides. Below the *dalishi* screen are two inset openwork *lingzhi* panels, beneath which are, aprons, fitted at an angle. The aprons are carved with a central decoration and foliage on the sides.

版画索引 WOODBLOCK ILLUSTRATIONS INDEX

p. 64

《北宋志传》焦赞怒杀谢金吾，明代讲史小说，万历四十六年 (1618) 刊本。
首都图书馆编《古本小说版画图录》上函第七册，线装书局，北京，1996，图版 468。

Bei Song Zhi Zhuan (Stories of the Northern Song), Ming dynasty historical novel, Wanli (1618) edition. See Capital Library (ed.), *Guben Xiaoshuo Banhua Tulu* (Woodblock Illustrations from Ancient Books), Xianzhuang Shuju, Beijing, 1996, case1, vol. 7, plate 468.

p. 64

《李素兰风月玉壶春》，元代杂剧类书籍，明刊插图。
陈崎编《元明清戏曲故事集》，上海辞书出版社，2003，页 28。

Lisulan Fengyue Yuhuchun (The Romance of Yuhu), Yuan dynasty drama, Ming dynasty illustration. See Chen Qi (ed.), *Yuan Ming Qing Xiqu Gushiji* (Selected Dramas from the Yuan, Ming and Qing Dynasties), Shanghai Cishu Chubanshe, 2003, p.28.

p. 86

《占花魁》种缘，清代剧本，改编自晚明小说《醒世恒言》中《卖油郎独占花魁》，明 崇祯 (1628–1644) 原刻本。傅惜华《中国古典文学版画选集》下册，上海人民美术出版社，1981，页 827。

Zhan Huakui (Tale of the Popular Courtesan), Qing dynasty drama, adapted from the late Ming dynasty novel *Xingshi Hengyan* (Lasting Words to awaken the World), Chongzhen (1628–1644) original edition. See Fu Xihua, *Zhongguo Gudian Wenxue Banhua Xuanji* (Selected Woodblock Illustrations of Classic Chinese Literature), Shanghai Renmin Meishu Chubanshe, 1981, vol. 2, p. 827.

p. 112

《金钿盒》插图，明代戏曲，明刊本。
朱家溍《明清室内陈设》，紫禁城出版社，北京，2004，页 32。

Jindian He (Inlaid Gold Box), Ming dynasty opera, Ming period. See Zhu Jiajin, *Mingqing Shinei Chenshe* (Interior Decoration in the Ming and Qing Dynasties), Forbidden City Publishing House, Beijing, 2004, p. 32.

p. 112

明 午荣编《鲁班经匠家镜》卷二，页二十七。
鲁克思《中华帝国晚期的木作和建筑：十五世纪工匠指南〈鲁班经〉研究报告》，荷兰 莱顿，1993，图版 II 61.

Lu Ban Jing Jiang Jia Jing (The Classic of Lu Ban and the Craftsmen's Mirror), Wu Rong (Ming period) (ed.), chapter 2, page 27. See Klaas Ruitenbeek, *Carpentry and Building in Late Imperial China: A Study of the Fifteenth-Century Carpenter's Manual Lu Ban Jing,* Leiden, 1993, plate II 61.

p. 134

《画中人》，明代传奇类书籍，崇祯 (1628–1644) 刻本。
傅惜华《中国古典文学版画选集》下册，上海人民美术出版社，1981，页 699。

Huazhong Ren (Beauty from the Hanging Scroll), Ming dynasty novel, Chongzhen period (1628–1644). See Fu Xihua, *Zhongguo Gudian Wenxue Banhua Xuanji* (Selected Woodblock Illustrations of Classic Chinese Literature), Shanghai Renmin Meishu Chubanshe, 1981, vol. 2, p. 699.

p. 134

《牡丹亭还魂记》插图，明代传奇类书籍，万历二十六年 (1598) 刻本。
George N. Kates, *Chinese Household Furniture*, New York and London, 1948, reprinted by Dover Publications, New York, 1962. 乔治‧凯茨《中国家居家具》，纽约、伦敦，1948，多佛尔出版重印，纽约，1962，页 47

Mudanting Huanhun Ji (The Peony Pavilion: Return to the Living), Ming dynasty novel, Wanli (1598) edition. See George N. Kates, *Chinese Household Furniture*, New York and London, 1948, reprinted by Dover Publications, New York, 1962, p. 47.

p. 134

《鼓掌绝尘》传幽谜半幅花笺纸，明代短篇小说，崇祯 (1628–1644) 刻本。
首都图书馆编《古本小说版画图录》下函第十一册，线装书局，北京，1996，图版 785。

Guzhang Juechen (Fantastic tales of Society), Ming dynasty short story, Chongzhen period (1628–1644). See Capital Library (ed.), *Guben Xiaoshuo Banhua Tulu* (Woodblock Illustrations from Ancient Books), Xianzhuang Shuju, Beijing, 1996, case 2, vol. 11, plate 785.

p. 138
p. 470

《西厢记》妆台窥简，元代杂剧类书籍，明 万历 (1573–1620) 刻本。
傅惜华《中国古典文学版画选集》上册，上海人民美术出版社，1981，页 472。

Xi Xiang Ji (The West Chamber), Yuan dynasty drama, Ming Wanli edition (1573–1620). See Fu Xihua, *Zhongguo Gudian Wenxue Banhua Xuanji* (Selected Woodblock Illustrations of Classic Chinese Literature), Shanghai Renmin Meishu Chubanshe, 1981, vol. 1, p. 472.

p. 138

《水浒传》插图，元末明初历史小说，明 崇祯 (1628–1644) 刻本。
首都图书馆编《古本小说版画图录》下函第十册，线装书局，北京，1996，图版 712。

Shuihu Zhuan (Outlaws of the Marsh), historical novel of the late Yuan to early Ming, Chongzhen period (1628–1644). See Capital Library (ed.), *Guben Xiaoshuo Banhua Tulu* (Woodblock Illustrations from Ancient Books), Xianzhuang Shuju, Beijing, 1996, case 2, vol. 10, plate 712.

p. 142

明 王圻、王思义编《三才图会》器用十二卷十五，明代绘图类书，万历三十七年 (1609) 前后刻本。影印本，中卷，上海古籍出版社，上海，1985，页 1330。

Wang Qi & Wang Siyi (Ming period) (ed.), *Sancai Tuhui* (Pictorial Encyclopedia of Heaven, Earth and Man), Qiyong (Utensils for Daily Life) vol. 12:18, Wanli (1609) (approx.) edition. Photocopy edition, Shanghai Guji Chubanshe, 1985, vol. 2, p. 1330.

p. 148

《新镌绣像小说清夜钟》黩父不为强生 淫儿终从横死，明代小说，南明隆武 (1645–1646) 刊本。首都图书馆编《古本小说版画图录》下函第十一册，线装书局，北京，1996，图版 743。

Xinjuan Xiuxiang Xiaoshuo Qing Ye Zhong (Alarm Bell on a Still Night), Ming dynasty novel, Southern Ming Longwu period (1645–1646). See Capital Library (ed.), *Guben Xiaoshuo Banhua Tulu* (Woodblock Illustrations from Ancient Books), Xianzhuang Shuju, Beijing, 1996, case 2, vol. 11, plate 743.

p. 148

《西湖二集》插图，明代话本，万历 (1573–1620) 刻本。
柯惕思《两依藏 黄花梨》香港，2007，页 140。

Xihu Erji (Two Collections of Stories of the West Lake), Ming dynasty drama, Wanli (1573–1620) edition. See Curtis Evarts, *Liang Yi Collection Huanghuali*, Hong Kong, 2007, p. 140.

p. 154

《赵盼儿风月救风尘》插图，元代杂剧类书籍，明刊插图。
陈崎编《元明清戏曲故事集》，上海辞书出版社，2003，页 10。

Zhao Paner Fengyue Jiu Fengchen (Rescue of Prostitute by Zhao Paner), Yuan dynasty drama, Ming dynasty illustration. See Chen Qi (ed.), *Yuan Ming Qing Xiqu Gushiji* (Selected Drama Stories from the Yuan, Ming and Qing Dynasties), Shanghai Cishu Chubanshe, 2003, p.10.

p. 158

《养正图解》插图，周至宋代传说典故解说，明 万历 (1573–1620) 刻本。
王正书《明清家具鉴定》，上海书店出版社，2007，页 210。

Yangzheng Tujie (Illustrated book of Educational Legends), Ming Wanli (1573–1620) edition. See Wang Zhengshu, *Mingqing Jiaju Jianding* (Identification of Ming and Qing Dynasty Furniture), Shanghai Shudian Chubanshe, 2007, p. 210.

p. 246

清 梁延年编《圣谕像解》感激力学，卷十五，清 康熙"上谕十六箴" 圣谕注释并配图，康熙二十年 (1681) 刻本，纽约市公共图书馆斯潘塞图书室藏影印本。

Liang Yannian (Qing period) (ed.), *Shengyu Xiangjie* (Imperial Edicts, Annotated and Illustrated), chapter 15, Kangxi period (1681), photocopy edition, Spencer Collection, New York Public Library.

p. 287

明 午荣编《鲁班经匠家镜》卷二，页三十。
鲁克思《中华帝国晚期的木作和建筑：十五世纪工匠指南〈鲁班经〉研究报告》，荷兰 莱顿，1993，图版 II 65。

Lu Ban Jing Jiang Jia Jing (The Classic of Lu Ban and the Craftsmen's Mirror), Wu Rong (Ming period) (ed.), chapter 2, page 30. See Klaas Ruitenbeek, *Carpentry and Building in Late Imperial China: A Study of the Fifteenth-Century Carpenter's Manual Lu Ban Jing,* Leiden, 1993, plate II 65.

p. 289

明 金忠编《御世仁风》富民非巳，卷一，页五，万历四十八年 (1620) 刻本，美国哈佛大学哈佛燕京图书馆藏影印本。

Jin Zhong (Ming period) (ed.), *Yushi Renfeng* (Tales of Benevolent Emperors) chapter 1, page 5, Wanli (1620) period, photocopy edition, Harvard–Yenching Library, Harvard University.

p. 290

汉 刘向撰，明 仇英绘画，明 汪道昆增辑《仇画列女传》周郊妇人，妇女传记，明 万历 (1573–1620) 刊本，中国书店，北京，1991，第二册，卷三，页二十一。

Qiuhua Lienu Zhuan (Biography of Women in Ancient China illustrated by Qiu Ying), Liu Xiang (Han period), illustrated by Qiu Ying (Ming period), supplemented by Wang Daokun (Ming period), Wanli (1573-1620) edition, Zhongguo Shudian, Beijing, 1991, vol. 2, chapter 3, p. 21.

p. 314

明 午荣编《鲁班经匠家镜》卷二，页二十三。
鲁克思《中华帝国晚期的木作和建筑：十五世纪工匠指南〈鲁班经〉研究报告》，荷兰 莱顿，1993，图版 II 51。

Lu Ban Jing Jiang Jia Jing (The Classic of Lu Ban and the Craftsmen's Mirror), Wu Rong (Ming period) (ed.), chapter 2, page 23. See Klaas Ruitenbeek, *Carpentry and Building in Late Imperial China: A Study of the Fifteenth-Century Carpenter's Manual Lu Ban Jing,* Leiden, 1993, plate II 51.

p. 314

《忠义水浒传》吴用智赚玉麒麟，元末明初历史小说，明 万历 (1573–1620) 刻本。郑振铎编《中国古代版画丛刊》卷二，上海古籍出版社，1988，页 836。

Zhongyi Shuihu Zhuan (Outlaws of the Marsh), historical novel of the late Yuan to early Ming, Wanli (1573–1620) edition. See Zheng Zhenduo (ed.), *Zhongguo Gudai Banhua Congkan* (Ancient Chinese Woodcuts), Shanghai Guji Chubanshe, 1988, vol. 2, p. 836.

p. 320
p. 372

《金瓶梅词话》真夫妇明偕花烛，明代长篇小说，影印本，文字用万历 (1573–1620) 刊本，插图用崇祯 (1628–1644) 刻本，文学古籍刊行社，册一，第九十七回。

Jin Ping Mei Cihua (The Golden Lotus), Ming dynasty novel, photocopy edition, text after Wanli (1573–1620) edition, illustrations after Chongzhen (1628–1644) edition, Wenxue Guji Kanxingshe, vol. 1, chapter 97.

p. 320
p. 418

明 午荣编《鲁班经匠家镜》卷二，页三十二。
鲁克思《中华帝国晚期的木作和建筑：十五世纪工匠指南〈鲁班经〉研究报告》，荷兰 莱顿，1993，图版 II 70, 71。

Lu Ban Jing Jiang Jia Jing (The Classic of Lu Ban and the Craftsmen's Mirror), Wu Rong (Ming period) (ed.), chapter 2, page 32. See Klaas Ruitenbeek, *Carpentry and Building in Late Imperial China: A Study of the Fifteenth-Century Carpenter's Manual Lu Ban Jing,* Leiden, 1993, plate 70, 71.

p. 323

《金瓶梅词话》杨姑娘气骂张四舅，明代长篇小说，影印本，文字用万历 (1573–1620) 刊本，插图用崇祯 (1628–1644) 刻本，文学古籍刊行社，册一，第七回。

Jin Ping Mei Cihua (The Golden Lotus), Ming dynasty novel, photocopy edition, text after Wanli (1573–1620) edition, illustrations after Chongzhen (1628–1644) edition, Wenxue Guji Kanxingshe, vol. 1, chapter 7.

p. 323

汉 刘向撰，明 仇英绘画，明 汪道昆增辑《仇画列女传》鲍宣妻，妇女传记，明 万历 (1573–1620) 刊本，中国书店，北京，1991，第三册，卷六，页二。

Qiuhua Lienu Zhuan (Biography of Women in Ancient China Illustrated by Qiu Ying), Liu Xiang (Han period), illustrated by Qiu Ying (Ming period), supplemented by Wang Daokun (Ming period), Wanli (1573–1620) edition, Zhongguo Shudian, Beijing, 1991, vol. 3, chapter 6, p. 2.

p. 323

汉 刘向撰，明 仇英绘画，明 汪道昆增辑《仇画列女传》侯氏才美，妇女传记，明 万历 (1573–1620) 刊本，中国书店，北京，1991，第四册，卷八，页二十三。

Qiuhua Lienu Zhuan (Biography of Women in Ancient China Illustrated by Qiu Ying), Liu Xiang (Han period), illustrated by Qiu Ying (Ming period), supplemented by Wang Daokun (Ming period), Wanli (1573–1620) edition, Zhongguo Shudian, Beijing, 1991, vol. 4, chapter 8, p. 23.

p. 338

汉 刘向撰，明 仇英绘画，明 汪道昆增辑《仇画列女传》沙溪鲍氏，妇女传记，明 万历 (1573–1620) 刊本，中国书店，北京，1991，第八册，卷十六，页五。

Qiuhua Lienu Zhuan (Biography of Women in Ancient China Illustrated by Qiu Ying), Liu Xiang (Han period), illustrated by Qiu Ying (Ming period), supplemented by Wang Daokun (Ming period), Wanli (1573–1620) edition, Zhongguo Shudian, Beijing, 1991, vol. 8, chapter 16, p. 5.

p. 408

《二刻拍案惊奇》吴宣教干偿白镪，话本小说，明 崇祯 (1628–1644) 刊本。
郑振铎《中国版画史图录》卷十五，中国版画史社，上海，1940–1942。

Erke Paian Jingqi (Amazing Tales–Second Series), Ming dynasty novel, Chongzhen period (1628–1644). See Zheng Zhenduo, *Zhongguo Banhua Shi Tulu* (An Illustrated History of Chinese Woodblock Prints), Zhongguo banhua Shishe, Shanghai, 1940-1942, vol. 15.

p. 412

《苏门啸》，明代杂剧，崇祯壬午十五年 (1642) 刻本。
周芜、周路、周亮编《日本藏中国古版画珍品》，江苏美术出版社，1999，页 423。

Sumen Xiao (Howling at Sumen Mountain), Ming dynasty drama, Chongzhen period (1642). See Zhou Wu, Zhou Lu, Zhou Liang (eds.), *Riben Cang Zhongguo Gu Banhua Zhenpin* (Japanese Collection of Ancient Chinese Woodcuts), Jiangsu Meishu Chubanshe, 1999, p. 423.

p. 412

《仙媛纪事》，明代仙道故事，万历 (1573–1620) 刻本。
陈同滨等主编《中国古典建筑室内装饰图集》，今日中国出版社，北京，1995，页 930。

Xianyuan Jishi (Chronicles of Immortal Beauties), Ming dynasty stories of celestial beings, Wanli (1573–1620) edition. See Chen Tongbin et al (eds.), *Zhongguo Gudian Jianzhu Shinei Zhuangshi Tuji* (Collection of pictures on Classic Chinese Architecture and Interior Decoration), Jinri Zhongguo Chubanshe, Beijing, 1995, p. 930.

p. 412

《醒世恒言》卷十五，明代小说，天启丁卯七年 (1627) 刊本。
周芜、周路、周亮编《日本藏中国古版画珍品》，江苏美术出版社，1999，页 510。

Xingshi Hengyan (Lasting Words to awaken the World), Ming dynasty novel, Tianqi period (1627). See Zhou Wu, Zhou Lu, Zhou Liang (eds.), *Riben Cang Zhongguo Gu Banhua Zhenpin* (Japanese Collection of Ancient Chinese Woodcuts), Jiangsu Meishu Chubanshe, 1999, p. 510.

p. 424

《征播奏捷传》礼集一卷 杨应龙偕鸾凤佳配，明代讲史小说类书籍，万历癸卯三十一年 (1603) 重刊本。周芜、周路、周亮编《日本藏中国古版画珍品》，江苏美术出版社，1999，页 226-227。

Zhengbo Zoujie Zhuan (Putting Down the Rebellion at Bozhou), Ming dynasty historical novel, Wanli period (1603). See Zhou Wu, Zhou Lu, Zhou Liang (eds.), *Riben Cang Zhongguo Gu Banhua Zhenpin* (Japanese Collection of Ancient Chinese Woodcuts), Jiangsu Meishu Chubanshe, 1999, pp. 226–227.

p. 424

《灵宝刀》青楼乞赦，明代传奇类书籍，万历三十六年 (1557) 刻本。
傅惜华《中国古典文学版画选集》上册，上海人民美术出版社，1981，页 414。

Ling Bao Dao (The renown knife Lingbao), Ming dynasty novel, Wanli period (1557). See Fu Xihua, *Zhongguo Gudian Wenxue Banhua Xuanji* (Selected Woodblock Illustrations of Classic Chinese Literature), Shanghai Renmin Meishu Chubanshe, 1981, vol. 1, p. 414.

p. 427

《南宋志传》插图，历史小说，明 万历（约 1618）刻本。
郑振铎编《中国古代木刻画选集》，人民美术出版社，北京，1985，第四册。

Nansong Zhizhuan (Historical Tales of the Southern Song), Wanli period (circa 1618) edition. See Zheng Zhenduo (ed.), *Zhongguo Gudai Mukehua Xuanji* (Selected Chinese Ancient Woodcuts), Remin Meishu Chubanshe, Beijing, 1985, vol. 4.

p. 438
p. 455

《西湖二集》三星照洞房 暮然间、得效鸾凤，明代话本，崇祯 (1628–1644) 刻本。
首都图书馆编《古本小说版画图录》下函第十册，线装书局，北京，1996，图版 696。

Xihu Erji (Two Collections of Stories of the West Lake), Ming dynasty drama, Chongzhen (1628–1644) edition. See Capital Library (ed.), *Guben Xiaoshuo Banhua Tulu* (Woodblock Illustrations from Ancient Books), Xianzhuang Shuju, Beijing, 1996, case2, vol. 10, plate 696.

p. 438
《郁轮袍》求配，明代传奇类书籍，崇祯 (1628—1644) 刻本。
傅惜华《中国古典文学版画选集》上册，上海人民美术出版社，1981，页 800。

Yulun Pao (The Tale of a Pipa Song), Ming dynasty novel, Chongzhen (1628–1644) edition. See Fu Xihua, *Zhongguo Gudian Wenxue Banhua Xuanji* (Selected Woodblock Illustrations of Classic Chinese Literature), Shanghai Renmin Meishu Chubanshe, 1981, vol. 1, p. 800.

p. 438
《画中人》插图，明代传奇类书籍，景明刊插图。
陈崎编《元明清戏曲故事集》册三，上海辞书出版社，2003，页 304。

Huazhongren (Beauty from the Hanging Scroll), Ming dynasty novel, illustrations after Ming edition. See Chen Qi (ed.), *Yuan Ming Qing Xiqu Gushiji* (Selected Dramas from the Yuan, Ming and Qing Dynasties), Shanghai Cishu Chubanshe, 2003, vol. 3, p. 304.

p. 450
《新刊出像补订参采史鉴唐书志传通俗演义题评》诸将佐具陈智略，明代讲史小说，万历二十一年 (1593) 刊本。首都图书馆编《古本小说版画图录》上函第五册，线装书局，北京，1996，图版 254。

Tangshu Zhizhuan (Romance of the Tang dynasty), Ming dynasty historical novel, Wanli (1593) edition. See Capital Library (ed.), *Guben Xiaoshuo Banhua Tulu* (Woodblock Illustrations from Ancient Books), Xianzhuang Shuju, Beijing, 1996, case 1, vol. 5, plate 254.

p. 452
明 王圻、王思义编《三才图会》器用十二卷十九，明代绘图类书，万历三十七年 (1609) 前后刻本。影印本，中卷，上海古籍出版社，上海，1985，页 1332。

Wang Qi & Wang Siyi (Ming period) (ed.), *Sancai Tuhui* (Pictorial Encyclopedia of Heaven, Earth and Man), Qiyong (Utensils for Daily Life) vol. 12:19, Wanli (1609) (approx.) edition. Photocopy edition, Shanghai Guji Chubanshe, 1985, vol. 2, p. 1332.

p. 455
《诗赋盟》饯别，明代戏曲类书籍，崇祯 (1628–1644) 刻本。
傅惜华《中国古典文学版画选集》下册，上海人民美术出版社，1981，页 807。

Shifu Meng (Alliance sworn with Poetry), Ming dynasty opera, Chongzhen (1628–1644) edition. See Fu Xihua, *Zhongguo Gudian Wenxue Banhua Xuanji* (Selected Woodblock Illustrations of Classic Chinese Literature), *Shanghai Renmin Meishu Chubanshe,* 1981, vol. 2, p. 807.

p. 455

《望湖亭》插图,明代传奇类书籍,景明刊插图。
陈崎编《元明清戏曲故事集》,上海辞书出版社,2003,页256。

Wanghu Ting (Lake View Pagoda), Ming dynasty novel, illustrations after Ming edition. See Chen Qi (ed.), *Yuan Ming Qing Xiqu Gushiji* (Selected Dramas from the Yuan, Ming and Qing Dynasties), Shanghai Cishu Chubanshe, 2003, p. 256.

p. 461

《琵琶记》对镜梳妆,元代南戏类书籍,明 万历 (1573–1620) 刻本。
傅惜华《中国古典文学版画选集》上册,上海人民美术出版社,1981,页128。

Pipa Ji (Story of the Lute), Yuan dynasty opera, Ming Wanli (1573–1620) edition. See Fu Xihua, *Zhongguo Gudian Wenxue Banhua Xuanji* (Selected Woodblock Illustrations of Classic Chinese Literature), Shanghai Renmin Meishu Chubanshe, 1981, vol. 1, p. 128.

p. 461

《双鱼记》观鱼,明代传奇类书籍,万历 (1573–1620) 刻本。
傅惜华《中国古典文学版画选集》上册,上海人民美术出版社,1981,页210。

Shuang Yu Ji (A Pair of Fishes), Ming dynasty novel, Wanli (1573–1620) edition. See Fu Xihua, *Zhongguo Gudian Wenxue Banhua Xuanji* (Selected Woodblock Illustrations of Classic Chinese Literature), Shanghai Renmin Meishu Chubanshe, 1981, vol. 1, p. 210.

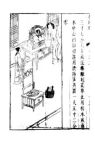

p. 461

明 午荣编《鲁班经匠家镜》卷二,页十九。
鲁克思《中华帝国晚期的木作和建筑:十五世纪工匠指南〈鲁班经〉研究报告》,荷兰 莱顿,1993,图版 II 41。

Lu Ban Jing Jiang Jia Jing (The Classic of Lu Ban and the Craftsmen's Mirror), Wu Rong (Ming period) (ed.), chapter 2, page 19. See Klaas Ruitenbeek, *Carpentry and Building in Late Imperial China: A Study of the Fifteenth-Century Carpenter's Manual Lu Ban Jing*, Leiden, 1993, plate II 41.

p. 470

《西厢记》玉台窥简,元代杂剧类书籍,明 万历 (1573–1620) 刻本。
傅惜华《中国古典文学版画选集》上册,上海人民美术出版社,1981,页107。

Xi Xiang Ji (The West Chamber), Yuan dynasty drama, Ming Wanli (1573–1620) edition. See Fu Xihua, *Zhongguo Gudian Wenxue Banhua Xuanji* (Selected Woodblock Illustrations of Classic Chinese Literature), Shanghai Renmin Meishu Chubanshe, 1981, vol. 1, p. 107.

p. 479
《杜蕊娘智赏金线池》元代杂剧类书籍，明刊插图。
陈崎编《元明清戏曲故事集》，上海辞书出版社，上海，2003，页 9。

Du Rui Niang Zhi Shang Jin Xian Chi, Yuan dynasty drama, Ming dynasty edition. See Chen Qi (ed.), *Yuan Ming Qing Xiqu Gushiji* (Selected Drama Stories from the Yuan, Ming and Qing Dynasty), Shanghai Cishu Chubanshe, 2003, p. 9.

p. 479
《金瓶梅词话》见娇娘敬济销魂，明代长篇小说，影印本，文字用万历 (1573–1620) 刊本，插图用崇祯 (1628–1644) 刻本，文学古籍刊行社，册一，第十八回。

Jin Ping Mei Cihua (The Golden Lotus), Ming dynasty novel, photocopy edition, text after Wanli (1573–1620) edition, illustrations after Chongzhen (1628–1644) edition, Wenxue Guji Kanxingshe, vol. 1, chapter 18.

p.479
《二刻拍案惊奇》撷草药巧谐真偶，话本小说，明 崇祯 (1628–1644) 刊本。
首都图书馆编《古本小说版画图录》下函第十一册，线装书局，北京，1996，图版 780。

Erke Paian Jingqi (Amazing Tales–Second Series), Ming dynasty novel, Chongzhen period (1628–1644). See Capital Library (ed.), *Guben Xiaoshuo Banhua Tulu* (Woodblock Illustrations from Ancient Books), Xianzhuang Shuju. Beijing, 1996, case 2, vol. 11, plate 780.

p. 482
p. 501
《忠义水浒传》梁山泊分金大买市，元末明初历史小说，明 万历 (1573–1620) 刻本。
郑振铎编《中国古代版画丛刊》卷二，上海古籍出版社，1988，页 864。

Zhongyi Shuihu Zhuan (Outlaws of the Marsh), historical novel of the late Yuan to early Ming, Wanli (1573–1620) edition. See Zheng Zhenduo (ed.), *Zhongguo Gudai Banhua Congkan* (Ancient Chinese Woodcuts), Shanghai Guji Chubanshe, 1988, vol. 2, p. 864.

p.482
《清夜钟》郡贤力扶弱主 良宦术制强奴，明代短篇小说集类书籍，崇祯 (1628–1644) 刻本。傅惜华《中国古典文学版画选集》下册，上海人民美术出版社，1981，页 795。

Qing Ye Zhong (Alarm Bell on a Still Night), Ming dynasty short stories, Chongzhen (1628–1644) edition. See Fu Xihua, *Zhongguo Gudian Wenxue Banhua Xuanji* (Selected Woodblock Illustrations of Classic Chinese Literature), Shanghai Renmin Meishu Chubanshe, 1981, vol. 2, p. 795.

p. 482
汉 刘向撰，明 仇英绘画，明 汪道昆增辑《仇画列女传》章穆郭后，妇女传记，明 万历 (1573–1620) 刊本，中国书店，北京，1991，第五册，卷十，页四。

Qiuhua Lienu Zhuan (Biography of Women in Ancient China illustrated by Qiu Ying), Liu Xiang (Han period), illustrated by Qiu Ying (Ming period), supplemented by Wang Daokun (Ming period), Wanli (1573–1620) edition, Zhongguo Shudian, Beijing, 1991, vol. 5, chapter 10, p. 4.

p. 501
明 王圻、王思义编《三才图会》器用十二卷十九，明代绘图类书，万历三十七年 (1609) 前后刻本。影印本，中卷，上海古籍出版社，上海，1985，页 1332。

Wang Qi & Wang Siyi (Ming period) (ed.), *Sancai Tuhui* (Pictorial Encyclopedia of Heaven, Earth and Man), Qiyong (Utensils for Daily Life) vol. 12:19, Wanli (1609) (approx.) edition. Photocopy edition, Shanghai Guji Chubanshe, 1985, vol. 2, p. 1332.

p. 501
《二刻拍案惊奇》神偷寄兴一枝梅，话本小说，明 崇祯 (1628–1644) 刊本。首都图书馆编《古本小说版画图录》下函第十一册，线装书局，北京，1996，图版 782。

Erke Paian Jingqi (Amazing Tales – Second Series), Ming dynasty novel, Chongzhen period (1628–1644). See Capital Library (ed.), *Guben Xiaoshuo Banhua Tulu* (Woodblock Illustrations from Ancient Books), Xianzhuang Shuju, Beijing, 1996, case 2, vol. 11, plate 782.

p. 504
《金瓶梅词话》薛媒婆说娶孟三儿，明代长篇小说，影印本，文字用万历 (1573–1620) 刊本，插图用崇祯 (1628–1644) 刻本，文学古籍刊行社，册一，第七回。

Jin Ping Mei Cihua (The Golden Lotus), Ming dynasty novel, photocopy edition, text after Wanli (1573-1620) edition, illustrations after Chongzhen (1628–1644) edition, Wenxue Guji Kanxingshe, vol. 1, chapter 7.

p. 504
《金瓶梅词话》草里蛇逻打蒋竹山，明代长篇小说，影印本，文字用万历 (1573–1620) 刊本，插图用崇祯 (1628–1644) 刻本，文学古籍刊行社，册一，第十九回。

Jin Ping Mei Cihua (The Golden Lotus), Ming dynasty novel, photocopy edition, text after Wanli (1573–1620) edition, illustrations after Chongzhen (1628–1644) edition, Wenxue Guji Kanxingshe, vol. 1, chapter 19.

引用文献 BOOKS CITED

中文书目
Chinese publications

中国国家博物馆编《简约·华美：明清家具精粹》中国社会科学出版社，北京，2007
National Museum of China (Ed.), *Jianyue · Huamei: Mingqing Jiaju Jingcui* (Simplicity·Opulence: Masterpieces of Ming & Qing Dynasty Furniture), Zhongguo Shehui Kexue Chubanshe, Beijing, 2007

中国嘉德《逸居—文案清供》北京，2015年11月14日
China Guardian, *House of Leisure — Scholar's Studio Objects*, Beijing, 14 November, 2015

中国嘉德《观华—明清古典家具及庭院陈设精品》香港，2012年10月7日
China Guardian Hong Kong, *Classic Furniture and Garden Ornament of Ming and Qing Dynasties*, Hong Kong, 7 October 2012

王世襄《明式家具珍赏》三联书店（香港）有限公司／文物出版社（北京）联合出版，香港，1985
Wang Shixiang, *Mingshi Jiaju Zhenshang* (Appreciation of Ming Furniture), co-published by Joint Publishing Co. (HK) / Cultural Relics Publishing House (Beijing), Hong Kong, 1985

王世襄《明式家具研究》图版卷，三联书店（香港）有限公司，香港，1989
Wang Shixiang, *Mingshi Jiaju Yanjiu* (Ming Furniture Research), Plates volume, Joint Publishing (HK) Ltd, Hong Kong, January, 1989

王世襄《明式家具研究》生活·读书·新知三联书店，北京，2007
Wang Shixiang, *Mingshi Jiaju Yanjiu* (Ming Furniture Research), SDX Joint Publishing Company, Beijing, 2007

王世襄《明式家具研究》生活·读书·新知三联书店，北京，2008
Wang Shixiang, *Mingshi Jiaju Yanjiu* (Ming Furniture Research), SDX Joint Publishing Company, Beijing, 2008

王世襄 袁荃猷《明式家具萃珍》美国中华艺文基金会 Tenth Union International Inc，芝加哥·旧金山，1997
Wang Shixiang and Yuan Quanyou, *Mingshi Jiaju Cuizhen* (Fine Examples of Ming Furniture), Tenth Union International Inc, Chicago and San Francisco, 1997

朱家溍《故宫博物院藏文物珍品全集 明清家具》上卷，商务印书馆（香港）有限公司，香港，2002
Zhu Jiajin, *The Complete Collection of Treasures of the Palace Museum, Furniture of the Ming and Qing Dynasties*, vol. 1, The Commercial Press (H.K.) Ltd., Hong Kong, 2002

伍嘉恩《中国古典紫檀家具—几件明及清初实例及其纵横探讨》，《中国古典家具研究会会刊》十二，1992年11月，北京
Grace Wu Bruce, *Zhongguo Gudian Zitan Jiaju - Jijian Ming Ji Qing Chu Shili jiqi Zongheng Tantao* (Chinese Classic furniture in *Zitan* - Some Ming and Early Qing Examples and Their Exploration), *Zhongguo Gudian Jiaju Yanjiuhui Huikan* (Journal of the Association of Chinese Classical Furniture), No. 12, November 1992, Beijing

伍嘉恩《明式家具二十年经眼录》紫禁城出版社，北京，2010
Grace Wu Bruce, *Two Decades of Ming Furniture*, The Forbidden City Publishing House, Beijing, 2010

伍嘉恩《明式家具二十年经眼录之四 桌类》，《紫禁城》第166期，2008年11月，紫禁城出版社，北京
Grace Wu Bruce, Two Decades of Ming Furniture Part IV: *Zhuo* tables, *Forbidden City*, issue 166, November 2008, The Forbidden City Publishing House, Beijing

伍嘉恩《明式家具经眼录》故宫出版社，北京，2015
Grace Wu Bruce, *Ming Furniture Through My Eyes*, The Forbidden City Publishing House, Beijing, 2015

伍嘉恩《从几件实例探讨中国古典紫檀家具》，《文物天地》第 213 期，中国文物报社，北京，2009 年 3 月
Grace Wu Bruce, *Cong Jijian Shili Tantao Zhongguo Gudian Zitan Jiaju* (Some Examples of Chinese Classic Furniture in *Zitan* Wood and Their Study), *Cultural Relics World*, issue 213, Zhongguo Wenwu Baoshe, Beijing, March 2009

吕章申主编《中国国家博物馆古代艺术系列丛书：大美木艺—中国明清家具珍品》北京时代华文书局，北京，2014
Lu Zhangshen (Eds.), *Zhongguo Guojia Bowuguan Gudaiyishu Xilie Congshu: Damei Muyi – Zhongguo Mingqing Jiaju Zhenpin* (Ancient Art Series of the National Museum of China: Wood Art – Fine Chinese Ming & Qing Dynasty Furniture), Beijing Shidai Huawen Shuju, Beijing, 2014

陈增弼《明式家具的功能与造型》，《文物》1981 年 3 月，文物出版社，北京
Chen Zengbi, *Mingshi Jiaju de Gongneng yu Zaoxing* (Functions and Styles of Ming Furniture), *Wenwu* (Cultural Relics), March 1981, Wenwu Chubanshe, Beijing

清 钱泳《履园丛话》清代史料笔记丛刊，中华书局，北京，1979
Qian Yong (1759-1844), *Lu Yuan Cong Hua*, *Qingdai Shiliao Biji Congkan* (Collected Discourses of the Lu Yuan), Zhonghua Shuiju, Beijing, 1979

双语书目
Bilingual publications

佳士得《奉文堂藏竹雕及家具》香港，2015 年 6 月 3 日
Christie's, *The Feng Wen Tang Collection of Bamboo Carvings and Furniture*, Hong Kong, 3 June 2015

香港艺术馆《好古敏求 敏求精舍三十五周年纪念展》香港，1995
The Hong Kong Museum of Art, *In Pursuit of Antiquities: Thirty-fifth Anniversary Exhibition of the Min Chiu Society,* Hong Kong, 1995

历史博物馆《风华再现：明清家具收藏展》台北，1999
Museum of History, *Splendor of Style: Classical Furniture from the Ming and Qing Dynasties*, Taipei, 1999

国家文物局《亚洲文明博物馆之中国文物收藏》新加坡，1997
National Heritage Board, *Asian Civilisations Museum: The Chinese Collection*, Singapore, 1997

嘉木堂《中国家具·文房清供》香港，2003
Grace Wu Bruce, *Chinese Furniture: Wenfang Works of Art*, Hong Kong, 2003

英文书目
English publications

Christie's, *Fine Chinese Furniture, Ceramics and Works of Art*, New York, 20 September 2001
佳士得《中国家具、陶瓷与工艺精品》纽约，2001 年 9 月 20 日

Christie's, *Fine Chinese Ceramics and Works of Art Part I*, New York, 24 March 2011
佳士得《中国陶瓷与工艺精品》纽约，2011 年 3 月 24 日

Christie's, *Fine Chinese Ceramics and Works of Art*, New York, 16 September 2016
佳士得《中国陶瓷与工艺精品》纽约，2016 年 9 月 16 日

Christie's, *Important Chinese Furniture, Formerly The Museum of Classical Chinese Furniture Collection*, New York, 19 September 1996
佳士得《中国古典家具博物馆藏珍品》纽约，1996 年 9 月 19 日

Christie's, *The Dr S Y Yip Collection of Fine and Important Classical Chinese Furniture,* New York, 20 September 2002
佳士得《攻玉山房藏中国古典家具精萃》纽约，2002 年 9 月 20 日

Christie's, *The Gangolf Geis Collection of Fine Classical Chinese Furniture,* New York, 18 September 2003
佳士得《Gangolf Geis 收藏之中国古典家具珍品图册》纽约，2003 年 9 月 18 日

Christie's, *The Mr & Mrs Robert P. Piccus Collection Fine Classical Chinese Furniture,* New York, 18 September 1997
佳士得《毕格史伉俪藏中国古代家具精品》纽约，1997 年 9 月 18 日

Clunas, Craig, *Chinese Furniture, Victoria and Albert Museum Far Eastern Series*, London, 1988
柯律格《英国国立维多利亚与艾尔伯特博物馆·东亚系列·中国家具》伦敦，1988

Ecke, Gustav, *Chinese Domestic Furniture,* Peking, 1944. Reprinted by Charles E. Tuttle, Rutland, Vermont and Tokyo, 1962
古斯塔夫·艾克《中国花梨家具图考》北京，1944。查尔斯·E. 塔特尔重印本，拉特兰．佛蒙特．东京，1962

Ellsworth, Robert Hatfield, *Chinese Furniture: Hardwood Examples of the Ming and Early Ching Dynasties*, Random House, New York, 1971
安思远《中国家具：明至清前期硬木例子》纽约，1971

Evarts, Curtis, "Classical Chinese Furniture in the Piccus Collection", *Journal of the Classical Chinese Furniture Society*, Autumn 1992, Renaissance, California
柯惕思《毕格史收藏中国古代家具》，《中国古典家具学会季刊》1992 秋季刊，加州文艺复兴镇

Handler, Sarah, *Austere Luminosity of Chinese Classical Furniture*, Berkeley, Los Angeles and London, 2001
萨拉·汉德娜《中国古典家具的简朴光芒》伯克利，洛杉矶，伦敦，2001

Journal of the Classical Chinese Furniture Society, Winter 1990, Renaissance, California
《中国古典家具学会季刊》1990 冬季刊，加州文艺复兴镇

Markbreiter, Michael, The Grace Wu Bruce Collection of Chinese Furniture, *Arts of Asia*, November – December 1987, Hong Kong.
迈克·马克布赖特《伍嘉恩中国家具藏品》，《亚洲艺术》1987 年 11-12 月，香港

Maudsley, Catherine (ed.), *Classical and Vernacular Chinese Furniture in the Living Environment*, Hong Kong, 1998
毛岱康编《中国古典家具与生活环境》香港，1998

Musée national des Arts asiatiques – Guimet, *Ming: l'Âge d'or du mobilier chinois, The Golden Age of Chinese Furniture*, Paris, 2003
吉美国立亚洲艺术博物馆《明·中国家具的黄金时期》巴黎，2003

The Oriental Ceramic Society of Hong Kong, *Arts from the Scholar's Studio,* Hong Kong, 1986
香港东方陶瓷学会《文玩萃珍》香港，1986

Piccus, R.P. Conference and Exhibition Review, *Orientations,* February, 1995, Hong Kong
毕格史《会议展览评论》，《东方艺术杂志》1995 年 2 月，香港

Ruitenbeek, Klaas, *Carpentry and Building in Late Imperial China: A Study of the Fifteenth-Century Carpenter's Manual Lu Ban Jing,* Leiden, 1993
鲁克思《中华帝国晚期的木作和建筑：十五世纪工匠指南〈鲁班经〉研究报告》荷兰 莱顿，1993

Skinner, *European & Asian Furniture & Decorative Arts featuring Fine Ceramics*, Boston, July 17, 2004
斯金纳《欧洲与亚洲家具及装饰艺术并瓷器精品》波士顿，2004 年 7 月 17 日

Sotheby's, *Fine Chinese Ceramics and Works of Art,* New York, June 3, 1992
苏富比《中国陶瓷与工艺精品》纽约，1992 年 6 月 3 日

Sotheby's, *Fine Chinese Ceramics and Works of Art,* New York, March 20, 2002
苏富比《中国陶瓷与工艺精品》纽约，2002 年 3 月 20 日

Sotheby's, *Fine Chinese Ceramics and works of Arts,* New York, 18, March, 2014
苏富比《中国陶瓷器工艺精品》纽约，2014 年 3 月 18 日

Wang Shixiang, "Additional Examples of Classical Chinese Furniture" *Orientations*, January 1992, Hong Kong
王世襄《古典中国家具其他例子》，《东方艺术》1992 年 1 月，香港

Wang Shixiang, *Classic Chinese Furniture: Ming and Early Qing Dynasties*, Han-Shan Tang, London, 1986
王世襄《古典中国家具：明至清前期》寒山堂，伦敦，1986

Wang Shixiang, *Connoisseurship of Chinese Furniture: Ming and Early Qing Dynasties,* vol. II: Plates, Hong Kong, 1990
王世襄《中国家具鉴赏：明至清前期》卷二图版，香港，1990

Wang Shixiang and Curtis Evarts, *Masterpieces from the Museum of Classical Chinese Furniture,* Chicago and San Francisco, 1995
王世襄 柯惕思《中国古典家具博物馆馆藏精品》芝加哥·旧金山，1995

Wu Bruce, Grace, "Classic Chinese Furniture in Tzu-Tan Wood", *Arts of Asia,* November-December 1991, Hong Kong
伍嘉恩《紫檀木造古典中国家具》，《亚洲艺术》1991 年 11-12 月，香港

Wu Bruce, Grace, *Dreams of Chu Tan Chamber and the Romance with Huanghuali Wood: The Dr. S. Y. Yip Collection of Classic Chinese Furniture,* Hong Kong, 1991
伍嘉恩《攻玉山房藏明式黄花梨家具：楮檀室梦旅》香港，1991

Wu Bruce, Grace, *Living with Ming – the Lu Ming Shi Collection*, Hong Kong, 2000
伍嘉恩《侣明室家具图集》香港，2000

Grace Wu Bruce Co Ltd, *Ming Furniture*, Hong Kong, 1995
嘉木堂《中国家具精萃展》香港，1995

Wu Bruce, Grace, *Ming Furniture, Selections from Hong Kong & London Gallery*, Hong Kong, 2000
嘉木堂《明朝家具香港伦敦精选》香港，2000

Wu Bruce, Grace, *On the Kang and Between the Walls: the Ming Furniture Quietly Installed,* Hong Kong, 1998
嘉木堂《炕上壁间》香港，1998

Wu Bruce, Grace, "Sculptures To Use", *First Under Heaven: The Art of Asia*, London, 1997
伍嘉恩《实用雕塑》，《天下第一：亚洲艺术》伦敦，1997

Wu Bruce, Grace, "Small Portable Treasures, Examples of Classic Chinese Furniture: (Ⅴ)", *Oriental Art,* Autumn 1993, London
伍嘉恩《经典明朝家具之五：轻巧袖珍宝》，《东方艺术》，1993 年秋季刊，伦敦

Copyright © 2017 by SDX Joint Publishing Company.
All Rights Reserved.
本作品版权由生活・读书・新知三联书店所有。
未经许可，不得翻印。

图书在版编目（CIP）数据

木趣居：家具中的嘉具 / 伍嘉恩著 . — 北京：生活・读书・新知三联书店，2017.9 （2017.12 重印）
ISBN 978-7-108-06066-2

Ⅰ . ①木… Ⅱ . ①伍… Ⅲ . ①木家具- 收藏- 中国- 图录 Ⅳ . ① G262.5-64

中国版本图书馆 CIP 数据核字 (2017) 第 195466 号

书名题签　　王世襄

木趣居——家具中的嘉具
The Best of The Best
The MQJ Collection of Ming Furniture

著　　者	伍嘉恩（Grace Wu）
责任编辑	曾　诚
装帧设计	李猛工作室
责任校对	夏　天
责任印制	卢　岳
出版发行	生活・讀書・新知三联书店
	北京市东城区美术馆东街 22 号　100010
图　　字	01-2017-5779
网　　址	www.sdxjpc.com
经　　销	新华书店
印　　刷	北京图文天地制版印刷有限公司
版　　次	2017 年 9 月北京第 1 版
	2017 年 12 月北京第 2 次印刷
开　　本	787 毫米 ×1030 毫米 1/16　印张 33
字　　数	520 千字　图 1091 幅
印　　数	10,001-16,000 套
定　　价	468.00 元（全二册）

印装查询 010-64002715　邮购查询 010-84010542